HE DO THE POLICE
IN DIFFERENT VOICES

HE DO THE POLICE
IN DIFFERENT VOICES

The Waste Land and Its Protagonist

CALVIN BEDIENT

THE UNIVERSITY OF CHICAGO PRESS

CHICAGO AND LONDON

CALVIN BEDIENT is professor of English at the University of California, Los Angeles. He is the author of *Architects of the Self: George Eliot, D. H. Lawrence, and E. M. Forster; Eight Contemporary Poets;* and *In the Heart's Last Kingdom: Robert Penn Warren's Major Poetry.*

The University of Chicago Press, Chicago 60637
The University of Chicago Press, Ltd., London
© 1986 by The University of Chicago
All rights reserved. Published 1986
Printed in the United States of America

95 94 93 92 91 90 89 88 87 86 12345

LIBRARY OF CONGRESS CATALOGING-IN-PUBLICATION DATA

Bedient, Calvin.
  He do the police in different voices.

  Includes index.
    1. Eliot, T. S. (Thomas Stearns), 1888–1965.
  Waste land. 2. Persona (Literature) 3. Point of view
  (Literature) I. Eliot, T. S. (Thomas Stearns),
  1888–1965. Waste land. II. Title.
  PS3509.L43W3627 1986   821'.912   86-11302
  ISBN 0-226-04140-9

To Ella Marie Bedient

CONTENTS

PREFACE

Two issues have continued to remain unresolved in the growing yet often largely repetitious commentary on T. S. Eliot's 1922 masterpiece—the quintessential poem of Anglo-American modernism—*The Waste Land*. One is that of the emotional, intellectual, and cultural disposition of the poem, its stance (if a simplifying figure may be used) toward history, modernity, erotic love, women, the metaphysical. Is it a poem, as many have thought, of despair? Or a poem, as others have believed, of heroically attained salvation? Or, as still others have suggested, of something peculiarly in-between, something baulked? This bewildering range of response—a result, in part, of the tricky reserve, the justifiably profound reticence, of Eliot's poem—characterizes the other major critical issue as well: that of the existence or nonexistence of a single protagonist; of the nature or purpose of the apparent medley of voices. Is it "Eliot" who speaks the work (or speaks in it)? Or a polyphony of equal voices? Or Tiresias? Or a nameless narrator-protagonist? Or still some other possibility?

The two issues are linked in that, until the second is really taken out of the storehouse to which it is usually confined and thoroughly aired, examined front and back, the first must remain subject to a chance accumulation of impressions taken from the poem, not to mention to the accidents of assumptions (that faith and modernism do not mix; that Eliot was not yet a supernaturalist; that Eliot was already the caretaker of the "European mind," and so on). If it can be argued in detail, in the closest listening to the text, that there is a single presiding consciousness in the poem, that of a poet-protagonist who is "dramatizing" (for want of a more exact word) the history of his own religious awakening, then the metaphysics of the poem (for the poem and the poet-protagonist would then be one), its relation to the past, to contemporaneity, to "the silence," to the possibility of salvation, indeed its very nature as a poetic performance and structure, could perhaps be determined with more exactness than has been demonstrated before.

As my title suggests, I argue for the view that all the voices in the poem are the performances of a single protagonist—not Tiresias but a nameless stand-in for Eliot himself—performances, indeed, of a distinctly theatrical kind, as I believe that Eliot's working title for the poem, which mine echoes, pointedly indicates. To ask why the pro-

ix

tagonist must be theatrical starts up a complex of topics: pre-Oedipal mimesis and uncertainty; Oedipal phobias; historical hyperconsciousness, hence heteroglossia and heteromodality; and a metaphysical critique of identity, consciousness, language, and voice. (To help unfold these I have enlisted the work of several authors, in particular Mikhail Bakhtin on genres, Julia Kristeva on abjection, and Angus Fletcher on allegory.) The gist of the matter, as I see it, is this: in the protagonist, both a psychoanalytical and a historical straying (the first the situation, perhaps, of every man, the second of every representative of Western "culture") come to crisis over against, and finally begin to find redemption in, an experience and cultivation of a metaphysical reality: a One transpsychic, transhistorical, and thus literally beyond words, though it may be the ultimate happiness of words to die into it.

I should perhaps add that my admiration for the genius of the poem has little to do with its metaphysics—stirring as metaphysics usually is to the imagination—though a good deal to do with an openness of temperament that perhaps accounts equally for its mimetic brilliance (the "doing" of the voices) and the protagonist's sympathy with aethereal rumors. I cannot believe, however, that the frequent resistance displayed toward this aspect of the work does justice to its metaphysical daring. This philosophically severe poem itself indicates how it should be read. That Eliot did not more directly state until later his supernaturalist and superhumanist allegiances should not, I think, prevent us from perceiving and granting the radical metaphysics of *The Waste Land.*

His earlier poems are in fact more of a piece with his later work than is perhaps generally acknowledged. Certainly his conversion to Anglicanism in 1927 did not mark a sudden dividing point, with nihilism on the youthful side and religious belief on the other. On the contrary, his Anglicanism was even a retrenchment from the metaphysical absolutism to which everything in *The Waste Land* refers (mostly, of course, by an acutely suffered or unwittingly abject banishment from it). In fact, the heroes of Eliot's two earlier masterpieces, "The Love Song of J. Alfred Prufrock" (1911) and "Gerontion" (1919), anticipate precisely the struggle both against and *of* faith in the protagonist of *The Waste Land.* In this regard, the three heroes form a progression. The "overwhelming question" that Prufrock cannot bring himself to face is a puritanical absolutism that, having already seeped into him, has destroyed his relations with women: he is more a man of faith than he knows, but, all the same, of a miserable reluctant faith, so that he can be decisive neither for the sensual nor for the unseen. Gerontion marks an advance in that, though more cynical than Prufrock—an Eliot prematurely aged by the Great War, by the

ashes of history raining on his hair—he is also more agonizingly restive, desperate to rationalize his failure to have lived by a faith that he
was nonetheless unable to deny: "I that was near your heart," he says,
addressing (it must be) "Christ the tiger," "was removed therefrom /
To lose beauty in terror, terror in inquisition." The protagonist of *The
Waste Land* differs from his predecessors simply in *acting* on his
faith—none too soon, and having to overcome a winter slumber of
inertia and unwillingness before doing it, but doing it—*doing* a voice
of conversion, and then a voice of (allegorical) highest pilgrimage.

Allegory is not a mode usually associated with modernism. Yet, as a
mode always to be equated with estrangement from the sensory world
and with a quest for purity, a mode almost openly artificial, confessing
at the outset the arbitrary nature of representations, it is exactly suited
to a representation of a conversion from this world—from history—
to the eternal silence. Of all literary forms, it is the least an offense to
this last, the most of an accommodation.

Throughout the poem, Eliot's "allegorical style" displays an intelligent economy of language that moves to check—by its chastity, its
formal arrangements—the forsaken babble of historical discourse. In
The Waste Land, poetry is mustered against both overweening literary
style and spates of narcissistic speech, even as both are richly, if ironically, represented. (Indeed, all style is here potentially ironized as pose
or mask.) The mercurial theatricality of the protagonist performs the
illusion of "being someone," indeed many, in a void in which identity
is a fiction. But what might at least approach purity is the right performance, a properly chastened one. In any case, the eternal silence cannot be conceived except in relation to temporal language, which,
though always based in abjection, can counter it through original dis-
ciplines of form. By 1921, allegory had come round again to freshness,
and, in any case, the severe splintering of literary form (that further,
pricking discipline) was in vogue.

So, again, this reading of the poem places emphasis on the self-
conscious if abysmal theatricality of a protagonist who, at first hardly
aware of it himself, is bent, however ambivalently, on transcending the
theater of consciousness altogether. It posits and traces a change within a poet-protagonist whose lugubrious and all-too-lyrical awareness
of abjection is, after an initial surprise assault by the Divine, gradually
lifted by more gentle intuitions of the inconceivable (because utterly
pure) Absolute: a protagonist not ineradicably steeped in nihilism,
after all, but, instead—openly likening himself to devious Hieronymo
in Thomas Kyd's *The Spanish Tragedy*—cunningly conscious of the
need to get round the hostile skepticism of the age by disguising an
extremism of faith with an apparent extremism of ironic disorder.

ACKNOWLEDGMENTS

Acknowledgment is made to Faber and Faber and to Harcourt Brace Jovanovich for their generous permission to quote the entire text of *The Waste Land,* and for their permission to quote, as well, from *The Waste Land: A Facsimile and Transcript of the Original Drafts Including the Annotations of Ezra Pound.* Acknowledgment is also made to Valerie Eliot for her share in the granting of these permissions.

Sloppy is a beautiful reader
of a newspaper. He do the
police in different voices.

Dickens, *Our Mutual Friend*

TITLE AND EPIGRAPH

The Waste Land

"Nam Sibyllam quidem Cumis ego ipse oculis meis
vidi in ampulla pendere, et cum illi pueri dicerent:
Σίβυλλα τί θέλεις; respondebat illa: ἀποθανεῖν θέλω."

For Ezra Pound
il miglior fabbro.

Metaphor and Metonym

The first metaphor of *The Waste Land*—and in both senses of "first"—
is its title. Already, as an allusion to the devastated land of Arthurian
Grail romance, it distances us from the putatively actual, secular, if
hardly less mythic city of Eliot's poem, with its London Bridge, Saint
Mary Woolnoth's, honking horns, drying combinations, gram-
ophones, cigarette ends, Shakespeherian Rag (an import from the *Ziegfeld Follies*), etc., etc. This presumptive metaphoricity continues within
the body of the poem itself, holds sway there—so that, for instance, the
phrase "A heap of broken images" anticipates by many lines a "naturalistic" itemization of the contents of the secular realm. Throughout,
the metaphors act like preventive medicine, giving us a measure of
immunity in advance to everything abject (which in this poem is everything we ordinarily think of as real).

What is the "place" of a title, inside or outside the work? *The
Waste Land* begins with a title in one sense as exterior to it as a handle
to a case but, in another sense, equally anchored to the work from
within. In sweeping up everything into its definite article, in pre-
categorizing and deciphering ahead of time the ideational significance
of the urban and contemporary specificities of the poem, the title *The
Waste Land* also requires that such specifics attract it right into the
poem, one by one and collectively, draw it in as by capillary action, till
it prove coextensive with the poem itself. When well along in the poem
the protagonist begins to flee the waste land, he might be trying to roll
the boulder of the title away from the work, which up to that point has
effectively imprisoned him—the fulcrum for that removal being implicit in the title itself, as a reference to an earthly barrenness for which
there is, at least in the fabulous pages of myth, a heavenly solution. But
what he would flee to—the Absolute—is just as imperious, pre-

I

emptive, and totalizing in relation to everything that is (and is not) as the title is at first in relation to everything in the poem—the title with its inert center lying in the desolation of "waste" and the heaviness of "land." "Power is everywhere; not because it embraces everything, but because it comes from everywhere."[1]

Reality, so the metaphoric tenor of the poem implies, is really something abstract, something to which one refers *away,* something free from the leaden weight of the concrete and all deathward motions. It is at the same time, as the real, piercingly present in a way that the word "abstract" hardly touches, and that "concrete" understates. But this complexity is not of so much moment here as the fact that—as in Yeats's "Byzantium," which is one of his counterparts to Eliot's poem—everything discrete is "image," and in that sense unreal, the Absolute alone being beyond imagination, and alone real. Within the broken world of images, the important distinction is between those "unpurged" and those purged. *The Waste Land* inscribes an inside movement from the realm of the first, which is "found," historical, secular, to that of the second, which is selected, allegorical, and sacred, a realm shaped by the poet-narrator of the poem. Beyond this shaper is, of course, Eliot himself, who shapes *everything* in the poem as purged image, since, thanks to his spirited intentionality (to me, Eliot's statement that "One doesn't know quite what it is that one wants to get off the chest until one's got it off" does not quite cover the case),[2] even the images of abjection are presented as just that, already judged, purified by art for an end supposedly beyond art, namely a spiritual quickening and cleansing.

Both "unpurged" and "purged" images can take the form of metaphor: "this stony rubbish" is metaphor yet an image of secular fallings-away from divine coherency. Metaphor asserts a dominance in the poem that is almost a tyranny: it signals over and over that the purging principle of art has already gone to work on the secular material. Metaphor, in the right hands, is a peremptory, dismissive figure, substituting one thing for another as if to repel it into a limbo of the not directly recognized, of what lies beneath mention. Wilhelm Worringer noted in *Abstraction and Empathy* (1911) that an artist's dread of reality—of its snakily entangled contingencies—urges his style toward abstraction: the framing, isolating, freeing of things, a redemption by stylization. Naturalism equates with one or another kind of

---

1. Michel Foucault, *The History of Sexuality,* vol. 1, *An Introduction,* trans. Robert Hurley (New York: Vintage Books, 1980), 93.

2. See *Writers at Work: The Paris Review Interviews, Second Series,* ed. George Plimpton (New York: Penguin Books, 1977), 97.

trust in nature, whereas a distorting stylization preempts the shaping and misshaping powers of reality, establishing, out front, the artist's will to mastery over the brute materials that life plants before him.[3] Its characters mostly mere types, its lilacs odorless, its "rat's feet" literary, its mountains made of papier-mâché, *The Waste Land* shows a will to abstraction that relents at only a few points, points where the body of the world, as if the mother's own body, or the father's (the lines on the Hofgarten and Marie and the lines on the lounging fishmen, respectively), is looked on, and heard with dispassion, compassion, or simple pleasure.

Eliot's most hauntingly beautiful poem, "Marina," catches reality just on the verge of its dissolution into grace: "What seas what shores what granite islands towards my timbers / And woodthrush calling through the fog / My daughter."[4] Only thus near the supernatural could Eliot relax his vigilance against brute reality and release his imagination to a passion of rhythm and sweet tone, as here, or of rhythm and sweet tone and vivid metaphor, as in the meditative response to the divine command, "Control," in part 5 of *The Waste Land.* For the rest, he is on guard, and his work has the hard coldness that, in praising Hawthorne, he declared a hallmark of all genuine art. Even "shores" and "granite islands," and so on, keep their distance from the gravitational pull of specific, geographical, contextually ensnared things and places. Until *Four Quartets,* the détentes with actual things are, as intimated, few, and the raptures look away, or inward, into the unseen.

And yet a peculiarity of *The Waste Land* is its freight of non-allegorical, metonymic grit.[5] Contemporary readers saw it as portraying, not a never-never-land of myth or metaphysical longing, but, more or less, their own world; its historical *applicability* was felt at once, never doubted. Besides, even "myth" in the poem proved—Eliot being, after all, a belated author who would nonetheless seek an original, in the sense of timeless, knowledge of the One—entirely mediated

3. Wilhelm Worringer, *Abstraction and Empathy: A Contribution to the Psychology of Style,* trans. Michael Bullock (New York: International Universities Press, 1953), 15–18.

4. T. S. Eliot, *The Complete Poems and Plays 1909–1950* (New York: Harcourt, Brace and Co., 1952), 73.

5. I rest on Roman Jakobson's by now well-known extension of the term "metonym" to cover relationships of contiguity and context (such as those dominant in "realistic" novels), as distinct from "metaphoric" relationships of resemblance. The recent efforts to break down the distinction between metonym and metaphor have not obviated the need for a practical distinction. See Roman Jakobson, "Two Aspects of Language and Two Types of Aphasic Disturbances," in *Fundamentals of Language* (The Hague: Mouton, 1971), 72–96.

through a "body" of European literature, as historical, if not as contemporary, as a gramophone or taxi. An allusion to a sylvan scene is not in the first instance an allusion to myth, but to Milton on myth, and Milton is in a metonymic, that is, contiguous and contextual, not a metaphoric, that is, mirroring relation to Dante, Shakespeare, Eliot himself. All told, Eliot's poem was as remarkable for its *novelistic* use of history and voices other than the poet's own as for its daring assumption, first in the title and many times thereafter, of governing and organizing metaphor. Yeats, when he wanted to evoke contemporary cosmopolitanism and time-shallow culture, mere fashion, spoke generally and precisely (in "Coole Park and Ballylee") of "fashion or mere fantasy," adding "We shift about—all that great glory spent— / Like some poor Arab tribesman and his feet." Eliot, treating the Elizabethans as a now "antique" "glory" of European culture (though hardly a perfect glory; everything cultural is relatively purged or unpurged) abruptly introduces "But / O O O O that Shakespeherian Rag— / It's so elegant / So intelligent," and the jazz age, with its frivolity and kick, its blithe idiocy and frantic high spirits, is suddenly before our ears.

Of course, Yeats himself moved from faery to fact, from moony dimnesses to harsh poetry, and in "Beautiful Lofty Things," for instance, is as much the memoirist, as concerned with historical metonymic context, as, say, Eliot in the passage on Countess Marie Larish. Differentiations among the modernists, even the poets, with regard to their transparency to history (their own, that of the past) pale beside their common achievement of a dance and balance between metaphor and metonym, or obvious figure and fact. How good they were at keeping each within reach of the other, at a brinded art; how good at a musicalization of fact and a journalization of music; how adept and how determined to avoid what Irving Babbitt, Eliot's mentor at Harvard University, had condemned as the contrary forms of romantic "excess": sickly dreaming and brute naturalism, or "escape from the world of fact" and "devotion to . . . fact."

Edmund Wilson's discussion of Yeats, Eliot and Joyce in *Axel's Castle* somewhat exaggerated their affinities with the French Symbolists ("escape from the world of fact"). Eliot himself showed a hard-headed approach even to the metaphysical, save in "Marina," an old man's privileged, happy, shocked dream of an imminent aetherealization, and "Ash-Wednesday," a studied religious meditation that has, for my taste, too little historical or autobiographical check or control. In the gradual progression from "The Love-Song of J. Alfred Prufrock" to "Gerontion" to *The Waste Land,* Eliot does not so much lift himself out of history into the unseen as broaden the base of his approach to each; there is *more* of history in the last poem than in the first, and *more* of the "overwhelming question," the superhuman, the supernatural. (Much the same sort of advance, on both fronts, is evident in Yeats.)

Not that Eliot, in *The Waste Land,* does not regard history as utterly abject (lacking, as he did, the "swordsman" element that quarreled with the "saintly" element in Yeats, though even the first could think of itself as a ditch-sleeping tramp: "A living man is blind and drinks his drop. / What matter if the ditches are impure?"). His attraction to it (for it amounted to that) is almost never less than guilty and self-berating—a willed masochism of conscious meanness. What had fallen off from transcendence—as became apparent from "Gerontion" on, and hindsight adds: "Even in 'Prufrock'"—at once seduced and horrified Eliot: the smell of steaks in passageways, yellow soles of feet clasped in the palms of soiled hands, the physical, the female, the vegetal, the mechanical. A high dream of purest coherence, living and ungraspable, swift and eternal, terrorized everything below it, everything of flesh and time and even everything lingual, even art, though the whole aim of Eliot's career was to perfect art to the point where it would be forgiven, maybe even graced, by the Absolute.

In *The Waste Land,* Eliot's protagonist (a smaller version of himself, having initially more to learn; a larger version, too, daring to break with society and women and cut a road to hermitic saintliness through his pain)—Eliot's protagonist will at length turn his back on the abject realm of history, with its heap of rubbishy metonyms, and head off into allegorical mountains of an interior region, in pursuit of—well, whether of a still more inviolable poetic voice (for the protagonist is a poet in his own right) or of " the silence" it would be hard to say. Here, only metaphor can help him to his meanings, intuitive correspondences between figurations and the Nonfigurable. Metaphor and its narrative forms of allegory and myth: he is, for instance, the Fisher King of the Grail romances, as described by Jessie Weston in *From Ritual to Romance* (1921): somehow the principle of life, but ailing; and he is the knight of purity and metaphysical daring who, after a period of trial and quest, is able to cure the sick king. Still, here there is no "grail," nothing so idolatrous—no Christian trappings, nothing that restricts one to doctrine. For just as the medieval romancers converted the pagan fertility materials (figures, rituals, narratives) to Christian fictions, so Eliot, in turn, converts the romantic Christianity of the legends (romantic in the sense of being emphatically strange, marvelous, miraculous) into a more austere and syncretic metaphysics of the Unnameable. (There are readers who think that Eliot goes back from the Christian rewrite to pagan values, that *The Waste Land* would promote natural and human fertility. But I believe that the poet fiercely nips in the bud [and the buds crop up, are there] any nostalgia for natural and human values—green growth, fruit, sex, love—in a ferocious dedication to the opposite of all such natural darkness, a devotion to "the heart of light.") Finally, Eliot dismisses myth, which he had used as being more universal, less schismatic, than a doctrinal religion, and less flatly abject than metonymic discourse, in favor of metaphor, which is in turn free of the narrative limits of myth (metaphors such as lightning, rain, thunder-speech, fishing, shoring and fitting) in a *bricolage,* an inspired multiplicity and harlequinade of approach to what can neither be narrated nor imaged, let alone understood. He sets out figural fragments like bread crumbs on a window ledge to attract the Bird of the Absolute. The bird does not come. But the crumbs have been laid out and the window is open. The poem has done that much, if no more. (I do not mean—what is often proposed—that the protagonist "fails" to find salvation. That is to put the emphasis in the wrong place. Rather, he succeeds in readying himself for a salvation that—such is Eliot's severe Easternized sense of the matter—can only really be attained by the purest death.)

The Epigraph: Between Metaphor and Metonym

As a figural strategy, the epigraph differs from the title precisely in being an epi-graph, a peripheral writing, a side-jotting; bottled away from the rest of the text, as the Sibyl of which it speaks is bottled away from passersby, yet able to be looked into within the poem itself and, conversely, seen through from inside, in a circular irony of perspectives. Poor Sibyl of Cumae, heroine, so R. P. Blackmur says, of all that is stupid and clutching in life,[6] how precipitate, how breathless it was of her to ask for immortal life but to forget to ask for eternal youth. Why, even the Thames-daughters in part 3 of *The Waste Land* are wiser than she was, and exactly to the degree that they are disillusioned with life. On the other hand, this greatest victim of the aging process, this taster and taster of the bitter draught of mortality, at last and at least has grasped something of the horror of life, and she is twisted away from the temporizing inhabitants of the waste land in an unassimilable, unmirrored anguish.

Unless the protagonist himself mirrors her, in a flash of horror, in

6. R. P. Blackmur, *A Primer of Ignorance,* ed. Joseph Frank (New York: Harcourt, Brace & World, 1967), 45.

the very moment he turns from the scattered hell-fires of the senses toward the narrow white road of an interior expurgation ("burning burning burning burning / O Lord Thou pluckest me out"). But whereas *his* horror is the black lining of his faith in the absolutely pure, hers begins and ends in negativity—is bottled up in her despair of ever escaping from mortal impurity. The Sibyl is pagan, her very gods are abject, they are in love with life, their glory is only abjection that does not apologize. Unlike the protagonist, she has no access to the Platonic antiworld of an ascetic metaphysics. She cannot cross the limits of her pagan text and become absorbed in the Christianized Eastern text of Eliot's poem, with its quasi-Gnostic revulsions against the witch's cauldron of *breeding* and *stirring* and *mixing,* much as she herself has been brought to a cognate aversion.[7]

Yet she is in as well as around the poem; unlike several other figures she is even more than alluded to, she is named and narrated, even if in another's, and foreign, words (but *The Waste Land* is anyway a poem in which the concept of a foreign language loses some of its cutting edge, since here all language is, in a current French conception, under erasure). Too, she is framed between the title and the principal text, and if the title is already the beginning of the poem, the threshold, then she is already inside, if off to the side, as if in a little room near the entrance that it is no good to enter. Her relation to the poem is one of an inner metonym, a loose part—even if, for a brief instant, the protagonist mimics her horror, even as he transcends it in something else, and she appears at last to find a *semblable* in the text, to serve as already failing metaphor.

What she is to the main text, Petronius' *Satyricon* is to the whole poem. The latter has been brought inside *The Waste Land* yet exists fully and simply only outside it, as itself and as part of literary history. Trimalchio's short account of having once seen the Sibyl of Cumae in person is fiction in itself, fact as literature.[8] It enters Eliot's own fiction as fact harboring a fiction; but in *The Waste Land* all fact is itself reduced to fiction (to images), at the same time that a "supreme" fiction, the protagonist's allegory of a mountain journey, climaxes the poem as the true representation of spiritual fact. This trap-door arrangement through which fiction-bearing fact falls into fiction and fiction into a profound, indeed "bottom" level of fact awaits every aesthetic work that the poem, whether through quotation or allusion,

7. For this divination of some of the connotations of the first participles in *The Waste Land,* I am indebted to my former student, Stephen Lester.

8. Petronius, *The Satyricon,* trans. William Arrowsmith (New York: New American Library, 1983), 57.

draws into its structure (David Perkins counts "at least thirty-seven").[9] Like the *Satyricon, The Waste Land* is Menippean (in Mikhail Bakhtin's term for the largely carnivalesque, mixed-salad sort of discourse stemming nominally from the Greek author Menippus), but of a different sort.[10] The former, with its philosophical dialogue, adventure, slum naturalism, fantasticality, parody, verse amid prose, is *straight* Menippea, bold, eccentric, high-spirited, tweaking system by laughter and by thrusting monologic authority into the shade. *The Waste Land* substitutes for the impudent marginality of laughter a poetics of banishment, in which numerous voices, styles, and generic registers conspicuously fill a void left by the missing All. Self-overcoming Menippia, it then stills all that babble, stops up the pollutingly overheard, and even all generic strayings, except for what it carefully and homiletically selects and combines in its now deliberate creation of an exemplary and allegorical fiction. *The Waste Land* is never really, and is finally far from being, carnivalesque; instead, it arranges the *appearance* of a riot of tones and images and languages with the cold cunning of a Hieronymo and with no less an intention than to silence the pretensions of language and literature once and for all (a suicidal mission that even *The Waste Land,* for all its severity, is unable to perform—indeed, it even gathers, just before the close, a heap of heterogeneous, quoted phrases like a squirrel hoarding nuts for the winter, and, in the same place, praises song).

The *Satyricon* is, then, both like and irrecoverably divided from *The Waste Land*. Here, on inspection, similitude fades to contrast, indeed, *The Waste Land* is so radical a work with regard to the status of literature itself—as what is always in quotation marks, an image of an image—that all other works fade to contrast beside it, even while it deliberately and even relentlessly recalls, as noted, a good many of them. The *Satyricon* cannot enter the poem except in an ironic, bottled state, as a metonymic presence, an internalized part of the contextual body of "tradition." Not also as a metaphoric presence? Like the Sibyl, only for the interval that it takes one to discern that Eliot would smash the bottle of Menippea beyond repair and let in "the silence" if only he could find a way to do so through a "mad" arrangement of words themselves.

9. David Perkins, *A History of Modern Poetry: From the 1890s to the High Modernist Mode* (Cambridge, Mass.: Harvard University Press, 1976), 511.

10. Mikhail Bakhtin, *Problems of Dostoevsky's Poetics*, trans. Caryl Emerson (Minneapolis: University of Minnesota Press, 1984), 133–34.

THE BURIAL OF THE DEAD

April is the cruellest month, breeding
Lilacs out of the dead land, mixing
Memory and desire, stirring
Dull roots with spring rain.
Winter kept us warm, covering
Earth in forgetful snow, feeding
A little life with dried tubers.
Summer surprised us, coming over the Starnbergersee
With a shower of rain; we stopped in the colonnade,
And went on in sunlight, into the Hofgarten,
And drank coffee, and talked for an hour.
Bin gar keine Russin, stamm' aus Litauen, echt deutsch.
And when we were children, staying at the archduke's,
My cousin's, he took me out on a sled,
And I was frightened. He said, Marie,
Marie, hold on tight. And down we went.
In the mountains, there you feel free.
I read, much of the night, and go south in the winter.

Heteroglossia

Who speaks the first seven lines? How persuasive are we meant to find them? And who speaks the next four, and the line in German? And who is the final speaker, this Marie who begins talking as if she needed no introduction?

No poem before ever started so, with an "overhear me," then an "overhear *me*," and the same again, and all the while a "never mind who, for it scarcely matters anyway."

It *is* going to matter who, and quite soon, but first the poem registers a crisis of heteroglossia, and, beyond that, a crisis of meaningless identity. This anatomy may coincide with modern clichés, but in fact terrible standards are being brought to bear, here, on human reality— the clichés of "lack of communication" and "lost generation" and so on have pitifully little application. *Of course* secular beings have nothing authoritative to utter, of course they do not know who they "are." Everything here below is unreal, hiding out from the One alone. Heteroglossia is Babel; God, or the Absolute, is "silence."

In the first verse paragraph, as occasionally later on in the poem,

9

the confusion as to who is speaking is greater than the difficulty of understanding what is being said. Gradually, identities do begin to emerge, the more readily under the hypothesis of a protagonist who "does" other voices as well as speaks in his own. This hypothesis satisfactorily deprives the procedure of the poem of an air of willful and cynical confusion. One is able to determine "that's *his* voice, straight," "that's him repeating Marie word for word," "that's him faking the collective voice of a weary war-torn generation," etc.

Still, the sheer number of voices and hence of styles, discourses, verbal ideologies, and even languages, is overwhelming in such a short space as the 434 lines of the poem, and a very queer thing to find in poetry at all. What does this multistylism and multivocality say? Where the unitary style of almost every other poem implies the *one* style of truth and feeling, the highest saying possible, the richest, the most moving, so that anything less or other would be a failed utterance, this polyvocalism and heteroglossia must mean just the opposite: that there is no unified sensibility, no truth to speak of; no, there is only speech, speech, speech. "The language of the poet," writes Bakhtin, "is *his* language, he is utterly immersed in it, inseparable from it, he makes use of each form, each word, each expression according to its unmediated power to assign meaning (as it were, 'without quotation marks'), that is, as a pure and direct expression of his own intention." Again: "the concept of many worlds of language, all equal in their ability to conceptualize and to be expressive, is organically denied to poetic style. The world of poetry . . . is always illumined by one unitary and indisputable discourse."[1] *The Waste Land,* even more than Pound's *Hugh Selwyn Mauberley* had already done, subjects poetry to the virus of quotation, till all appears cancerous, wild. For the most part, it compounds the injury to the sanctified idea of poetry as "one unitary and indisputable discourse" by omitting the quotation marks, so given over is it to the idea that all speech freely collapses into an indiscriminate heap, not even a medley but a linguistic morass.

The originality of the poem is one with its novelization, which is extreme—more than Ivy Compton-Burnett, if not more than William Gaddis, extreme. It is as if a novelist were to omit, at the outset of a novel, and in every subsequent chapter, the descriptions and names of the characters, who appear only as speech, and to suppress, besides, all pointing *he said's* as well as the hour and place. As if we were simply

---

1. Mikhail Bakhtin, *The Dialogic Imagination: Four Essays,* ed. Michael Holquist, trans. Caryl Emerson and Michael Holquist (Austin: University of Texas Press, 1981), 285–86.

to hear a series of unidentified duologuists—duologuists who, however, are never answered, whose words would be entirely absorbed into the cotton wool of the white spaces surrounding them or the great wads of cotton wool in the protagonist himself, if it were not for the reader, a being absolutely essential to their retrieval even if the reader, too, leaves the speeches unanswered.

In *The Dialogic Imagination,* Bakhtin declares that "the stylistic uniqueness of the novel as a genre consists . . . in the combination of . . . subordinated, yet still relatively autonomous, [stylistic] unities (even at times comprised of different languages) into the higher unity of the work as a whole; the style of a novel is to be found in the combination of its styles; the language of a novel is the system of its 'languages.' "[2] This comes so near to being true of *The Waste Land* that the difference is perhaps not worth defending—the difference that lies in the protagonist's studied control, as internal representative and surpasser of the poet himself, over the words that he *brings over* from other styles to echo in the bleak chamber of his chagrin and irony. Does the protagonist even *have* a style of his own? Like Joyce's mercurial narrator in *Ulysses,* like Joyce himself, overexposed as it were to the radiation from the accumulated conglomerate of mutually relative prose styles in English, the protagonist is a chameleon and *bricoleur* of styles, a post-stylist condemned to show some style. He is almost never free of echoes of others, we know him best by his "purified" directness, as when he says, "I sat upon the shore / Fishing," the least personal of declarations, a neutral allegorical style. Or we know him through the chaste style of the absolutely economical statement, as when he says, "Then a damp gust / Bringing rain."

In the novel, as Bakhtin remarks, various verbal ideologies, disguised as characters, clash with one another, competing to see which will be the most persuasive. The internally persuasive discourse of the novel is like the squabble of turkey vultures over a scrap of carrion, the carrion of "you're right," compared to the churchly or royal feast, ritually laid out and partaken, that was once the "authoritative word." This last, the word of the fathers, a word *already* acknowledged in the past, always "a dead quotation," was situated "in a distanced zone" that was hierarchically higher than the "zone of contact with unresolved contemporaneity."[3] But the novelist and his characters cannot have it, even *will* have none of it, being rebelliously and rawly contemporary.

2. Ibid., 262.
3. Ibid., 342–36.

Heteroglossia: language up for grabs. Awash without authority. Modernist "experimentation" was a response to the lost authority of words, words, words. With both nostalgia for unself-conscious stylization and irony toward all style, *The Waste Land* and *Ulysses* alike lift the lid on a trans-epochal and transcontinental Babel, the first with fascinated mistrust and the second more ludically, in connoissseurship and amusement, also more masteringly, in encyclopedism and rivalry. Word-animals themselves, Joyce and Eliot, the chief modernists to write in English (or Irish English and American English) delighted in the remanipulation and reanimation of the written discourse of the others; but in *The Waste Land* this activity is at the same time a sickness of words, a nausea and disease of them, an argument, finally, for a chastening "silence."

In both *The Waste Land* and *Ulysses,* Menippea and heteroglossia finally perish in a "yes," though a "yes" to opposite things within the scale of the fertile and wonderful: Eliot's poem to the unfleshy, and even unpsychic, Absolute, Joyce's novel to Eros and the worldly arrangement of marriage (Yes, Molly Bloom says, not to Sex or Love, exactly, but to a proposal). But meanwhile, at the outset of Eliot's poem, we hear a no, a complex no to the negation of a No already declared through, and by, a long winter of maintaining, by choice, a "dull roots" existence. In 1917, Eliot wrote to his father: "Everyone's individual lives are so swallowed up in the one great tragedy [the war] that one almost ceases to have personal experiences or emotions, and such as one has seem so unimportant." After quoting these words, Alfred Kazin comments that in *The Waste Land* Eliot was "no longer making grisly fun of himself, as in 'Prufrock'; he was trying to put into one framework the desperate voices of a war-torn civilization."[4] Yet if the war had the effect of fusing Eliot weakly and compassionately with others in "the one great tragedy," he reacted, perhaps first less out of spiritual fastidiousness than from a need to keep himself purposeful and sane ("I have a lot of things to write about," he adds in the same letter to his father, "if the time ever comes when people will attend to them"), into critical apartness, indeed, the severity of an Old Testament prophet. What explains the heteroglossia in his poem is perhaps less compassion than, on the one hand, an incorporative hysteria (replete with revulsion) and, on the other, the unsympathetic aim of exposing speakers through their words: in all, an unstable and formidable mix. Eliot was not so much offering generous space next to his own voice to desperate postwar voices as gathering them like spec-

4. Alfred Kazin, *An American Procession* (New York: Alfred A. Knopf, 1984), 316.

imens of a world that, because of its own unreality rather than for any active evil, is about to become extinct.

First the protagonist does a voice perhaps more suited to a T. S. Eliot than to the hypothetical average man of the postwar years, but a voice pitched, all the same, to awaken sympathetic vibrations in anyone who felt that he or she had been through too much, and wanted out. It evokes the suffering not of wartime in particular but of desire always—desire that cannot be satisfied, that is an agony of disappointment; desire that, mixed with the further self-absence constituted by memory, is deadly, though we call it a sign of spring; desire that would return us, circularly, to the place of starting, which is already a place of being cast out, since desire circles around the impregnable fortress of incest and all-consuming "demand" (in Jacques Lacan's view of it);[5] or, as Foucault puts the psychoanalytical position, "you always rediscover in your innermost selves your Object-Mother or the sovereign sign of your Father: it is through them that you gain access to desire"—gain it too late, and under the sign of castration.[6]

This speaker would not again be "sick with desire," as the aged speaker in Yeats's "Sailing to Byzantium" would no longer be. And ultimately, like Yeats's speaker, he will choose "God's holy fire" and the selflessness attributable to a work of art as compensation for being a "dying animal" and cure for the sickness of desire. Only, unlike Yeats's speaker he will not allow the second to take precedence over the first: he will juggle the two until, in the very last line, he will catch the *holy* sphere in his hand and hold it for the close (to be sure, the close of a work of art): the sphere of "the silence" and not of "O when may I be like the swallow [and sing]" (*Quando fiam uti chelidon*).

Now, according to the inspiration of the poem, the protagonist is right to resist, to distrust, desire. Desire has such a good lobby in this lingeringly romantic century that many readers, perhaps most, conclude that there must be something sick about the protagonist's preference of dullness over "breeding" and "spring," and they are helped to this impression by the bias of the fertility cults underlying—but in truth already subverted by—the Christian Grail romances. But in *The Waste Land* the nature myth is a paled-out and distanced and at best nostalgic flap through which one is conducted into regions of lifegiving asceticism. Thoreau's words perfectly put the case:

5. Jacques Lacan, *Ecrits: A Selection*, trans. Alan Sheridan (New York: W. W. Norton, 1977), 286.

6. Michel Foucault, *The History of Sexuality: An Introduction*, vol. 1, trans. Robert Hurley (New York: Vintage Books, 1980), 113.

The generative energy, which, when we are loose, dissipates and makes us unclean, when we are continent invigorates and inspires us. Chastity is the flowering of man; and what are called Genius, Heroism, Holiness, and the like, are but various fruits which succeed it. Man flows at once to God when the channel of purity is open. . . . He is blessed who is assured that the animal is dying out in him day by day, and the divine being established.[7]

Eliot is equally (and more consistently) austere. The protagonist is sick because he feels, despite himself, desire, and desire is a disease of un-cleanliness, having no relation whatever to purity ("all sensuality is one, though it takes many forms; all purity is one"—Thoreau). But "dullness" is not purity, either; it is a sensuality of torpor. The "gener-ative energy" that, when we are continent, "invigorates and inspires us" has not yet been bred in it, stirred.

The voice we hear in the first seven lines of the poem is "of" the waste land, not dissociated from it, unless through the very perfection of its eloquence. Neither Marie nor the woman who first appears as the protagonist's girlish sweetheart, a mythical ingenue, nor any of the other contemporary characters shows the slightest comparable power of conception, feeling, phrase. Hindsight shows us that this speaker is already an *exceptional* representative of the waste land, and not least in being a lyrist; he is already (and more or other than he knows) profoundly apart, apart because profound, quick with potential, full of the spiritual promise of agony. His extraordinarily beautiful words, words unexceptional in themselves but ravishing in their combination, these are not the confessional formulas of the speaker himself, who is anything but dull or evasive, but of a race of the dull and evasive for whom he momentarily takes it upon himself, no doubt out of a genu-ine complicity, to speak. At this point the speaker lags far behind his author in enlightenment, just as he is assuredly in advance, on that score, of a Marie or a hyacinth girl, and just as he will by the end seem to have gone farther along a purifying hermitic path than Eliot himself apparently ever did on his own, that is, without his character's gener-ous and imaginary help.

Is this speaker not affected in the way he works the vein of the disturbed "little life" for all the interest of pathos that it will yield? Still weak, sensual, undecided, the protagonist evidently decides to make the most of a collective disillusionment, enjoying its melancholy and resignation but, even more, the sensuality that awakens within it and contradicts it and corrupts it. (Involved here is the sexual excite-ment of a feigned resistance to sensuality.) In this *incipit* the waste

7. *The Portable Thoreau*, ed. Carl Bode (New York: Viking Press, 1947), 466.

land itself is granted its greatest, almost its only, seductive appeal. To feel as this speaker does! To know the really poignant mixture of nostalgia and boredom, experience the tussle between inertia and the great annual stirring of nature! We are almost ready to drink from this cup, rather than to recognize it as poison.

Lyricism is not the dominant tonality of *The Waste Land,* and for a reason: lyricism itself is disease. Or there is lyricism and lyricism, and this initial vein of it carries subtle impurities. Enacting conflict between "I'd rather not" and "Oh, can I hold out against desire any longer?" the lines are structured like a torture apparatus but a rather delicious one, withal. On the one hand, the two sentences together show a rearward pull from "April" to "Winter," from the revolutionary present to the conservative past; and the formal phonemic patterning, telescoping "Lilacs . . . dead" into "land" and alliteratively binding pairs of words—"mixing / Memory"; "Winter . . . warm"; "roots . . . rain"; "little life"—this strategy holds back any element of excitement. The imitation in the second sentence of the caesural and syntactic patterns of the first, down to the terminal participles, is a further attempt at *not moving.* On the other hand, the alliteration (to return to that) itself suggests breeding, coupling. And the protagonist gives himself, gives his syntax, almost willingly, masochistically, to the wrack formed by the first series of terminal (as if unsubduable) present participles, "breeding," "mixing," "stirring." He is lyrical, after all, because he feels movement within him, inertia being the "anti-poetic *per se,*" as Ortega y Gasset put it.[8] The caesuras before the participles seem both to drag against them and to be kicked away by them, and the line breaks protest against them rather feebly, as if knowing the futility of resistance. Then, although the impersonal diction, which is almost all distancing metaphor, lends its own resistance to the mad desire to breed, to mix sex with sex, identity with identity, the metaphor itself is an erotic interbreeding of objects, or states, and images.

No, the protagonist is *sensually* lyrical, not purely so, and his lyricism is to that extent suspect if judged by the most ascetic standards, standards that are indeed applied in the poem, and almost cripplingly, so that it is all the poem can do to *be* a poem against them, or all the protagonist can do to express a desire—as though in flouted, defiant sensuality—to sing like Philomel (if, to be sure, inviolably) or praise a structure like Wren's interior of St. Magnus Martyr, not Quaker-plain but an "inexplicable splendor." What is at fault—luringly so—is feel-

8. José Ortega y Gasset, *Meditations on Quixote,* trans. Evelyn Rugg and Diego Marín (New York: W. W. Norton, 1963), 136.

ing that feeds on itself narcissistically, as here, in contrast to feeling that is, to borrow an expression from Eliot's doctoral dissertation, which was published under the title *Knowledge and Experience in the Philosophy of F. H. Bradley,* "the adjective of some transcendental self."[9]

Still, as noted, signs of detachment and hence of a potential *ascetic* regeneration in the protagonist already appear in this *incipit.* For instance, in the critical edge of "Dull" and a "little life," and the deliberate perversity of the paradox "Winter kept us warm," and above all the awareness that desire is not good for you, is part of a dying seasonal round. Yes, he senses that it is wrong to reduce oneself, dwindle down, to "Dull roots," wrong to try to live without an intolerable happiness. But he has yet to know this as knowledge and faith, yet to find the right jouissance.

Heteroglossia and Metastasis

What follows, in the next four lines, without even so much as the switch-signal of a typographical gap, is a different voice, a new style: "Summer surprised us, coming over the Starnbergersee / With a shower of rain," etc. Whose voice is this, so socially easy and graceful, so far from pain? Is it now the protagonist's own, as against his brilliant simulation of the voice of a generation? It is, rather, the sociolect of the memoir, the comfortable conversation, the letter; generic, giving nothing away, it simulates phatic happiness. Here, not private anguish projected as Everyone's Predicament, but a simple personal reminiscence that is curiously unashamed (considering that it occurs in a poem) to be merely that, leaking in like someone else's call on a long-distance telephone conversation, mixing a gay superficial chatter with a choked misery. As before, the verse is repetitive in structure, showing a marked caesura in the middle of each line:

> Summer surprised us, coming over the Starnbergersee
> With a shower of rain; we stopped in the colonnade,
> And went on in sunlight, into the Hofgarten,
> And drank coffee, and talked for an hour.

But here the effect is altogether different, a lovely casual saunter. The stops and starts are unresented. The depressed feeling is gone. And although the brief summer shower has no apparent agricultural importance (it is slight and freakish, out of season, a surprise), no normal generative impulse seems wanting. The people themselves are not

9. T. S. Eliot, *Knowledge and Experience in the Philosophy of F. H. Bradley* (London: Faber and Faber, 1964), 21.

rooted, but moving, in a rhythm of musical pause and flow; language itself flows; and summer comes over the mountains as if it were happy to be nothing more than a flotilla of moisture-bearing clouds.

Not only the tone and movement are different, the matrix of the diction is too; the poet has dipped into a different bin of words. No longer elevatedly metaphoric, the discourse is now unanxiously and banally metonymic, happy in its consciousness of spatial and temporal continuities, the this and that and here and there and now and then of the world, genial toward differences, open, not closed in. Here the external world, rather than subjective feeling, is the focus. Everything is literal and specific. An object-concrete word like "coffee," a place-specific word like "Hofgarten," would violate the tenor of the initial discourse, which is insularly figurative in style, disguising feeling in seasonal imagery, painting feeling as if it were a subject to be framed and hung for display.

How much of the original discourse is literal? April, lilacs, spring rain, no doubt. But a particular April or every April from time immemorial? Lilacs with an odor or lilacs as a badge, not even a purple badge, or a white badge, of spring? The frankly figurative "Dull roots" makes us wonder retroactively about the literalness of, at the least, "dead land." And the transfer of the adjective "forgetful" from the mind to "snow" subdues the season to an illustrative role, giving peremptory primacy to a state of feeling. "Summer," by contrast, is unequivocally a certain summer, implicitly datable, and dated, and the Starnbergersee stands in its own geographical space. So with the colonnade, the hour, the talk. Significations here are single-leveled. Firm. Trustworthy. The "world" of the first seven lines is patently a fictional construct, a molecular model of a certain state of feeling; this other world is what, by another fiction, we agree to call the real world. Eliot will undercut this "reality," but not yet; here it only lies on the surface of discourse like a cup of coffee on a table. Look at it. Take hold. It is there.

As suggested, the intrinsic distance between the metaphoric texture and the literal subject of the initial discourse was a technique for lending persuasion to the claim of a "little life." The language occluded "reality." How much more of life is conveyed by the contrasting metonymic style? Here language is less fraught with significance, but neither is there a pressure on it—wincing, edgy—to signify. Drinking coffee is distinguishable from "feeding / A little life with dried tubers" not least in being happily ordinary. The frightening, the macabre irony of feeding a little life (to keep it little) is gone. Looking back on the experience in Munich's Hofgarten, the protagonist (for it must be he who has this convincingly specific reminiscence) might be ready to classify it under the rubric "A little life," but, if so, the classification doesn't appear, on the face of it, dismissive. The reminiscence gives off a tinkle like a triangle, but that is not a disagreeable sound, and in any case what is one to do, condemn the summer, the colonnade, the garden, sociality?

Two puzzles are involved here: the how and the why of this passage, its manner of introduction and placement, on the one hand, and its "meaning" on the other. The "how" is metastasis, as when a disease shifts from one part of the body to another; the "why" is the intention to show the disease of life in another form from the initial one. For this hour or so in the Hofgarten is not so innocent as it at first seems—is not even the innocence before a fall. The social discourse is fallen per se; it is of the world, worldly. Measure the movement into and out of the colonnade, out of the rain and into the sunshine, and toward the cafe table, against the allegorical journey of part 5 of the poem, with its inner mountain and rain-freighted thunder, and it is as the inching of pettiness against heroic strides. A harsh measure, but one the protagonist will increasingly inflict upon himself, and already in this instance on a memory without even quite knowing, as yet, how infinite the measure involved.

We may hypothesize that his discourse on a "little life" has, as if by an inevitable association, caused him to think of the moment in the Hofgarten (which is later to be implicitly measured against the moment near the Hyacinth garden and the protagonist's first—or earliest confessed—mystical experience of the infinite). Here in the Hofgarten is a life in which desire is subdued to dormancy, not even *sub rosa;* here is escape from April's cruelty and spring rain. This second discourse is much the more "forgetful" of the two, the first being all sorrowful, perversely witty realization. The new style is itself a graph of a little life, but is free of disappointment. Here we find life at least not being consciously cruel to itself, bitter over the nothingness of desire.

Metastasis—in Fritz Senn's gloss, "derived from a verb *methistanai* (to place in another way, change), it means 'change, shift, removal, transformation,' [and] in particular as used in classical rhetorics, it means a rapid transition from one point of view to another"[10]—metastasis carries here the same stigma as, just as it coincides with, heteroglossia, the stigma of arbitrariness, only at the level of "point of

10. Fritz Senn, *Joyce's Dislocutions: Essays on Reading as Translation,* ed. John Paul Riquelme (Baltimore: The Johns Hopkins University Press, 1984), 139.

view" rather than that of linguistic register or "system." We are shunted on the rails of our "reader's voice" (in Eudora Welty's term) from one mental set to another as if it did not really matter to which we harkened, if either—as from the inconceivable "point of view" of the Absolute it conceivably would not. This, again, is harsh, but the order of this poem—the order of its apparent disorder—is not humanistic, but ironic, and what it says, over and over, is that there *is* no authoritative point of view of a secular stamp, there are only broken angles of vision, splinters of mood, tinkles or other tones of discourse that fall and die far outside the Eternal Silence of the Fullness of God, the *Om* of Eastern meditation.

Instinctively, the protagonist seems to realize this; as autobiographical hero, he may suffer this knowledge, endure the shift from the first to the second style, his voice virtually breaking on him with the embarrassing "surprise" of an adolescent boy's. Or that is one hypothesis to entertain. He could not in any case use the first style for the second subject, use a silver mesh to grate a carrot. Subject matter dictates style, in conjunction with a dialogic situation (the real or supposed audience); the "levels" of experience foster their own heteroglossia, layers of discourse that do not touch, that float in disrelation from one another. From having been the preternatural voice of a society, the protagonist becomes, in line 8, socially ordinary, and his style follows after this change without so much as a blink of the eye, and without missing a beat, as if it were instinctive with the superficial changes of a superficial, because conscious and careening, existence, a chameleon, a prestidigious tongue. By contrast, as poet and arranger, as subtle educator of the reader, operating independently of and as it were ahead of the autobiographical hero (who still has so very much to learn), the protagonist, a surrogate for Eliot, wants *us* to experience the brokenness of secular life directly through the splintered medium of his discourse, his discourses. His metastases—as inflicted by him, not suffered by him—prick our supposed assumption that human lives and discourses, our lives, our discourses, are reasonably coherent and coherently rational.

As we read on we come to still a third discourse in the paragraph, not counting the wild-card line in German, namely Marie's monologue, and here we are made aware of, made to hear, metastases within a single, and fairly ordinary, discourse. We see that the few lines of narrative reminiscence—those of the second discourse—are intended to set the stage for this third one, though not merely intended for that, and that the first two discourses, if related to one another, are in themselves coherent compared to Marie's artless broken monologue, to leave aside the art that the protagonist, or Eliot, used to fake it.

Marie, Marie (Heteroglossia, Metastasis, Woman, and Abjection)

Suddenly, the tape of that conversation in the Hofgarten, over coffee, begins to replay, and in mid-sentence (though perhaps Marie is always more or less in mid-sentence). Unaware that she is performing in another's monologue, let alone T. S. Eliot's poem, Marie does not introduce herself to the reader, she is found in the *medias res* of her own primary and indeed exclusive monologue. For the protagonist, whether he cannot help it or because he chooses to have it so, she is abruptly heard again, as if breaking in on the band of his own consciousness, a competitive frequency. Nor is she the first to usurp *his* monologue, which was, to begin with, virtually self-usurped, self-subverted, then distracted by a line of apparently overheard conversation, "Bin gar keine Russin, stamm' aus Litauen, echt deutsch." The "original" of Marie, Countess Marie Larisch (née Baroness von Wallersee) was not Lithuanian, but, instead, Bavarian, nor would it make much sense for her to shift as conversationalist from German to English in two successive lines, though it makes sense when Eliot does it *as poet*. The line in German betrays a petty, in fact false concern with worldly purity, purity of race, national clean and proper boundaries, a concern that, in the context of a poem in which the only clean and proper self is one unbounded before the Divine, is alone sufficient to explain its inclusion.

Once Marie herself is tracked in, she babbles on with childlike breathlessness: "And when we were children, staying at the archduke's, / My cousin's he took me out on a sled, / And I was frightened," etc. Marie, it is clear, could quickly become tiresome, her discourse is the opposite of the relentlessly summatory discourse of the *incipit*, proceeding as it does in low, metonymic skips and skids ("And"), and without the gracious fluidity of the no less metonymic discourse just before it.

Marie is "immediate" in the sense that we are granted no abstract approach to her, she just begins to talk, and not to us (whereas the protagonist had tacitly been addressing the reader). There is a correspondence between the way she appears to us and the way reality appears to her: both seem to come from nowhere, from around the corner, and to lack an organization, a center. Marie herself seems to know better who she *was* than who she is (like the German speaker, a prey to the political passion for mastery of boundaries, the countess, who was raised in the Hapsburg court, would become, in postwar years, a few years after Eliot met her in Munich, a general servant to a struggling Jewish family in Berlin).[11]

This person, who seems to be displaced from her own life and who speaks only after a voice in German protests being misplaced through the wrong national labelling, speaks again to the protagonist over an indefinite displacement of time and space, emerging out of the hinterlands, the no-man's-lands of memory. But she does not realize all this pathos of displacement, nor even that which she *could,* if a more honest and acute person, realize, that which she rather unwittingly divulges. Instead, she refuses the pathos of recognitions, even as she makes them available to us. She rushes into speech as if it were a train that would take her to a destination, to herself, but her identity is enfolded in her own memory, in a familial, noble, national cocoon and, a limp butterfly, she cannot find her way back. In contrast to the protagonist, who seems never to have been a child, who never hints of any existence prior to the adult experiences narrated in the poem, Marie is a stray outside her own childhood. That, at least, was *her.* That was real.

Now undefended except for a certain green obtuseness, now forlorn and only just realizing it, Marie drifts both in her speech and in her life, a diminished female analogue of Eliot's famous male drifters and strayers—Prufrock, Gerontion. She has only one subject, herself, because she has never quite found out what that is, or has forgotten what it was. Autobiographical like the earlier discourses but more decidedly the typical expression of a discrete personality, her discourse is pegged to a naïve "I" that is at once dominant and obliquely apologetic. The earlier plural pronouns are replaced by singular personal ones; the only "we" Marie acknowledges belonged to her childhood ("And when we were children"). Marie is forlorn exactly to the degree that she is stuck in personal pronouns. She has no inkling, surely, of the opposite of "I" and "me" and "my"—the "Thou" of the sacred. Delmore Schwartz depicted Eliot as "the international hero," oddly, since Eliot clearly equated internationalism with deracination. The true heroism, for Eliot, was to "question" the Absolute, however overwhelming the task, however incongruous in view of human vanity and abjection (Eliot himself sportively and youthfully wrote that he was the first-born child of the Absolute, turned out neatly in a flannel suit). Marie is international, but no heroine. The only true heroism is devo-

11. See William Empson, *Using Biography* (Cambridge, Mass.: Harvard University Press, 1984), 190.

tional. Marie is a waif with regard to the metaphysical. Indeed, perforce, since she is a woman: women, Eliot thought, are enemies of the Absolute, as are both society (though society in this poem is mostly women) and time.[12] Women, as Eliot portrays them in *The Waste Land,* are relentlessly self-referenced, whirlpools of vanity, Ophelias on their way down in their own nothingness.

So it is that, in the total context of Marie's monologue, the archduke's instruction, "Marie / Marie, hold on tight," appears ironic. Marie seems unable to let go of herself, at the same time that she is a deject from her own childhood. Marie cannot say from what she feels excluded, but the childlikeness of her discourse—the breathless polysyndeton of the first lines, the flit-brained parataxis of the final ones—reveals what it is, namely the excited openness of childhood. This openness is originally the mother, or it is she who defines it by giving it something to frame. In spitting out the mother, in becoming a "self," the child ultimately becomes, by the law of its own concern for a clean and proper identity, its own growth, an orphan. "I expel *myself,* I spit *myself* out," as Julia Kristeva puts it in her psychoanalytical essay on abjection, *Powers of Horror,* "I abject *myself,* within the same motion through which 'I' claim to establish *myself.*"[13] For psychoanalysis, and certainly for Eliot, abjection is the female not quite purified out of the self; and that female is, in the first instance, and perhaps in all, the mother. To be abject is to be born of a woman, born to die, incestuously hungering to return to the mother's body yet dreading the death that her body is, even its powers of reproduction, which would give still more life over to nothingness.

Abjection is a synecdochic crisis. A blur of separation/connection. Something both empowering and deadly has been refused. This results in the feeling both of being (at last) clean and proper, safely across the border from all that mires and compromises strength of self (the abject being "what disturbs identity, system, order. What does not respect borders, positions, rules")[14] and of being forlorn. The abject "becomes what culture, the *sacred,* must purge, separate, and banish so that it may establish itself as such in the universal logic of catharsis."[15] The writing of abstract discourse, with its clean symbolicity, its ab-

12. See Lyndall Gordon, *Eliot's Early Years* (New York: Oxford University Press, 1977), 23.

13. Julia Kristeva, *Powers of Horror: An Essay on Abjection,* trans. Leon S. Roudiez (New York: Columbia University Press, 1982), 3.

14. Ibid., 4.

15. Julia Kristeva, "Psychoanalysis and the Polis," in *The Politics of Interpretation,* ed. W. J. T. Mitchell (Chicago: University of Chicago Press, 1983), 96–97.

sence of breath (as distinct from Marie's breathlessness, as mimed by a fearlessly mimetic kind of writing), is one such catharsis.

What the protagonist responds to in Marie, the reason he gravitates toward her after attaining a certain metaphoric complicity with abjection (dull roots in the body of mother earth) is a soft, fuzzy, and innocuous image of his own abjection—his twinned sense of estrangement and of necessary, if costly, purge. He, too, is an outcast from something all-founding, real, by comparison with which the boasted "I" is always on the verge of give-away desperation. Is it the mother from whom he has strayed, or is it the Divine? He has strayed from the mother, but the mother herself, because the source of cyclical life, has strayed from the Divine. The way to the Real, to Being, is not back through the mother but further along the cruel, estranged path leading from her—along lines laid out by the father: lines of writing, asceticism, identity, order, positions, rules—toward the ideal, which is neither maternal nor paternal, which transcends the paternal roost of the superego as it does the mire of human veins, which has no bounds yet is perfectly pure, in a paradox that conscience (the consciousness of abjection) cannot understand. It combines the sentiment of Being originally connected with the mother and the purifying incorporeality of paternal Law into a single beatific whole.

In Marie's monologue itself, the ostensible figure of nostalgia is not the mother but a male figure, the masterful and royal cousin who feeds her instructions (as the Thunder will instruct the protagonist in part 5, which is also set in the freeing mountains). This cousin steers the sled (as later the Divine will navigate the "boat" of the protagonist's heart). In his company, which triangulates her relation to her mother, Marie is happy. Here is her rescuer, she feels free, she comes "alive" in his presence, under his direction (as, again, the protagonist *lives* only in his "surrender" to the Absolute). Marie's innocent babble enfolds a paradigm of what the protagonist seeks, a release, through "masculine" energies and guidance (the written discourse he quotes from is almost all by men), from the abjection of mortal necessity.

Abjection is synecdoche in that the "abject, not yet object, is anterior to the distinction between subject and object in normative language"[16]—the abject is, from the beginning, a grounding, and cannot be entirely abrogated: the "I" cannot take its base in thin air. "The nonobjectality of the archaic mother, the locus of needs, of attraction and repulsion, from which an object of forbidden desires arises,"[17] the

16. Ibid., 96.
17. Ibid.

abject is in one sense the "whole" that can never be successfully *seen,* or wholly felt, only felt like a dark fertile shadow on one side of one's being, the side opposite where the cold sun lights a path into the day, the city of men, the city of God. The protagonist will eventually choose between the "heart of darkness" (and Conrad had shown how abominably abject that could be) and the "heart of light." But for the time being, here in the capriciously sunlit past, he merely lounges in the superificial seasonal light of earth, listening to a woman who scarcely threatens his male composure (she is too much the child: and her model, Countess Marie Larisch, was roughly twice Eliot's age); who wants nothing from him as a man, except sympathy for her own crisis of living across the border from the archaic ground of being. Once she seemed to be rescued by a male, but down she went, down the slope of self-consuming sensation ("And down we went"). Still, the protagonist is sensitive enough to his likeness to Marie (though ultimately he himself will ascend into the mountains along a slope of asceticism) to recall her years later as an accidental female mirror of his own estrangement from the archaic mother and indeed from that rescuing knight, the father.

Synecdoche is the site of pathos, weakness is *the not being free* and *the not being happily held.* A synecdoche, as Paul de Man writes, is a "borderline figure"—one that "creates an ambivalent zone between metaphor and metonymy."[18] It knocks in vain on the door that leads from association to the self-same, a door in which metaphor stands expectant, arrested.

The anonymous aggregate of individuals evoked in the first seven lines of the poem is prodded by the spring rain into the ache of synecdochic connection, through memory and desire—desire itself being a circular return from regressive memory, a going forward to find what the incest taboo shrilly declares is not back there, in the dark. The gone and the dead talk, would breed with the present and the living: even sexless Marie plucks the protagonist back to attend, reattend, to her baffled desire. What she perhaps misses ("I read, most of the night, and go south in the winter") is sex, but sex as Foucault says recent centuries have formed it, as "the most speculative, most ideal" element in a secular deployment of sexuality:

It is through sex . . . that each individual has to pass in order to have access to his own intelligibility (seeing that it is both the hidden aspect and the generative principle of meaning), to the whole of his body (since it is a real

18. Paul de Man, *Allegories of Reading: Figural Language in Rousseau, Nietzsche, Rilke, and Proust* (New Haven: Yale University Press, 1979), 63n.

and threatened part of it, while symbolically constituting the whole), to his identity (since it joins the force of a drive to the singularity of a history). Through a reversal that doubtless had its surreptitious beginnings long ago . . . we have arrived at the point where we expect our intelligibility to come from what was for many centuries thought of as madness; the plenitude of our body from what was long considered its stigma and likened to a wound; our identity from what was perceived as an obscure and nameless urge. . . . Hence the fact that over the centuries it has become more important than our soul.[19]

In the next verse paragraph, the protagonist will record his own recoil from the usurpation of the soul's supreme and ideal position by secularly magnified and idealized sex. In Marie, he simply attends to the pathos of its installment in the individual as an internal, imaginary element, as "the desire for sex," sex "as something desirable." It is with admirable delicacy that Eliot conveys *her* share in the belief that sex is "a truth every bit as precious as the one [people] had already demanded from the earth, the stars, and the pure forms of their thought" (Foucault). A cousin, a plummeting sled, a nostalgia for freedom in the mountains, a cold unanalyzable restiveness, and it is done. And through her share, the protagonist's, which is shakier, more tattered, ready to drop off like rags from a lean hermitic disposition.

Abjection and desire (as always a half-absence) are thus both from the mother: "There is nothing like the abjection of self," writes Kristeva, "to show that all abjection is in fact recognition of the *want* on which any being, meaning, language, or desire is founded."[20]

In *The Waste Land* the soul plies its way between two "unnameable" powers: on the one hand, the archaic mother, the darkness of the feminine, and on the other the pre- and transobjectal Absolute, the hermaphroditic or neuter heart of light.

But only the protagonist is a soul (in the allegory of part 5 he becomes its very type). That is, only he is conscious of the high dream that can replace the low dream of sex. More of the women in this poem are disenchanted with sensual romanticism than the men are, but they merely fall away from the low dream, lie inert like dropped puppets at its periphery, or pace about there in a baffled way. The "news" of the high dream never reaches them. Marie has come down from the heights of the low dream and cannot find her way up to anything else. She was moved by an invisible impersonal force, the exciting but lowering force of sex, at least losing ego-confinement in

19. Foucault, *The History of Sexuality*, 155–56.
20. Kristeva, *Powers of Horror*, 5.

that rush. Conversely, the protagonist will, in part 5, seek to lose himself in an unseen power through a transcendence of the low dream, an antisexual, anchoritic quest. So it is that the poem works and reworks its images, cleansing them of abjection through repeated washings, turning "Lilacs" into heroic "roots that clutch," a child's fear and joy into ecstatic terror of the sacred, a shower into heavenly rain, coffee into a sacral flow of the spirit, sunlight into the heart of light, broken speech into the Silence.

Meanwhile, Marie's speech is broken indeed. Not only does it begin abruptly (if with a pseudo-smoothing connective); once it gets started, it darts, and darts again, like a minnow that has lost its school. *Non sequitur* governs her monologue, just as it does the three- (or four-) discourse structure of the paragraph. Paradox and *non sequitur* between them divide up the opening block, the first saying that "happiness" (the low dream) is misery; the second, that a secular existence does not add up. Under the aegis of the first, the lovely *incipit* of Chaucer's *Canterbury Tales* (virtually the *incipit* of English poetry) is turned on its head in "April is the cruellest month." To rhyme "April" with "cruel"! April breeds lilacs out of the "dead land"? Isn't that a black magic? "Winter kept us warm"? Here logic grimaces. There is logical chagrin, too, in the fancy of feeding a little life with dried tubers. This approaches conundrum, a mad science. In all, a topsy-turviness. Even English prosody is queered as the first three lines fall a syllable short of iambic pentameter, in a resistant way, and the fourth—with its stubborn pull and push of monosyllables, "Dull roots with spring rain"—seems intractably to stop at the halfway point of a decasyllabic. The accentual tug and clot of "Dull roots" tries to hold its own against the resonant drumming of "spring rain," with only the filmy, flimsy "with" to stand in between. Deceptive Chaucerian beauty of measure is flouted, no line is an "expected" English line, love itself is not what the "dark shimmer of sex" portends.

Non sequitur surprises us with "Summer surprised us," imitatively in step. Here subtle scissors begin to cut away connections. Summer surprised us, yes, but with rain, not summeriness. We stopped? "And went on." The conjunction "and" seems absent-minded. Went on, moreover, "in sunlight." A sequence, then, of deadpan surprises. Reversals are simply not indicated as such, apart from the keying word "surprised." One thing at a time. And drank coffee. And talked for an hour. Nothing need, and nothing intends to, follow.

"Bin," for instance. The statement it introduces, "Bin gar keine Russin, stamm' aus Litauen," forms a "that's that" until we reach "echt deutsch"; there are Lithuanians who consider "echt deutsch" anything but Lithuanian. Political temporization? In any case, Marie, all temporization, does not follow from the German with her "And," nor her talk of the fright of sledding that leads, abruptly, to "In the mountains, there you feel free." Marie examines nothing; she only declares, and serially. The race-ahead-and-back-up grammar of "In the mountains, there you feel free" suggests—if not a too-literal translation of a German commonplace—a mind unused to thinking things through, to building syntactic scaffolds of order.[21] "I read much of the night" does not follow from "there you feel free" except at a level Marie in effect refuses to articulate. She rejects the chains of perceived connections: not "But now I only read,"; instead, "I read." Even the rhythm of the last line disavows any relation to the previous one: the excited jounce of "In the mountains, there you feel free" gives way to the nervous twinge of interruption in the bored, dismissive rhythms of "I read, much of the night, and go south in the winter." "Read" takes a somewhat embarrassed stress, whereas "there" in "In the mountains, there you feel free" rejoices in its accent. So, she reads much of the night. What does she do during the day? Her "and" makes as if to tell, but, instead, she appends "go south in the winter," a baffling shift from the diurnal to the seasonal. The final line is even out of sorts with itself. Why does Marie (or the protagonist for her) set off "much of the night," but not the parallel phrase "in the winter"? The architecture of the sentence appears "forgetful." Marie shelters in the unreal, the chaotic, the loose-leaved. "The real is the organized," Eliot remarks in *Knowledge and Experience.* "And this statement is metaphysics."[22]

Marie is not to be heard from again, even though she has the last word in the paragraph. She is not answered by the protagonist, rather she is contained by him, he has incorporated her: his memory like an infant's mouth sucking at his own experience. Marie is known only through her speech; for the protagonist her being is entirely verbal (and, oral, regressive, she too lives off of memory). Whereas the polyphonic writer "proceeds from an assumption of *equal rights* for simultaneously existing, experiencing persons," or so Bakhtin would say,[23] Eliot is really no more polyphonic than he is Menippean, which is to say he appears to be either only if his protagonist is denied his meta-

21. The Marie of Countess Marie Larisch's *My Past: Reminiscences of the Courts of Austria and Bavaria; Together with the True Story of the Events Leading up to the Tragic Death of Rudolph, Crown Prince of Austria* (New York: G. P. Putnam's Sons, 1913) is what used to be called a simple soul, as her gushy title indicates, but less childlike than Eliot's character, and somewhat more coherent at narrative.

22. Eliot, *Knowledge and Experience,* 82.

23. Mikhail Bakhtin, *Problems of Dostoevsky's Poetics,* ed. and trans. Caryl Emerson (Minneapolis: University of Minnesota Press, 1984), 37.

physics, his organization, his subordination of everything in the poem
to the story (though at first it hardly seems a story) of his own soul.
Marie is in the poem, his poem, because she means something to him
(even in the sentimental sense of the phrase: surely William Empson is
mistaken to conclude that Eliot despises her and sums her up as "stony
rubbish," a phrase that may apply, but not in the sense of a thrown
stone; a phrase that lies far to the other side of yet another, and this
time typographically marked, metastasis). Marie is the pathetic female
counterpart of the protagonist's own secular estrangement, a soft version not particularly upsetting to contemplate, a gentle introduction to
the still more bleak-voiced women in the poem, a retardedly youngish
version of them, a slow start.

What Are the Roots That Clutch

What are the roots that clutch, what branches grow
Out of this stony rubbish? Son of man,
You cannot say, or guess, for you know only
A heap of broken images, where the sun beats,
And the dead tree gives no shelter, the cricket no relief,
And the dry stone no sound of water. Only
There is shadow under this red rock,
(Come in under the shadow of this red rock),
And I will show you something different from either
Your shadow at morning striding behind you
Or your shadow at evening rising to meet you;
I will show you fear in a handful of dust.
               Frisch weht der Wind
               Der Heimat zu
               Mein Irisch Kind,
               Wo weilest du?
"You gave me hyacinths first a year ago;
"They called me the hyacinth girl."
—Yet when we came back, late, from the Hyacinth garden,
Your arms full, and your hair wet, I could not
Speak, and my eyes failed, I was neither
Living nor dead, and I knew nothing,
Looking into the heart of light, the silence.
Oed' und leer das Meer.

The Poem's Crux

This second paragraph (etymologically, a peripheral writing, a writing
aside, as all writing in *The Waste Land* is) develops, by dramatizing,
what is implicit in the first one: the protagonist's piercing disenchantment with human beings as objects of demand and desire, in particular

with the waste place of romantic entanglements. The protagonist recalls a fatal moment when he felt cut off from a woman, indeed from all women, through an inexplicable metaphysical castration. This lesson in the desolation of human and natural love, the total demand of Divine love—for it came to that—was a seed that fell on ground ready for it, but a strange seed that would require darkness in which to grow. Having looked into the "heart of light" and been blinded by it, the protagonist has no choice but to let the "roots" of his new spiritual life clutch, its "branches" grow, in a fertile area of himself to which his arid conscious mind has little access. This benighted conscious mind, this mind too much in the hot ordinary light, is first addressed by its own sacral depths as "Son of man." (The protagonist is at least canny enough about himself to accomplish *that*.) Then this conscious mind, still that of a young man courting the hyacinth girl, recalls an incident a year in the past, the instant when, outside the Hyacinth garden, the supernatural seed fell into the soil of his soul, the moment when abjection was made speechless in him by a loving call from the infinitely eloquent Eternal Silence.

Guilt was tacit in the way Marie had reentered the protagonist's consciousness—the guilt of a mother's child, guilt over a careful remoteness from, indeed an abandonment of, women: one that does not at all keep him from lingering near them, as if still hoping, against all odds, to eradicate, with their help, his primal want. (Eliot, or so notes his biographer Peter Ackroyd, turned morose when deprived of the company of women.)[24] Marie, who was once partnered by a male in a rush of physical sensation, once alive, once thrilled, now appears to live and travel alone, untouched at night, a woman in whom desire is almost successfully repressed, her very search for warmth a routine ("I . . . go south in the winter"). As for the "hyacinth girl," she whose arms the protagonist first loaded with cut hyacinths a year ago, she is abandoned, as it were, before our very eyes, and by a man who can no longer either see or know her, a man to whom she has become, precisely, nothing, her youth and beauty and vivacity no more to him than drops of dew or rain accidentally clinging to hyacinths, those symbols of a startled blackout and subsequent surprised resurrection into the blaze of spring light.

The framing lines from Wagner's libretto for *Tristan und Isolde* provide compass points for interpretation. In the first, beginning "*Frisch weht der Wind,*" a young sailor at the start of act 1 sings the song of a sailor who pities the woman ("Mein Irisch Kind") who

24. Peter Ackroyd, *T. S. Eliot: A Life* (New York: Simon and Schuster, 1984), 59.

vainly awaits his loving return: "Woe, ah woe for my child!" (Wehe! Wehe, du Wind / Weh'! Ach wehe, mein Kind!")[25] Woe, too, to the hyacinth girl, she who does not know what catastrophe awaits her in and because of love. As for the final line from the libretto, "*Oed' und leer das Meer,*" it reports the finding of the shepherd set to look for the ship bearing Isolde with her healing arts to the fatally wounded Tristan: empty and waste the sea. A woman's love cannot save a man, nor a man's love a woman, human love will not cure mortality, the only heart that *will* sail triumphantly on eternal seas is one navigated by the Divine: "The boat responded / Gaily, to the hand expert with sail and oar / The sea was calm, your heart would have responded / Gaily, when invited, beating obedient / To controlling hands" (part 5).

Even without these hints, the passage declares itself unequivocally against the natural and the human orders. Their fusing representative, that pseudo-floral nymph the "hyacinth girl"—what is she that she should captivate the protagonist, bind his soul? Listen to her speak: "You gave me hyacinths first a year ago: / They called me the hyacinth girl." Those are the only words the protagonist recalls from their conversation, and they are strategic for establishing that the relationship has had some duration and is already marked, weighed down, by the repetition of the natural cycle (for he has evidently given her hyacinths once again)—the cycle that the opening lines of the poem groan to acknowledge. They are merry words, but touched by anxiety. Already she is nostalgic for that fresher time, that "first" time, that moment pristine with the Edenic earliness of flower gathering and giving, and with Adamic naming ("They called me the hyacinth girl"). Already her happiness is referred away from the present. Has she sensed, latterly, a withdrawl in the protagonist (as his subsequent confession/disavowal suggests she ought to have)? Perhaps only just: her words instinctively act to call him back, back to the last moment when he seemed normally (with normal illusionism) near. But her words accomplish more than that—they are also instinct with abject narcissism. How she babbles on, he gave her *this* and they called her *that.* Her unbroken lines drop plumb into a vacuum of vanity. Less subtle than Marie, but hardly less childlike, she calls attention to herself as an object to be looked at, adorned, and, so to speak, dechristened and renamed as a pagan goddess. She is all complicity with the protagonist's instinct to "place" her beauty as one with the voluptuously vital and corruptible earth. She delights in her apotheosis as a vegeta-

25. Richard Wagner, *The Authentic Librettos of the Wagner Operas* (New York: Crown Publishers, 1938), 312.

tion nymph, she agrees to be this charming creature, this fertile object (a contradiction in terms), this paragon and natural wonder, the "hyacinth girl."

Unwittingly, she thus associates herself (as the protagonist's floral giving had associated her) with the tabooed mother object, the "object of forbidden desires" that emerges from "the nonobjectality of the archaic mother." And the mother means castration and death, the first doubly, because, "castrated" herself, she further castrates her son, and again doubly: through threatening to reabsorb him, unman him, and through his fear of punishment for forbidden desires. The mother is, in any case, the queen of the realm of objects. D. W. Winnicott traces awareness of objects to the child's slipping symbiosis with the mother. What he calls a "transitional object"—the first real kind of object—is symbolically mother-and-me, but mostly uncathected thing.[26] Thenceforth object relations become melting ice cubes. Always they threaten to return the "subject," now self-realized through knowing a world of objects, to a fund of anguish, the *want* of which objects are the unsympathetic outer face. The object relation, observes Lacan, is always "a means of masking, of parrying the fundamental fund of anguish."[27] Narcissism *is* this want, the hyacinth girl could not do more than she does to alert the protagonist to her own fund of anguish, to her inability to wipe out his. Like Marie, she is a nothing who asks for attention from a nothing. She does not feel naturally full and fertile, rather she asks to be invested with this feeling; she looks at it, enviously, from outside.[28] Fill my arms with hyacinths. Call me the hyacinth girl. To which the protagonist, up to a certain failing point, was responding, Be for me the hyacinth girl, flourish for me, stimulate me, bear triumphantly from the natural garden an armful of indomitable phalli. But as a sort of reaper of phalli, she cannot fail to arouse his incest and castration dread. And as a nature goddess, she cannot fail to attract his nausea for the cyclical naughtening (in Heideggerean parlance) of nature, which erects only to bring down. Metonymic adjuncts to begin with, floral metaphors, the flowers take her over, smother her humanness, till she becomes an expression of them, a nymph, or rather a would-be nymph, a theatrical one, breathlessly remarking: If only it *could* be so!

Thus self-exposed, the hyacinth girl ceases to enchant the pro-

26. D. W. Winnicott, *Playing and Reality* (New York: Basic Books, 1971), chap. 1.
27. See Kristeva, *Powers of Horror,* 33.
28. "Abjection is therefore a kind of *narcissistic crisis:* . . . abjection gives narcissism (the thing and the concept) its classification as 'seeming'" (Kristeva, *Powers of Horror,* 14).

tagonist (though he could not have *put* it quite so, he *shows* it as such). Whether as a direct result of discovering the nothingness of romantic love (its foundation in two narcissistic wants), or coincidentally, through an accident of timing he then discovers the Absolute, or it discovers him with a sudden blow comparable to the one Yeats depicts in "Leda and the Swan." Rushing in to fill the vacuum left by human relationships, it attacks his senses and his psyche—to both of which it is entirely foreign, being neither natural nor mental—with a merciless dismissal and offers instead, *is*, a powerfully attracting numinous fullness and love, Being Itself. The protagonist's natural and human faculties cannot adequate the supernatural and the superhuman, and that is why he cannot see, speak, understand, is neither alive nor dead. It is something else in him that looks into the heart of light, that hears what cannot be heard, the silence.

So I would reverse the usual reading, which indicts the protagonist for a failure to love naturally and humanly, and note of the passage that it marks a metaphysical success—one involving only a *due* failure of natural and human powers. Brief as it is for the protagonist, and baffling, it is also wonderfully founding, he *sees* being, and as a slip-about heteroglossic theater of words, he knows the absoluteness, at last, of the pre- and transverbal, the comparative nothingness of language. Robert Langbaum's suggestion that *The Waste Land* is about "sexual failure as a sign of spiritual failure" should thus be stood on its head. The poem, I believe, is about spiritual success which renders sexual failure nugatory, indeed, expects it.

"Sex and religion," Langbaum elaborates, "spring from the same impulses"; "sexual and religious fulfillment are related."[29] Yet Eliot's sense of the matter was I think directly opposite, traditionally ascetic and not romantically heretical, neo-pagan. Eliot's use of what began as nature-cult material must not mislead us on this point. Pagan and ascetic metaphysics do not mix, "the heart of light" does not fall on hyacinth gardens, the silence cannot hear the words "I love you." Between the vital and the Absolute there can be no relation; the soul is founded in a categorical either/or. On this the ancient wisdom of East and West agree, O Lord Thou pluckest me out, burning burning burning burning.

29. Robert Langbaum, "New Modes of Characterization in *The Waste Land*," in *Eliot in His Time: Essays on the Fiftieth Anniversary of the Waste Land*, ed. A. Walton Litz (Princeton: Princeton University Press, 1973), 113. Compare A. D. Moody: "[The protagonist's] mind, that would be whole and entire in love, becomes intensely aware of being out of love, dissociated, and unable to achieve the mysterious sea-change" (*Thomas Stearns Eliot: Poet* [Cambridge: Cambridge University Press, 1979], 87).

Eliot had rehearsed the protagonist's peripeteia near the garden in "La Figlia che Piange," a poem of callow brilliance included in his youthful 1917 collection, *Prufrock and Other Observations*. There, in hysterical stage direction, a voice instructs a girl to "Clasp your flowers to you with a pained surprise," adding, "So I would have had her stand and grieve, / So he would have left / As the soul leaves the body torn and bruised, / As the mind deserts the body it has used."[30] This tentative element of "would" becomes a "done" in *The Waste Land,* though one that—after the first as-it-were unearned transcendence—takes some doing on the protagonist's part, some self-examination (as in the interrogation of himself as "Son of man," of which more in a moment). In the other direction chronologically, Eliot declared unequivocally in his essay on Baudelaire, in 1930, the inadequacy of human relations to human passion, the consequent sadness of romantic poetry, which disbelieves "in any further object for human desires than that which, being human, fails to satisfy them."[31]

The hierophany that the protagonist experiences near the garden shatters his youth. It establishes Reality as the One, and so renders unreal everything palpable, everything multiple. (Eliot had rehearsed this idea in his paraphrase of Bradley: "Reality is one. It must be single, because plurality, taken as real, contradicts itself." But whereas Bradley's Absolute cannot be apprehended, the protagonist's is mystically revealed.)[32] The hyacinths are mythically allied to the protagonist, not the girl, in his hidden figuration as the hyacinth boy: caught in a rivalry among three doting gods for his love—the sun god Apollo, the wind gods Boreas and Zephyrus—Hyacinthus was killed, so the story goes, when the wind gods blew on a discus Apollo tossed to the youth, causing it to strike his head. From the spilt blood grew the flower that bears his name. So it was that, looking at a disc thrown by the sun the youth felt his eyes fail, he knew nothing, and was thenceforth neither alive nor dead. And so with the protagonist, his human capacity for relationship dies when a jealous God dazzles his faculties with a blow of unearthly light.

The protagonist is thus brought—for an immeasurable moment, or eternity—to the end of desire. But "Desire itself is movement / Not in

30. T. S. Eliot, *The Complete Poems and Plays 1909–1950* (New York: Harcourt, Brace and Co., 1952), 20.

31. T. S. Eliot, *Selected Essays* (London: Faber and Faber, 1958), 428.

32. For a recent discussion of Bradley's conception of the Absolute, see Michael H. Levenson, *A Genealogy of Modernism: A Study of English Literary Doctrine 1908–1922* (Cambridge: Cambridge University Press, 1984), 177–78.

itself desirable," in the words of "Burnt Norton." What is superior to
it is "Love," for "Love is itself unmoving, / Only the cause and end of
movement." In the aspect of time Love is "Caught in the form of
limitation / Between un-being and being."[33] Neither living nor dead.
All the same, caught between un-being and being though the protagonist himself might be, he is opened, for an instant, to the purely
spiritual: to a heart made of light. In an essay on Dante, Eliot takes
note of "that imagery of *light* which is the form of certain types of
mystical experience" and praises Dante's ability to "realize the inapprehensible in visual images."[34] "Heart of light" is a lovely invention,
it seems visual but cannot be visualized. The lines in "Burnt Norton"
on the pool that "filled with water out of sunlight," its surface glittering "out of the heart of light," preserve the ambiguity. Light issues
from a "heart" that is itself "of light" yet more than light, a heart,
unwordable Love. Again: "After the kingfisher's wing / Has answered
light to light, and is silent, the light is still / At the still point of the
turning world."[35]

"Objects cannot arise without names," Eliot observes in *Knowledge and Experience,* but on the other hand "names never spring up
without objects" and what is objectal about "the silence"?[36] The Absolute is not a *that* (though it might be called a Thou, the word is more
Western than Eastern and Eliot has spiritually journeyed to the East in
this poem, without, as will be elaborated, renouncing altogether his
Christian sense of beauty, or the Bible). In Bradley's words, the Absolute is a "positive non-distinguished non-relational whole," the only
real "immediate experience"—for Bradley, an experience at best only
approximated through the correctional maneuvers of consciousness,
maturing ideas into concepts.[37] Not the unconscious but, Eliot says,
the "not conscious": "Experience, we may assert, both begins and
ends in something which is not conscious. And that this 'not conscious' is not what we call 'unconscious' should be sufficiently obvious. For what we term unconscious is simply an element *in*
experience which arises in *contrast* to other elements in experience. It
refers either to certain supposed mental entities which guide or influence our conscious actions . . . . [or to] that which as 'feeling' melts
imperceptibly into a physiological background."[38] Here Eliot is cau-

33. Eliot, *Complete Poems and Plays 1909–1950,* 122.
34. Eliot, *Selected Essays,* 267–68.
35. Eliot, *Complete Poems and Plays 1909–1950,* 118, 121.
36. Eliot, *Knowledge and Experience,* 133.
37. Ibid., 31.
38. Ibid., 28–29.

tiously tracing out and agreeing with Bradley, keeping clear of mystical terms but perhaps not of the thing itself. In *The Waste Land* he is
less cautious, the "not conscious" becomes the silence, the heart of
light.

Art and Silence

But perhaps Eliot's order is the truly climactic one, beginning with the
light and proceeding to the silence. For the silence is the harder
positivity to conceive. It not only chastises human complacencies of
speech in a manner that "the heart of light" does not so rudely effect
in relation to the lusts of the eyes; it taxes the human imagination as to
what Fullness, what Being, might be. Language, a fetishism (as Kristeva suggests)[39] disguising a fundamental want, fumbles in the
vicinity, which is actually everywhere, of the Absolute, and speaks of
looking into "the silence," and hesitates, too, over distinguishing the
"silence" from "the heart of light," virtually making a synesthesia of
light/silence to express the inexpressible. Confronting what is not articulated in itself but wholly one and the same throughout, and the
complete antithesis of want, syntax hesitates, phrases turn into puzzles. "To transcend humanity," said Dante in regard to Beatrice, "may
not be told in words."[40] What, then, of this Beatrice of light and silence, this further Beatrice, this reality that admits only the personification of "the heart," if even so much.

The Waste Land subscribes to, cultivates, what Susan Sontag calls
the second and more recent version of the modern myth of art (the first
being the treatment of "art as an *expression* of human consciousness,
consciousness seeking to know itself"): namely, the myth that "art is
not consciousness per se, but rather its antidote—evolved from within
consciousness itself," and serving "the mind's need or capacity for
self-estrangement.":

The newer myth, derived from a post-psychological conception of consciousness, installs within the activity of art many of the paradoxes involved
in attaining an absolute state of being described by the great religious my-
stics. As the activity of the mystic must end in a *via negativa*, a theology of
God's absence, a craving for the cloud of unknowing beyond knowledge and

---

39. "A representative of the paternal function takes the place of the good maternal
object that is wanting. There is language instead of the good breast. Discourse is being
substituted for maternal care . . ." (Kristeva, *Powers of Horror*, 45). Again, "is not
exactly language our ultimate and inseparable fetish. And language, precisely, is based
on fetishist denial ('I know that, but just the same,' 'the sign is not the thing, but just the
same,' etc.) and defines us in our essence as speaking beings" (ibid., 37).

40. Quoted in Eliot, *Selected Essays*, 265.

for the silence beyond speech, so art must tend toward anti-art, the elimination of the "subject" (the "object," the "image") . . . and the pursuit of silence.[41]

Of course, as Sontag adds, "the 'spirit' seeking embodiment in art clashes with the 'material' character of art itself. Art is unmasked as gratuitousness . . . the artist's activity is cursed with mediacy. Art becomes the enemy of the artist, for it denies him the realization—the transcendence—he desires." The curse of mediacy is illustrated, and all but advertised, by the clumsiness of the expression "looking into the heart of light, the silence." In this poem, Eliot's apparent "reluctance to communicate," his apparent ambivalence about being understood (his imitation of Hieronymo in Thomas Kyd's *The Spanish Tragedy*, who "fits" his despised audience through a deceptive play of many unknown tongues) is part and parcel of his attempt to turn art itself into a deliverance from words, an exercise in asceticism. "The characteristic aim of modern art," writes Sontag, "to be *unacceptable* to its audience, inversely states the unacceptability to the artist of the very presence of an audience—audience in the modern sense, an assembly of voyeuristic spectators."[42] In *The Waste Land* this aggression against audience, medium, "art"—deployed through allusions, metastases, unknown tongues, startling addresses to the reader, cryptic forms such as allegory (a genre of retreat from the outer world), dismantlings of narrativity—transmutes a phobia of abjection, transmutes objection, into a classical taciturnity, a queasily seductive intricacy and maze that would leave the reader either bewildered by the signs of abjection, at best shocked by recognition, or purged, released by art.

Is it not rash to conclude that Eliot succeeds as an artist to the degree that he fails of transcendence? Kristeva comments:

> The various means of *purifying* the abject—the various catharses—make up the history of religions, and end up with that catharsis par excellence called art, both on the far and near side of religion. Seen from that standpoint, the artistic experience, which is rooted in the abject it utters and by the same token purifies, appears as the essential component of religiosity. That is perhaps why it is destined to survive the collapse of the historical forms of religions.[43]

What is art, then, a gestural or a substantial purification? Built of elements of symbolicity, it stands over against the world on a raised

41. Susan Sontag, "The Aesthetics of Silence," in *Styles of Radical Will* (New York: Delta, 1970), 4–5.
42. Ibid., 8.
43. Kristeva, *Powers of Horror*, 17.

ground. It purifies the senses in the unifying, self-ordering, and where language is concerned abstract medium of the imagination. Conversely, it purifies ideas by running them through the refreshing stream of the senses. The mind and the senses die in one another's life, each sacrificing to the other, balancing obedience with power. This order of catharsis is only a halfway measure compared to the highest goal of asceticism, the most backward of analogues and imitations. Still, it doesn't altogether make of art "a false way." Art is, rather, a half-step.

Ascetic art both courts and forestalls, or displaces, "the silence." *The Waste Land* is nothing but words, nor are many of the words new—they make other voices, texts, sound again, increasing the din of art, multiplying art within a single work. On the other hand, the words are arranged reticently, silence is invited to take up quarters in the interstices between blocks of lines. The metastases are internalized representations of asceticism—fasts of discourse (of narrativity, mental understanding); art's own self-reductions, its sacrifices in the name (if the name only) of silence. The same is true of the ambiguity with regard to the speaking "subjects," these subjects seeming already impoverished as "identities," already estranged through a helpless drift into anonymity, or, as in the cases of Madame Sosostris and the protagonist, already self-confessedly arbitrary, a matter of role-playing. The slashes in the discourse of the poem would let in the silence, the light of otherness. At least—as a more practical aim—it would discipline and keep back language's immodest program of competence. (Here the *new* competence lies, in part, in the elisions and cryptifying arrangements of "irrepressible" spurts of language.)

The poem thus dramatizes the polarity of silence that is always implicit in language, and without which, as Sontag says, "the whole system of language would fail." "Silence remains, inescapably, a form of speech . . . and an element in a dialogue." It "never ceases to imply its opposite and to depend on its presence."[44] In order to perceive silence, we must retain an acute sense of the speech (or music) that marks it off. Ascetic art thus not only displaces the silence, but empowers it. The more *The Waste Land* makes us attend to its words—and it is a machine for eliciting such attention—the more it edges them with silence. We feel the strain they endure under their own suspicion that (in Samuel Beckett's words) "there is nothing to express, nothing from which to express, no power to express, no desire to express, together with the obligation to express." They must try to stimulate us to an awareness of a potentially crushing or swallowing silence, but can only do so through speech (the conjuration of Voice), since, as Sontag

44. Sontag, *Styles of Radical Will*, 11.

says, "silence doesn't exist in a literal sense . . . as the *experience* of an audience. It would mean that the spectator was aware of no stimulus or that he was unable to make a response. But this can't happen; nor can it even be induced programmatically. . . . As a property of the work of art itself, silence can exist only in a cooked or nonliteral sense."[45]

So, a dialectical project, *The Waste Land* speaking in contrast to silence (a full and pure silence) for the sake of the illumination of contrast.

Son of Man (Phobia and Speech)

Meanwhile, the protagonist is still very much a man of words, poet and poem at once. And how admirable seems his verbal dexterity as, having already forged (in both senses) three styles in the first verse paragraph, he here creates three more, again throwing in German lines, as well. He may try to evade the limitations of discourse by means of these stylistic, language, and vocal shifts, but a chameleon is a chameleon whether red, brown, or green, indeed all but a *number* of chameleons, a colorist crowd.

"The writer," notes Kristeva, "is a phobic who succeeds in metaphorizing in order to keep from being frightened to death; instead he comes to life again in signs." It is "want that positions sign, subject, and object." Not only is the phobic object "a proto-writing"; "phobia does not disappear but slides beneath language." "Any practice of speech, inasmuch as it involves writing, is a language of fear."[46] "An overmastery of the linguistic and rhetorical code"—what is this but mere "know-how" where phobia is concerned? Still it cannot utter what is "not yet a place," the "no-grounds" of fear. We cannot tell what assurance of being himself the protagonist can possibly entertain, what "untouchable, unchangeable, immortal" *being* he can imagine himself to have, when his voice dips now into this watercolor and now into that and the self-portrait is streaking down the page. Nor can we tell what must now frighten him most, the abysmal abjection of the archaic mother (including the "nothing" of the maternal phallus, the woman as phallic reaper), or the sensual devastations practiced by a terrorizing beyond. The Nothing and the All bracket his life, x's barbing it from opposite sides, keeping him from peace as and in "himself," goading him into seeing the arbitrariness and fragility of borders.

For the second and last time he structures a paragraph—if "structure" is not too clumsy, too old-fashioned, too orderly a word—in

45. Ibid., 9–10.
46. Kristeva, *Powers of Horror*, 38.

two contrasting master styles: one, again, all lifted, transmuted voice, and the other, again, colloquial, and divided and varied between a pair of voices in miscarried dialogue. One of the latter is, still again, quoted, carried into the text by a breeze of memory, and soon blown away. While it lives, it is entirely a presence, present tensed: socially projected, vivacious, in a way the protagonist's own voice is not (could hardly rise or deign to be). The latter narrates again conventionally in the past tense, scene-setting and now drama- and soul-sketching, too. The protagonist speaks in the past tense as if somehow posthumous (or neither living nor dead). By contrast, the voice that addresses him in the opening portion, booming, awful, is quick with the present tense, articulating the secret part of him that is indeed alive.

What the protagonist in some way saw (beyond seeing, beyond knowing) in the fading natural light of day was a no-thing before which the hyacinths, blazing badges of spring, hence of natural resurrection, and the hyacinth girl, their attendant genius of vain beauty and buoyant freshness, were yet jointly exposed as a desert. More than an oasis of metalight, it was, so it seems, the loving heart of everything—Primal Freshness, Loveliness purified of all voluptuousness, Intelligence too perfect, too indivisible, for articulation: forever silent. What was then set stirring in him may be figured by a new growth, borrowed from the fertility cults, but cannot be *named* by it, and exists across an absolute, nature- and mind- obliterating gap from it such as T. E. Hulme, to Eliot's approval, insisted always lies between the vital and the religious (quasi-geometrical) realms.[47]

The question he asks himself is rhetorical, punitive: "What are the roots that clutch, what branches grow / Out of this stony rubbish?" *Of course* the profane part of him does not know, nor can guess. Or put it that the latter does not want such knowledge, fearing its consequences: fear in a handful of dust, carnal deprivation, the sensory waste-ground that forms the green spring of the spirit. What is Not Conscious in the protagonist reproves what is cravenly conscious (and not). The God in him addresses the man, the life in him the murderous aridity, the living coherence the rubbish he is as a historical being, his heteroglossic heap of discourses.

The reticent scorn of the prophetic voice is the other side of the evasions of its addressee: the minatory mystery of the first mocks and increases the phobias of the second. "Know ye not, that so many of us as were baptized into Jesus Christ were baptized into his death? There-

<hr />

47. See T. E. Hulme, *Speculations* (New York: Harcourt, Brace [first pub. 1924]), 11.

fore we are buried with him by baptism into death: that like as Christ was raised up from the dead by the glory of the Father, even so we also should walk in newness of life"—the prophetic voice does not say anything so reasonably clear as these words of Paul's (Romans 6:3–4) but, instead, speaks cryptically of "your shadow" and a "red rock" and "fear in a handful of dust." Phobia clings to the "your" if not to the "shadow"; phobia cringes at the "red"; phobia always *knew* it was from the dust and to dust would return. The knowing voice (the protagonist ambushing his phobias in an attempt to frighten them into wisdom) is all forked tongue, part threat, part lure. So in the line "Come in under the shadow of this red rock," Isaiah's harsh command, "Enter into the rock and hide thee in the dust, for fear of the Lord" (Isaiah 2:10) fights for dominance with his eloquent and consoling "And a man [Christ] shall be as . . . rivers of water in a dry place, as the shadow of a great rock in a weary land" (32:2). The red rock, then, might be the oven of the mother's body, thus death, or it might be the blood sacrifice of Christ, and thus a different death, and the protagonist is saying to himself, "Choose between death and Death, life and Life. More: "how leave the new stirrings in yourself in so waste an internal region? '[God] is green before the sun, and his branch shooteth forth in his garden. His roots are wrapped about the heap, and seeth the place of stones' (Job 8:16–17): as God, so you. Clutch and grow."

Out of This Stony Rubbish

The stony rubbish, overwhelmingly negative though it seems, bears a potentially redemptive meaning: that of a *chosen* desolation of the senses. Just here, in this hardest of places, this landscape of "no relief," a saint might thrive, the roots of his faith clutching despite the barren soil prepared by history, the inevitably failing soil of the senses; its branches growing despite the extreme heat of a wholly material sun, antithesis of the Son, fiery emblem of cyclical mortalities, births back into sidling deaths.

The doubleness of "this red rock" is thus matched by that of "stony rubbish," for everything is double where, on the plane of imagery, an elective and a natural wastefulness (of what is of no heavenly use) overlap. The desert opposes the illusory garden of sensory happiness as, on the one hand, its inevitable consequence and, on the other, as the only site of spirituality. It is both the truth behind the mirage of the oasis of human sexual love and refuge from the unintended barrenness and disorder of a life lived (or died) outside the One.

The heap of broken images falls from off the idolatrous shelf where the senses had placed the hyacinth girl. It holds the rubbish of once-intact, *holding* female images, or so suggests the passage in Ecclesiastes that is paraphrased here, with its golden bowl and pitcher broken at the fountain (just as Eliot's cricket comes from Ecclesiastes' grasshopper, his dead tree from its flourishing almond). The female vessel (the womb, female sanctity, life) cannot remain whole, cannot hold the formless waters of the Spirit. It is to Formlessness itself that one must go (more strictly, to its hidden "heart") if one would drink of the Fountain. What had been half-revealed near the garden was the substance of the preacher's counsel, "Remember now thy Creator in the days of thy youth, while the evil days come not, nor the years draw nigh, when thou shalt say, I have no pleasure in them," with its addendum, "and desire shall fail" (Ecclesiastes 12:1,5). The protagonist appears now to be in the desert both of his inattention to the mystical illumination and, precisely, of his almost unwitting obedience to it, his inability to be sensual in good conscience (not that this particular sensibility could ever have been that), his awareness, such as it is, of inexplicable growth somewhere in the vicinity of his conscious death.

Student of both the Bible and Jessie Weston's *From Ritual to Romance* as he is, the protagonist may find even in the epithet "Son of man" an occasion for hope, belief in his capacity to climb out of the rubbish. Not only did Christ seem to speak of himself once as the Son of man (Matthew 8:19–20); Jessie Weston notes that Hippolytus, bishop of Portus in the third century, spoke of the Naasenes, one of the earliest Christian sects, as honoring "Man, and Son of Man," as "the Logos of all universals." "They think," Hippolytus added, "that the Gnosis of this Man is the beginning of the possibility of knowing God, saying, 'The beginning of Perfection is the Gnosis of Man, but the Gnosis of God is perfected Perfection.'" And the central doctrine of the Hellenistic mysteries, according to Reitzenstein (whom Weston also quotes), is that "Man, the Heavenly Man, the Son of God, . . . descends and becomes a slave of the Fate Sphere," and needs, in consequence, to win back his own freedom.[48] Insofar as Eliot is "Christian," he is Gnostically so, at least in *The Waste Land*. But with what nausea he seems to look across the chasm between "Son of man" and "Son of Man." "The beginning of Perfection is the Gnosis of Man"—how this assertion contradicts his experience of man as all lost from perfection.

48. Jessie Weston, *From Ritual to Romance* (Garden City: Doubleday, 1957), 151–54.

Hence his need of the less indulgently anthropomorphic theology of the East. His blistered and blistering antihumanism, his disenchantment with all that "man" conveys, required this passage to India.

Less than a slave of the Fate Sphere, man himself is part rubbish, stonily resistant to the solvents of Perfection. Shape-surrendering water, inhuman water, not the Christ, is the image of perfection required to chasten him. Even the image of a desert tree is preferable, with the understanding that its roots and branches belong not to nature but to what Hippolytus (telling of Phrygian mysteries) called "the Blessed Nature above of the super-Cosmic." In lower fertility worship, Generation made love to the Soul (Aphrodite desires Adonis). But in the higher cults, the god is emasculated, the Mother of "Aeonian space. . . calls back the masculine power of Soul to herself."[49] Castration here, Life there. With branches already shooting forth from the ruins of Generation.

You Cannot Know (Heteroglossia)

Here, then, is "authoritative speech"? If "the silence" sets the (inhuman) criterion of truth, then speech can only fake authority. Perhaps that is why this half-biblical voice is theatrical: it persuades of its "absolute" authority through techniques of intimidation. In fact, it is a species of social discourse. "Verbal discourse," as Bakhtin writes, "is a social phenomenon—social through its entire range and in each and every of its factors."[50] The admonitory voice may be nondialogic, it may not expect *back* talk, but, patterned on biblical prophecy, on the mediation of Divine Displeasure through social dialect, it knows its audience, means to strike fear into it, to prompt obedience, to be inscribed in the memory. Addressing "Son of man," a cryptic telescoping singular that virtually implicates every male listener, disallowing exception, it lies on the page like an open trap, awaiting its victims indiscriminately. The protagonist may aim it all toward himself, but not toward any accidents of personality, rather toward his natural and human (historical) status as Son of man.

While foregoing special script, this "authoritative" speech nonetheless comes to us, to "you," across a magisterial distance and as a "compact and indivisible mass," in Bakhtin's description of such speech; yet it shifts about in taunting, ambushing ways, is insidiously mobile rather than "static and dead."[51] An allusive authority? Practicing indirection? The "elitist" Eliot in prophetic form? Yes, this voice is

49. Ibid., 155.
50. Bakhtin, *The Dialogic Imagination*, 259.
51. Ibid., 342–43.

out of the same modernist cavern as the other voices in the poem, but what they achieve in combination, a glancingness of meaning, it achieves on its own. Echoic (and not only of itself), it is as full of paraphrase and quotation as daily speech is, and even more full of the Bible than nineteenth-century American literature is. (And *The Waste Land*, in its "open" religious quest, its Orientalizing, its high seriousness, its mobile and multiplied structure, harks back, like the rest of modernism, to American writers such as Thoreau, Melville, Dickinson, Whitman—early journeyers in English back to origins, "new" questers.) The major exception to biblical echo comes with Eliot's recasting of lines from Beaumont and Fletcher's *Philaster:* "How all the good you have is but a shadow, / I' the morning with you, and at night behind you / Past and forgotten"—lines plucked out of their romantic context and extended and straitened in sense, so made to yield a perfect diagram of existential illusion and disillusion: ignorance in youth of what Heidegger calls one's ownmost death, "Your shadow at morning striding behind you," and preoccupation with it in later years, "Your shadow at evening rising to meet you."[52] For the rest, this voice—at once far off and near, strange and close—mimics biblical discourse as no doubt the inevitable native model for scarifying conscience, for the therapy of dread and catharsis. "Son of man," God says to Ezekiel, "stand upon thy feet, and I will speak unto thee" (2:1), and, in effect, this is what the protagonist as prophet says to the protagonist as lagger, bestirring him. Again God asks Ezekiel, "Son of man, can these bones live?" (37:3). Confronted, questioned, challenged, the "son of man" is he who may yet attain to the miracle of Life. Thanks to his nuclear memory of the social feignings of God's speech in the books of Ezekiel, Isaiah, Job, and Ecclesiastes, the protagonist is enabled to speak God, at least to *play* God in the inner theater of his own verbal discourse of salvation.

This "authoritative speech" is not so much a pastiche of biblical style as a biblically shaded modern style, history-spanning. It begins biblically enough, with an arresting interrogative (compare "Who is as the wise man? and who knoweth the interpretation of a thing?" [Ecclesiastes 8:9]), and of course "Son of man" is biblical parlance; but the diction is otherwise contemporaneously blunt ("You cannot

---

52. Grover Smith, who notes the source in *Philaster*, believes that "in some tangential way the symbol of the shadow relates to sex and to the woman with whom the quester fails." But what Eliot's lines on the shadow indicate, I think, is a grasp of life as what must turn to the after-life, or the above-life, not "sex," for a solution to a conquering earthly shadowiness. See T. S. Eliot's *Poetry and Plays: A Study in Sources and Meaning* (Chicago: University of Chicago Press, 1974), 73–74.

say, or guess"), and the rhythm contemporaneously brisk. "A heap of broken images" recalls "her sins are heaped high as heaven" from the Revised Standard Version of the Bible, but not "For her sins have reached unto heaven" in the King James version (Revelation 18:5). "Heap" has scant biblical use, in either version, and Eliot's phrase manages a wholly contemporary force. The generic, imposing "the" is biblical—"the cricket," "the dead tree"—being peremptory, summatory, sharply accusing. And the cataloging polysyndeton is biblical, too. Yet, as against the luxurious measure of, say, "And the doors shall be shut in the streets, when the sound of the grinding is low, and he shall rise up at the voice of the bird, and all the daughters of musick shall be brought low" (Ecclesiastes 12:4), the protagonist's polysyndeton is nervously drawn up, cut into by comfortless asyndeton: "where the sun beats, / And the dead tree gives no shelter, the cricket no relief, / And the dry stone no sound of water." This quicker, more wasted rhythm tells of parched tension, dissatisfaction. The polysyndeton of "And went on in sunlight, into the Hofgarten / And drank coffee, and talked for an hour" was, by comparison, peace itself. Eliot's knobbly positioning of "only"—both in "for you know only / A heap" and "Only / There is shadow under this red rock"—is not biblical; nor is the almost coy "And I will show you"; nor the badgering repetitions: nor the parenthesis.

The modernization of biblical style effected here adds persuasion— a more archaic style would have run the risk of making Authority itself appear obsolete; a merely virtuosic exercise in pastiche had to be eschewed. A system of minatory, obscure memory traces was all that could be accommodated. The flesh of biblical language had to be implanted with excruciated modern nerves, even as the tone remained severe.

A more archaic style would also have split apart, and beyond bridging, the two major divisions of the paragraph, whereas the modernized biblical language is that of the "metaphysical" passage with an addition of prophetic tonality. The two styles must be allied in order to bear out the causal connection between the experience near the garden, which comes first in time, as seed, and the formal self-reproach, which marks the failure of that earlier moment to alter the conscious mind (which then "knew nothing" and still knows nothing) and, at the same time, is proof of a hidden development of gnosis within the protagonist himself.

In contrast to the lilting iambic naïveté of the hyacinth girl ("You *gave* me *hy*-," "They *called*," etc.)—an effect enhanced by slightly breathless tripping successions of slacks (*"hyacinths first"*; *"called* me the *h*yacinth *girl"*), the two "masculine" styles are crammed with stern contiguous accents. The first has *"what branch*es," *"You can-not," "you know only,"* "the *sun beats,"* "the *dead tree gives,"* "the *dry stone," "this red rock"*; and the second *"came back, late," "could not," "eyes failed,"* and *"knew noth*ing." The run of stresses and slacks is tossed-wave rough in "*What* are the *roots* that *clutch, what branch*es *grow* / *Out* of this *stony rub*bish? *Son* of *man,* / *You can*not *say,"* and so on. The rhythms are cruelly decisive. There is in such writing no blur or shadow in which to hide, to dream. It says, "At-tend." There is, however, understandably more rhythmic ease in the second section, even apart from the hyacinth girl's rather wide-eyed and wide-spaced measure:

> You GAVE me HY a cinths FIRST a YEAR a go;
> They CALLED me the HY a cinth GIRL.

The accents in *"Your arms full,* and *your hair wet"* sound sweetly affirming, nostalgic. Besides, the syntactic/metaphysical ambiguity of the flowing "Looking into the heart of light, the silence" offers its own kind of relief from the earlier harsh contours of discourse. Even the negating clots of accents in *"could not* / *Speak" "eyes failed,"* *"knew noth*ing," lack the punitiveness of the authoritarian style. The grim-mer use of stresses in this last is like a bullying outgrowth of the hard accents of the metaphysical lesson inflicted on the protagonist near the garden, a drubbing that he now administers, imitatively, in quasi-trau-matic repetition, to himself, exasperated as he is by his continued spir-itual backwardness.

The two masculine monologues are further linked by their common use of troubled polysyndeton. The pattern of "I could not / Speak and my eyes failed, I was neither / Living nor dead, and I knew nothing" parallels that of "where the sun beats, / And the dead tree gives no shelter, the cricket no relief, / And the dry stone no sound of water." The first, however, is not stopped at the end, but spills over with para-disal bewilderment into "Looking into the heart of light, the silence," with its refreshing liquid slacks, and the verbal and metaphysical plen-ty of the doubled phrase, "the heart of light, the silence."

This releasing flow is enhanced by a climactic coloration formed by the union of long *i* and *l*. These last, having replaced the groaning *o*'s of the first discourse ("grow," "know," "only," "stone," "show," and so on), first appeared separately, the *i* sounding half like a pro-noun in "hyacinths" and "eyes," as well as being one in "I," and the

I's vainly trying to brim, or brim over, in "called," "girl," "failed," "Living," and so on (liquid spread that each is). Beautifully, only the absolutist words, "light" and "silence," receive the combined blessing, mutually enhancing, lifting, easing, of both. Here, and not in "das Meer" or the wet Hyacinth garden, rises the hidden water of renewal.

This last discourse of the paragraph is a decimated Bible paraphrase, too. "And the eyes of them that see shall not be dim," Isaiah says in the verse immediately following the one on a great rock in a weary land, "and the ears of them that hear shall harken. The heart also of the rash shall understand knowledge, and the tongue of the stammerers shall be ready to speak plainly." Eliot's protagonist is forced to undergo the contradiction of this glad prophecy—paradoxically, precisely because, more apprehended than apprehending, he *is* absorbed in the Divine. In Eliot's inversion of Isaiah, only the organic and psychic functions, negated, relegated outside the charmed circle of mysticism, survive: "I could *not / Speak,* and my *eyes failed,* . . . I *knew nothing.*" Isaiah adds—suggestively, in relation to *The Waste Land*—that "the multitudes of the city shall be left: the forts and towers shall be for dens for ever, a joy of wild asses, a pasture of flocks: Until the spirit be poured upon us from on high, and the wilderness be a fruitful field." Yet even this beautiful passage is an earthly complacency compared to the lesson of the action of Eliot's poem, which is that the city shall be left, and be for dens for ever, for the spirit is other and elsewhere, and the wilderness everything that can be known, everything that can be fingered by the mind and senses.

Interruption

The lineation of the protagonist's final speech is appropriately mazelike. "Not" becomes imitatively dissociated from "Speak." "Neither" is dysfunctionally distanced from "Living." Caesuras multiply like shortness of breath. All this to show that the sensory world is—despite its splendid spatial extension—foldable, fundamentally abject. "The space that engrosses" the deject is, in Kristeva's words, not "*one,* nor *homogeneous,* nor *totalizable,* but essentially divisible, foldable, and catastrophic."[53] The heterogeneous discourse and disjunct constitution of the second paragraph spread out a few of the cards the protagonist holds as a player (actor, gambler) in a game he cannot win, unless he folds up the cards and leaves the game, reducing himself

53. Kristeva, *Powers of Horror,* 8.

from the many to the one. Meanwhile he suffers the Absolute as an interruption of his sensual play, and sensuality as a straying from the Absolute: Prufrock's dilemma, only drawn to greater extremes, at once sweetened and more tortured owing to the protagonist's recent history of winning near the goals of both love and Love, goals so like yet so effectively antithetical.

The disruptions of discourse in this paragraph, as throughout the poem, seem negative arguments for the necessary or ideal existence, far to the other side of words, of a living silence. What seems mockingly near to the other side of words, just to their backside, is the protagonist's own irony toward language. (And no wonder: if in this paragraph speech first clouts him, in the subsequent lines silence clouts him.) Untranslatable, reducing all speech and writing to what cannot be translated into truth (that is, *the silence*), this X beyond language secretly commands much of the protagonist's sympathy, and all his respect, explaining his animus against speech, and predisposing him to secretive, arcane, and difficult discourse. Turn about is fair play. If we do not know who speaks at the beginning of the paragraph, neither in a sense does he, nor did he know what declined to speak, could not even begin to diminish or sever itself into speech, near the garden. He is beset by the nontranslated. No surprise, then, that Eliot fails to translate the interruptive German verse (even in the officially documentary notes)—words, to begin with, in which a sailor addresses a girl who cannot hear him, and never will.

The paragraph is full of refused or unyielded translation, undelivered messages, blocked speech. The protagonist is first asked a question but not expected to answer it, in fact told that he would not know how. Wagner's shepherd mutters the untranslated "*Oed' und leer das Meer*" to himself—comfortless words, in any case. The hyacinth girl announces her delight in her epithet as if unable to contain her joy; the speech does not ask for a response, but is a fountaining of vanity. Still, gallantry would have responded, whereas the protagonist, wrenched out of all *courtesie,* responds only with a "Yet" that, unlike her own words (so the fiction goes) is first uttered, and in written not spoken form, in a poem, not for her ears. How, in any case, speak to her, this voluble, charming girl, about an experience in which speech failed? Her language is that of the senses, of narcissism, emotion, nature, myth, phatic words, while his is shadowed by the silence, and would be vatic. (The language of flowers, of the cut and resurrected, is his strongest speech to her.) In sum, the paragraph throughout wants a refreshing circulation of either language or silence.

Marks

The dash before "Yet" rescinds (recuts) the protagonist's tie with the hyacinth girl. A mark of pure alienation, a sudden straitening, it divides the two inexorably; is full of departure, of a brutally suffered farewell.

Opposite in thrust is the parenthesis "(Come in under the shadow of this red rock)," which makes a little verse den, a father's arms, out of the interruption promised to the protagonist's life in his own shadow. Christopher Ricks penetratingly notes a mild violence in this use of parenthetical marks as what Puttenham called a "first figure of tollerable disorder." Here the disorder is marked yet subtly bent on order:

What happens if we exclude Eliot's intercluded parenthesis?
                                 Only
          There is shadow under this red rock,
          And I will show you something different . . .
The sense is so precarious as to sound deranged, so a reader is pressed to let the words "(Come in under the shadow of this red rock)" come in, or come out from the shadow of their brackets, in order that there may then be the sane sequence: "Come in under the shadow . . . And I will show you."[54]

The parenthesis is a beckoning that will not be denied. It insinuates itself inescapably into the main development of the syntax, so that to pass it by is to imperil the sense: the very message that the passage as a whole carries with regard to *its* bearing on the conduct of life.

Shadows and Echoes

Just as the structure of this paragraph echoes that of the first, so it is internally echoic, self-shadowed. Here, spaced, pilloring verbal repetitions are marked, as in "What . . . what" in the first line, "You . . . you" in the third, "no . . . no" in the fourth. Particularly sinister is the fourfold repetition of "shadow": first (and twice) as what is under "this red rock," and as what a man would be "under" there, and second (and again twice) in "Your shadow," a treacherous death-sign that finally rises to meet you as if eager to coincide with you perfectly. The phrasal construction "Your shadow . . . you" reads like an indictment of "your" insubstantiality (the more severe because, as Dante's Statius says, it is vanity to "treat the shadows like the solid thing"). Shadows are visual echoes; and echoes, audible shadows. A voice is heard, inviting the protagonist to come in from out of the harsh place where individual shadows are cast, where sounds echo. This voice

54. Christopher Ricks, *The Force of Poetry* (Oxford: Clarendon Press, 1984), 308.

is already inside the privileged refuge, and if it, too, speaks repetitively it is to give clout to certain words ("shadow," "this red rock"). The echoic method thus remains consistent throughout the first discourse (it will recur with the girl's use of "hyacinth" and "me"), whether it enacts the static and sensational life or the peaceable life in the shadow of the One. The protagonist himself escapes the repetition only when held mystically fast by what is eternally the same and eternally refreshed.

MADAME SOSOSTRIS, FAMOUS CLAIRVOYANTE

Madame Sosostris, famous clairvoyante,
Had a bad cold, nevertheless
Is known to be the wisest woman in Europe,
With a wicked pack of cards. Here, said she,
Is your card, the drowned Phoenician Sailor,
(Those are pearls that were his eyes. Look!)
Here is Belladonna, the Lady of the Rocks,
The lady of situations.
Here is the man with three staves, and here the Wheel,
And here is the one-eyed merchant, and this card,
Which is blank, is something he carries on his back,
Which I am forbidden to see. I do not find
The Hanged Man. Fear death by water.
I see crowds of people, walking round in a ring.
Thank you. If you see dear Mrs. Equitone,
Tell her I bring the horoscope myself:
One must be so careful these days.

Flashes, Enigmas

So far, then, a story all intermittences, like pulse-takings. A once upon a time; a return, ominously late, from the Hyacinth garden, resulting in the shock of a double revelation, both negative (the heresy and nothingness of romantic love) and positive (the sacrality and Everything of the unseeable Light, the unhearable Silence). The aftermath: the absence of a "living" cultural tradition to fall back on, love having fled—a surround of "stony rubbish": flight from the witch's cauldron of natural regenerative forces, obscure sensings of inner change. And now, in the third paragraph, the protagonist's conscious search for enlightenment, if in a consciously wrong place (or so his defensively clever tone suggests): his almost willfully credulous expectation that Madame Sosostris, famous clairvoyante, will be able to see into his future. His own eyes having failed, the silence having remained silent (for all that the authoritative voice tried to speak it), he turns to another for second sight, for words of wisdom. He would "guess"— better, have someone "say"—what clutches in him, grows.

The protagonist has been remarkably indifferent to a linear presentation of his "story," to narrativity as an emplotment of time: stories humanize, he would transcend the human (escape the natural seasons, the clock, biography, history). So his story must emerge as it can, and as it must. His "biography" is an accident of his enforced spiritual change, not a narcissistic enterprise. The links do not matter, the shape does not signify. What can be "shown" is only the negative of what cannot be developed in the "unreal" world of natural and artificial light.

The poem is thus emerging as a monologue (however diversified as such and loaded with secondary monologues) which appears oblivious, from paragraph to paragraph and even from subparagraph to subparagraph, to what has already constituted it. On the surface, nothing is connected with nothing (to echo one of the Thames daughters in part 3: "I can connect / Nothing with nothing"). The divisions are like Madame Sosostris's cards: they are not, on the face of it, part of a coherent story; nor, up to this point, have they been laid out in proper sequence (the sequence proper to a chronological reading of the psychological and spiritual events signified by the paragraphs). So, a critical reshuffling (synthetic as much as analytical). The introduction of hypotheses. A humanization of what writhes to escape that stigma, that enchainment to time, that banality.

A poem, then, as a reluctant "montage trope," in Eisenstein's term: dispensing with detailed, explanatory, stepwise development of action and feeling; presenting, instead, isolated individual stages of them, the total sum of which is the equivalent of a narrative, a concept.[55] This "cut-up" method makes a virtue out of a merely superficial incoherence: it simultaneously increases the illusion of mimesis (in the sense of a "showing," a dramatic immediacy, the opposite of a diegetic "telling") and broadens the scope of possible presentation, allowing for the Hofgarten and Marie, for Isolde and Isaiah—for the utmost heterogeneity within a peculiarly concentrated psychospiritual history. No ordinary psychological subject, the protagonist is yet the coherence of the poem, which is his story even in its apparent incoherence, its shudders that shake loose the linchpins of narrativity, its strayings that stray right into the heart of unfreedom.

The Waste Land is an extreme instance of the disjunctiveness that acute abjection inflicts—like winces, attempted withdrawals—upon the flesh of narrative. Kristeva remarks:

55. On montage trope, see Sergei Eisenstein, *Film Form*, trans. Jay Leyda (New York: Meridian Books, 1958), 240.

Not until the advent of twentieth-century "abject" literature (the sort that takes up where apocalypse and carnival left off) did one realize that the narrative web is a thin film constantly threatened with bursting. For, when narrated identity is unbearable, when the boundary between subject and object is shaken, and when the limit between inside and outside becomes uncertain, the narrative is what is challenged first. If it continues nevertheless, its makeup changes: its linearity is shattered, it proceeds by flashes, enigmas, short cuts, incompletion, tangles, and cuts. At a later stage, the unbearable identity of the narrator and of the surroundings that are supposed to sustain him can no longer be *narrated* but *cries out* or is *descried* with maximal stylistic intensity.[56]

Eliot's protagonist negotiates a passage from unbearable identity to the unapprehensible. "Completion" is possible at neither extreme, at least not where language is still applicable; stylistic intensity is thus imposed at each end and, as well, along the rapids in between. The unspeakably abject and the inarticulably Omnipotent alike challenge the tongue.

Still, this passage from the unsustaining to the All-sustaining is itself a coherency, considered from a sufficient distance (that afforded by the larger structure of the poem). It is even (unasked-for by the conscious intelligence as it is) a destiny imposed upon the protagonist. The illumination near the garden (the garden-annihilating glimpse of the single Oasis of numinous light) is the true origin of his story (it is what allows him to begin to reduce the waste land to his background, to the apocalyptic backlighting of his own salvation)—just as it reveals his true Origin. The "plot" is already underway by the beginning of the second paragraph, and, through flashback, its seed-time is recalled in the closing half. Now Madame Sosostris is called upon to advance it by foretellings, by cryptic but accurate namings—a descrial dim and fragmented, but true.

Anything is possible, even magic. The world itself is the darkness of miracle.

Parroting, Quotation, Monologue

Like "Summer surprised us," "Madame Sosostris, famous clairvoyante"—an oddly gay if pompous line of iambic pentameter—begins another brief narrative introduction to a monologue, a monologue that, like Marie's and the hyacinth girl's, rides piggyback on the protagonist's own. This introduction is laced with the parroted babble of—of whomever would become excited over a famous clairvoyante. Once

---

56. Kristeva, *Powers of Horror*, 140–41.

again, the protagonist appears uninterested in guarding himself against being taken wrongly—as if to say, "How can my words possibly falsify who I am (for who am I)?" He satirizes, thus, not only his gullibility but his absurd concern (absurd where all is abject) for a clean and proper self. If originality is, in Emerson's definition, "being," then does he have any to protect?[57] Again, in Wallace Stevens's words, "Originality is an escape from repetition,"[58] and there is in the protagonist much of Tiresias, that abject bundle of repetitions, as he will later confess. In fact, original roots *are* astir in him, but as yet he scarcely knows of them, and nothing of their "how." So he is inclined to quote indifferently, albeit with a malicious subversion of what he quotes; he separates off from his own monologue the words of neither Madame Sosostris nor her admirers. Here comes everybody, he seems to say, if in a way that makes everybody afraid.

That they have reason to quail is displayed in the opening lines. These lines contain a hidden dialogue, with one voice saying—enthusiastically—"famous clairvoyante" and the other adding mischievously "Had a bad cold," then adding, too late, "nevertheless." The first, again, remarking effusively "the wisest woman in Europe" and the second, around the smirk of the line break, muttering "With a wicked pack of cards" (quoting, in "wicked pack," the fortune-teller's admirerers, if not Madame Sosostris herself). The protagonist thus simulates prattle while undercutting and dismissing it, liquidating voice by voice, tone by tone.

After this pretense at breathlessness (the second line, "Had a bad cold, nevertheless," being short, its eight syllables divided equally between the sorry monosyllables of "Had a bad cold" and the recuperative, racing "nevertheless"), Madame Sosostris herself, rather abruptly, speaks. In the first lines, diegesis veers toward mimesis (the telling is half a showing); then, as with Marie, an audio tape is replayed, another voice is directly "heard"—speaking in all innocence of any audience save that of the protagonist himself. With "Here, said she / Is your card," the fortune-teller launches into her professional monologue with no more ceremony—indeed with less—than Mr. Scogan uses in Aldous Huxley's novel *Crome Yellow*, when dressed up as the hag Sesostris, the Sorceress of Ecbatana, to command a booth at the annual Crome Fair, he receives all clients "in mysterious silence, indicating with a movement of the finger that they [are] to sit down

57. Ralph Waldo Emerson, "Quotation and Originality," in *The Portable Emerson*, ed. Mark Van Doren (New York: Viking Press, 1946), 301.

58. Wallace Stevens, *Opus Posthumous*, ed. Samuel French Morse (New York: Alfred A. Knopf, 1972), 177.

opposite."[59] Again dialogue dies on the vine: what Madame Sosostris wants from the protagonist is not his speech but his money—"Thank you"—plus a favor: "If you see dear Mrs. Equitone, / Tell her I bring the horoscope myself" (a request that places the protagonist as part of an all too equal-toned, indeed Prufrockian, set). Madame Sosostris's speech is in the authoritative mode; she is an emissary of the Fates.

Tireless monologuist that the protagonist himself is, he breaks in parenthetically with his own borrowed gnomic wisdom, "Those are pearls that were his eyes. Look!" He responds less to what she has said than to what she has shown; and he would show in turn ("Look!")— for, indeed, she does not see all that he sees, namely the possibility of a marvelous transformation, rich and strange, to be won from death. (He who could see, with second sight, roots that clutch among stony rubbish can see, as Ariel sees, the precious gain to be tortured from loss.) The excited interruption is clearly his; it is out of key with the clairvoyante's phlegmatic pronouncements. It has the note of genuine enthusiasm; her tones are all those of bored expertise (which here is something less than an expert tease).

Names (Metonyms/Metaphors)

If the Absolute is the pre-nominal, names are badges of abjection. "Marie"? Ejaculated in "Marie, Marie, hold on tight," the name shrilly and thinly inhabits, with almost conscious diminutiveness, a sphere of physical and psychological dependency. In effect, it is a parody of "crying on the name of Mary" (*Purgatorio*), though even such crying entails the desperation of the nominal.

By contrast, the appellation "the hyacinth girl" may seem a triumph of unification, an erasure of boundaries. But it marks a prodigious exclusion—that of the supernatural and the superhuman. Something "other" than the natural and the human in the protagonist challenges the exclusion.

With its international heteroglossia, the name Madame Sosostris, conjunct with the geographical epithet "the wisest woman in Europe," places the fortune-teller as at once worldly and a fantasy of history, a piece of patchwork. Her name belongs to the echoic order that rules out originality; it suits her routine reading of pre-read cards. With darkly intuited justice, her mirroring office as one who reflects back, however brokenly, the narcissistic concerns of those who consult her, as well as her own reduction of the world to mirrors, is echoed by the first five letters of both "Madame" and "Sosostris," which read the

59. Aldous Huxley, *Crome Yellow* (New York: Harper & Row, 1983), 121.

same in reverse. Each name bears a hidden figure of narcissistic chiasmus (*palindromos,* "running back again"). The name "Belladonna" at once elaborates and deforms the same visual pattern, clustering subordinate vowels around twin consonants.

As for the names of the tarot (and pseudo-tarot) cards,[60] they drape identity on a hook of circumstance; metonymic fetterings, they limit the spirit to contingency (the Lady *of the Rocks,* the man *with three staves,* and so on). Yet metaphoric, as well, they confer on the card figures a quasi-archetypal stature. All seem potent epitomes. The Phoenician Sailor? The carnal self ventured upon the currents of the Unreal. Belladonna? The Siren in the same waters. The Hanged Man? The sacrificed phallus, or the scapegoat god.

In a tarot discourse, capitals are expectable, so "the Lady of the Rocks" is only routinely imposing. More significant is the turnaround to lowercase in "the lady of situations," which amounts to a deflating comment. The Lady suffers a fall from Archetype to mere type, to wholly impure contingency. Perhaps "the man with three staves" could have supported capitalization; Eliot associated the card, as his note indicates, with the (capitalized) Fisher King. But capitals might have given an unduly portentous significance to the Three Staves, whereas in point of fact it hardly matters whether there was one stave, or two, or three. Similarly, "One-Eyed Merchant" would be a needless Gothicism. "Wheel," on the other hand, rightly towers with the superficially imposing large scheme of the natural cycle—much as this last proves a mere runaround, and runaground, of desire, and as well a nauseating, endless carnival ride of reincarnations. As for "The Hanged Man," it is justly capitalized, vertical with empowering catastrophe.

That "drowned" is not capitalized in "drowned Phoenician Sailor" properly prevents the drowning from appearing final. What remains literally uppermost is "Phoenician," with its Weston-secured links to the ancient sources of the grail myth, and "Sailor," a figure that, according to the original draft of part 4 of the poem, "Retains, even ashore, . . . / Something inhuman, clean, and dignified." To be a Phoenician Sailor is to be engaged not only in trade (as the protagonist will prove to be through his work in the City) but in the highest mysteries of transmogrifying renewal (as witnessed by "Those are pearls

60. According to Grover Smith, "the Tarot contains no drowned sailor or blank card," and the one-eyed merchant is the Fool. "Belladonna . . . is perhaps the Empress" (*T. S. Eliot's Poetry and Plays,* 77). See also Eliot's note to line 46, beginning "I am not familiar with the exact constitution of the Tarot pack of cards, from which I have obviously departed to suit my own convenience."

that were his eyes," evidence of the protagonist's own faith-finding, faith-serving gloss of his "card").

The final name in the paragraph, "Mrs. Equitone," is so patently allegorical that it might be still another tarot card, however comic in cast. In the context ("Tell her I bring . . . "), it suggests a stay-at-home upper-middle-class woman so neutral that her voice never rises or sinks—the mechanical voice of one of the lost who does not perceive that, "so far as we are human, what we do must be either evil or good." Equitone sounds like a brand of audio equipment. It tells of a woman equal to every occasion because to her they are all the same.

Woman, the Enemy of the Absolute

Irreverently patterned after Bertrand Russell, Huxley's Mr. Scogan advocates setting up a plastic bubble of reason, a dome of intelligence, inside a meaningless world: "After all, we all know that there's no ultimate point."[61] Though constrained to dress as a gypsy woman, he protestingly adopts a masculine name, Sesostris, after an Egyptian king. Men reason; women dabble in the mysteries, with which their supposed intuitions are confused.

Lyndall Gordon observes that Eliot's friends "would have recognized Bertrand Russell" in Eliot's "bogus clairvoyant,"[62] but unlike Russell (unlike Sesostris) Madame Sosostris is as credulous as she is mercenary; she appears to have devoted her life to reading the cards ("famous clairvoyante"); she moves about briskly among the mysteries. Insofar as she springs from Crome Yellow (Eliot acknowledged the influence of this delightfully clever novel published in 1921, the year he completed The Waste Land),[63] she takes her substance from Priscilla Wimbush, who greets the young hero, Denis, with the words, "You find me busy at my horoscopes." "Such a pity you don't believe in these things, Denis, such a pity," she soon observes; she loves keeping "in tune" with the Infinite, "and then there's the next world and all the spirits, and one's Aura, and Mrs. Eddy and saying you're not ill, and the Christian Mysteries and Mrs. Besant. It's all splendid. One's never dull for a moment."[64] If Madame Sosostris is kept relatively

61. Huxley, Crome Yellow, 133.
62. Gordon, Eliot's Early Years, 110.
63. Eliot may have been returning a salute, for Huxley had written at the outset of chapter 4: "Denis . . . decided to wear white flannel trousers—white flannel trousers and a black jacket, with a silk shirt and his new peach-coloured tie." "You have a bad habit of quoting," his friend Anne says to him a few pages later. "As I never know the context or author, I find it humiliating." Denis apologizes: "Things somehow seem more real and vivid when one can apply somebody else's ready-made phrase about them" (Crome Yellow, 17).
64. Ibid., 8.

laconic, it is because she is in business and would make short work of it, and because she must proficiently provide the dots that the rest of the poem must connect into a semblance of plot.

Bogus? Yes and no. Mistress of the visible signs of the future, at least as provided by the tarot deck (a deck that Eliot modifies to suit his purposes), she accurately foresees (again to suit Eliot's purposes) certain figures, patterns, and episodes in the protagonist's life. She understands nothing of this, or too little to matter, but she does what she is paid for. Hers not to comprehend, but to see foreseeingly. She turns up pictures of the heterogeneous and untotalizable, *predictive* pictures, but without any talent for resolving them into the singleness of a story, let alone the absolving and dissolving purifications of the One.

Commenting on the female capacity to wreck the infinite, Céline notes: "It would be hard to find a woman who is neither a bitch nor a ninny—if so, she will be witch and fey."[65] Madame Sosostris has pretentions to being a witch (hence her all-too-titillating "wicked pack of cards"), but the protagonist is inclined to regard her as a ninny (hence his suspicion that her second sight might be all too subject to a viral clouding). This last is a defence against the first, her aspect as London Sibyl, her subtle access as a female to oceanic knowledge, treacherous depths, rocky oppositions to male courses, the wheel of the natural cycle, "situations." She is the Mother Goddess who deals out death when she creates life, whose words transport one like the bubbles of a drowning. She represents the archaic abjectness that has always the power to draw one back and in, incestuously lost as one's bones are picked over in whispers. Hence the protagonist's hostile tones. "*Want* and *aggressivity*," Kristeva notes, "are chronologically separable but logically coextensive. Aggressivity *appears* to us as a rejoinder to the original deprivation felt from the time of the mirage known as 'primary narcissism'; it merely takes revenge on initial frustrations."[66] A luring emptiness, a false plenitude, Madame Sosostris (with her forbidding name) admonishes: "Fear death by water"—but what's the good of that after she has pronounced "the drowned Phoenician Sailor" to be one's card? Sailors, take warning. Men, fear women. Arm yourselves with the three staves.

Here again Woman is vaingloriously one with the visible, space her toilette. Seeing, she says, is believing. The aesthetic is the true. "Here . . . / Is, . . . / Here is . . . / Here is . . . and here . . . / And

---

65. Quoted in Kristeva, *Powers of Horror*, 157.
66. Ibid., 39.

here . . . and this card . . . / I see crowds of people": the fortune-teller's authority lies in a series of visual assaults, imperatives to "look." She peeps, her eyes raven. Her province is not the Unseen, but the foreseeable; figural seeing of the figurable. (To her, seeing even seems a single, indiscriminate activity: "I see crowds of people. . . . If you see dear Mrs. Equitone. . . .") The protagonist, catching the infection, adds his own "Look!," ironically exhorting regard of what has lost the vanity of seeing.

The original mother-glow cools and disintegrates into objects, mother-substitutes, mother's orphans. Language condones and fosters this process. Taking the word "object" in its "strongest acceptation— as the correlative of a subject in a symbolic chain," Kristeva comments: "The paternal agency alone, to the extent that it introduces the symbolic dimension between 'subject' (child) and 'object' (mother), can generate such a strict object relation."[67] What the protagonist *objects* to is not so much objecthood per se as his subjecthood in relation to a tormenting, never-satisfying world of objects. He will not be at rest until blind as pearls, until his carnal restiveness has died back into amniotic slumber. But even that will not be the peace that passes understanding. Beyond the mother's tropical tides, beyond even His verbalizable Will, lies the undisturbable, unimaginable element of the Eternal Silence.

What makes Madame Sosostris objectionable is not only her own meretricious objecthood—as the marketable product labeled "Madame Sosostris, famous clairvoyante"—but her vain, vulgar relation to reality as a system of readable (and profitably readable) object-signs. She sits down to her work as to a dressing table, the cards adorn her. What unites her with the hyacinth girl is an implicit demand to be seen (even as she is in the act of seeing). If there is something she is "forbidden to see," the stress must fall, titillatingly, on the specific prohibition (*she* is *forbidden* to see it), not on the extent of the mystery, which indeed is both ruthlessly flattened into a visual "blank" and, through an allusion to the Phoenician traders who spread the higher mystery cults, demoted to a portable product that can be packed ("something he carries on his back"). The same self-flattering and lucrative sort of titillation is implicit in the scare tactics of "Tell her I bring the horoscope myself: / One must be so careful these days."

The narcissistic object-woman reappears in the passage in Gothic form as Belladonna, the Lady of the Rocks. As with the hyacinth girl, so again, Woman adorned with flowers or floral products: the

67. Ibid., 44.

woman-flower, the natural wonder. Oceanic, all the same, with narcissism (narcissism tending, in Kristeva's words, toward "the unleash-
ing of drive as such, without object, threatening all identity, including
that of the subject itself"). At the least, treacherous with hidden gra-
nitic reserves of it, a wrecker of both the paternal "symbolic dimension between 'subject' (child) and 'object' (mother)" and the
transnominal, transobjectal Infinite.[68]

Heteromodality

The paragraph is in the mode of satiric realism, to which the reading
of the cards adds an exotic element of allegory—an element then oddly continued, as noted, in the fortune-teller's parting reference to Mrs.
Equitone. This modal doubling and blend testifies to the always relative and shiftable ground of discourse and representation. If *The
Waste Land* gravitates toward allegory, it is to adopt a mode of feign-
ing that is frankly that, and, moreover, chastely that, free of the phobic
smears and shadows of the Gothic surreal mode and the deceptive
reality of the "objective" repertorial mode. Allegory reduces the "outer" world to the status of a toolchest for representation. It implies that
the world itself is not real. It is the inevitable mode for Eliot's metaphysics of the One Alone.

Eliot's quarrel with Romanticism is, on the literary plane, a quarrel
with "symbol" and, on the metaphysical plane, a quarrel with "objects." The symbol is synthetic in intent, fusing "inner" and "outer."
It implies the reality of objects, and exalts a subject-object synthesis.
What Eliot would exalt is the preobjectal. The Absolute is neither external nor internal, but transcends all such dichotomies and boundaries, as the Alone Real and the All Real. There is no need to go to
school to landscape, like the Romantics; rather, landscape may be
faked, like papier-mâché topography, to provide the ground of a ficti-
tious journey toward the Nonrepresentable—the highest use of literature, even if still a concession to the backward child in the soul.[69]

But the protagonist has much to work through before he can begin—as a voluntary act, a discipline—his "journey," and so before the
poem can try to settle (it is not to prove more than a try) into allegory.
Allegory proper begins in part 5 (then fluctuates); meanwhile, as said,

---

68. Ibid.

69. In his essay "The Rhetoric of Temporality," Paul de Man effects a partial re-
alignment of Romantic literature with allegory, but not in a way that affects the present
argument. See Paul de Man, *Blindness and Insight: Essays in the Rhetoric of Contemporary Criticism*, 2d ed. revised (Minneapolis: University of Minnesota Press, 1983), 187–
228.

Eliot introduces through Madame Sosostris's card language a sort of allegorical kit, an unassembled allegory of the protagonist's future story. If the cards foretell his life, it is in a choked, nonnarrational manner. Yet after this local brief shower of atomistic allegory, a smell of the Higher Representation lingers in the air. "Unreal City" in the next paragraph adds to and takes advantage of this atmosphere.

The protagonist, having first allegorized himself as "dull roots," then more positively as "roots that clutch," is then allegorized by Madame Sosostris. And all along he himself is an allegory of Eliot. As Helen Vendler notes in *The Poetry of George Herbert*: "To allegorize oneself is different from writing about Everyman: it means to take one's own personality, exaggerate it, broaden it, delete its more eccentric specificities while retaining its individual character. . . . A self-allegory is recognizable as an individual person, yet not as wholly identical with the author."[70] Eliot's "individual character" remains so much a matter of hints, inferences, obscure grumbles, that, despite the undoubted exaggeration and broadening of the poet's own qualities, his surrogate, the protagonist, seems to be playing hide-and-seek in his own story. In the process he darts behind the words of others, and his self-portrait is so defensive and at the same time so distanced that it is scribbled over with multiple fugitive disguises. But this only makes the poet/protagonist more representative of the humanity of his time and place. The deletions of "eccentric specificities" is compensated for by a harlequinade of poses, quoted words, depictions of others, public scenes, and a continual tremor of implicitness, proving in several ways more gain than loss.

Eliot was to damn Shelley with the faint praise that he was "the one English poet of the nineteenth century who could even have begun to follow [Dante's] footsteps."[71] Given the subsequent burnout of Romanticism, could not the right poet actually begin to follow those steps? The goal of *The Waste Land* might be said to be exactly this: even down to and despite agreement with Dante that "to transcend humanity cannot be told in words."[72] Had not Dante shown how far one could go toward allegory and still represent the spiritual emptiness of a particular age?

A Virgil who never enters the poem, Eliot effectively conducts his protagonist from abulia to beatitude, apportioning out hell, purgatory, and paradise (if, to be sure, little of this last) in various scenes and

70. Helen Vendler, *The Poetry of George Herbert* (Cambridge, Mass.: Harvard University Press, 1975), 92.
71. Eliot, *Selected Essays*, 264.
72. Ibid., 265.

images. The very title of the work suggests comparisons with Bunyan's Vanity Fair or Herbert's "the wilde of Passion, which / Some call the wold; / A waste place, but sometimes rich." The plot itself might be Bunyanized as follows: After suffering a loss of Romantic belief in the vicinity of the Hyacinth Garden, Pilgrim, hearing a voice reproach him with being the Son of man, and uncertain of his way, visits the fortune-telling booth in Vanity Fair, and is warned to Fear Death by Water. Heeding this baneful advice, he walks round and round in Hell in the Unreal City, where only the crowds flow, sharing their quiet desperation. He marries Belladonna, the Lady of the Rocks—a fiery Medusa who turns his penis to stone—and wanders the banks of the Thames, a voyeur of slimy rats' bellies, cigarette ends, horny London traffic, typists scarcely forced. At length, no longer able to bear the absence of the Hanged Man, weary of the Blind Seers and Fake Goddesses of Vanity Fair, he ascends the Mount of Voluntary Dryness, praying for rain. Successfully meeting the challenge of the Perilous Chapel, he receives a sign of acceptance from the Heavens, and with Divine Help gathers wisdom for a further purification. At the end, he sits fishing on the Shore of Beatitude, the Arid Plains safely behind him, his line baited for God-food.

Of course this abstract and translation, this Writing in Caps, neglects much that gives the poem its complexity and vitality: for instance, the varied chorus of unsinging voices, the metastatic shifts, the multimodality (the range from "metonymic realism" to fable, to stop there), the historical in-gatherings constituted by the allusions. No single description of what the poem is—unless *mixed*—seems to suffice. Showing and telling, "faithful" and fanciful representation go round and round in it, not so much fighting for supremacy as finding little will to resistance in any of the opposition—till finally certain kinds of fanciful representation, particularly allegory and fable, take on strength, dominate, stiffen themselves to greet the Silence. But without the progress from unreality to reality that this growing hegemony, together with the allegorizable plot, observes, the poem would emerge as no more than a pointless exercise in melancholic brokenness, which indeed it is often celebrated for being. It is more than that, a twentieth-century poem of the (Dantean, indeed Eastern) high dream.

Allegorical Style

Eliot was to declare that "the poetry of Dante is the one universal school of style for the writing of poetry in any language," citing Dante's "allegorical method," which he appears to equate with a certain intelligent "lucidity of style." The allegorical method, he asserts, "makes for simplicity and intelligibility."[73] It derives from a "practical sense of realities," that is: "not to expect more from *life* than it can give or more from *human* beings than they can give; to look to *death* for what life cannot give."[74] So the "practical" coincides with the visionary, both being comprised by a (Catholic) philosophy of "disillusion."

Now, "simplicity and intelligibility" are not the first words most readers would associate with *The Waste Land;* yet I think they apply, one clears a way through to them. For all its vanguardism, the poem is a classical, chaste invention. It is free of flashing "romantic" expressiveness. It is a marvel of "practical" lucidity.

Eliot associated "lucidity of style" with a *"visual* imagination": "allegory means *clear visual images*."[75] Eliot himself has struck few as visual: it is his clear, haunting, exact rhythms that stay with one. Yet not only is there a distinctive spare visuality in Eliot; what he himself means by the "visual imagination" is roughly "vision." In praising Dante's implementation of the *"high dream"*—and opposing this last to the *"low dream"* of which alone "the modern world seems capable"[76]—Eliot notes that it merges "an idea . . . in images," which is what makes it allegorical: "in our awareness of the images we must be aware that the meaning is there too," however elusive. So "visual" comes to mean the expression of intelligent disillusionment in images, except where it actually blossoms into vision, as in certain passages in part 5 of *The Waste Land.*

What Eliot says of Dante's poem, that "we cannot extract the full significance of any part without knowing the whole," is true of his own. His style, too, is intelligent (allegorical). He, too, avoids local metaphors (for "allegory and metaphor," he notes, do not get on well together"). His style, too, is intensive, rather than expansive like Shakespeare's. With him, too, a purposeful concentration "simplifies the diction," making "clear and precise the images." He too "employs a very simple language." His too is "a *poetic* as distinguished from an *intellectual* lucidity": "the thought may be obscure, but the word is lucid, or rather translucent." Only in his poem, what is at first obscure might better be called the purport of the whole and hence of the part.

English words, Eliot adds, have "a kind of opacity which is part of their beauty . . . a kind of local self-consciousness, because they are the growth of a *particular* civilization," as opposed to the European

73. Ibid., 242.
74. Ibid., 275.
75. Ibid., 242–43.
76. Ibid., 262.

culture of Dante, the culture of a Europe "mentally more united than we can now conceive." Yet despite this limitation, Eliot's English is lucent: the language of "April is the cruellest month," of "I read, much of the night, and go south in the winter," of "A heap of broken images," of "You gave me hyacinths first a year ago," of "Tell her I bring the horoscope myself," is as near to simple, unself-conscious plainness—to prose—as English poetry is ever likely to get.

Whether auditory ("Fear death by water") or that and visual too ("I see crowds of people, walking round in a ring"), the power of Eliot's lines is invariably formal and moral as well—the first because the economy of the whole makes taut every part, and the second because Eliot's imagination is never preoccupied with anything less than happiness or the lack of it, and this for him is a moral issue, the only real joy being a pure joy, a joy in purity. Eliot's formal economy and beauty derive from his passion for sanctity. It is as what A. Alvarez calls "a supreme interpreter of mediated experience" that Eliot places language under a peculiar control, and the reader along with it. "Finally, with practice," Alvarez adds, "the obscurity [is] seen to be a matter of the economy and delicacy with which the argument [is] pushed forward,"[77] and this economy, in turn, represents the rigor of an allegorizing imagination, which remorselessly applies its high dream to everything human. Edmund Wilson spoke of Eliot's "exquisite phrasing in which we feel that every word is in its place and that there is not a word too much." This exquisiteness, I am suggesting, must be linked with what Wilson—quoting Eliot on Blake— called Eliot's "peculiar honesty" in "exhibiting the essential sickness or strength of the human soul"—an honesty that "gives him a place among those upon whose words we reflect with most interest and whose tones we remember longest."[78]

UNREAL CITY

Unreal City,
Under the brown fog of a winter dawn,
A crowd flowed over London Bridge, so many,
I had not thought death had undone so many.
Sighs, short and infrequent, were exhaled,
And each man fixed his eyes before his feet.
Flowed up the hill and down King William Street,

---

77. A. Alvarez, *The Shaping Spirit: Studies in Modern English and American Poets* (London: Chatto & Windus, 1958), 23–26.

78. Edmund Wilson, *Axel's Castle: A Study in the Imaginative Literature of 1870–1930* (New York: Charles Scribner's Sons, 1953), 130–31.

To where Saint Mary Woolnoth kept the hours
With a dead sound on the final stroke of nine.
There I saw one I knew, and stopped him, crying: "Stetson!
"You who were with me in the ships at Mylae!
"That corpse you planted last year in your garden,
"Has it begun to sprout? Will it bloom this year?
"Or has the sudden frost disturbed its bed?
"Oh keep the Dog far hence, that's friend to men,
"Or with his nails he'll dig it up again!
"You! hypocrite lecteur!—mon semblable,—mon frère!"

Refusal and Unreality

"Unreal City": the yawning capitalized adjective and the monumental capitalized noun lord it over the province of the paragraph. For a moment there is nothing but this Unreal City, which lies grammatically and lineally inert, inescapable, a paralyzing nomination.

An "O" would have made it a proper apostrophe, animated it; and indeed, till Pound cut into it, it *was* an apostrophe, a dull apprising: "Unreal City, I have sometimes seen and see / Under the brown fog of your winter dawn / A crowd flow," and so on.[79] What remains is, by contrast, ambiguous: the most reluctant of invocations, a dispirited sidelong address, a start that is already a dead end, both summation and indictment. So the syntax hesitates between calling upon this City to heed the speaker's witness of what occurs in it and merely naming it, with an exhalation like a short sigh, realizing that it *cannot* be addressed, *must* not be addressed, for it represents the refusal of all intelligent realization.

And so the story advances: by now the spring torment of youthful love has passed, and the protagonist has settled into a job in the City, joining the crowd walking a daily round, just as Madame Sosostris had foreseen (though her word "ring" had suggested a paddock, if not a circus). Winter has come round again and is still a condition of being "Under," but not as one is under the shadow of a red rock, of the real, but under a layer of insulation from reality: earlier, forgetful snow; now, more rememberingly, a brown fog of commercial secularism that is like a sighing up of the heavy color of the earth into the air, a mist formed by the lingering dissolution of the sense of the absolute. What the fog both coweringly and despondently obscures is the heart of light. The protagonist's mood has changed since the opening of part 1:

79. T. S. Eliot, *The Waste Land: A Facsimile and Transcript of the Original Drafts Including the Annotations of Ezra Pound*, ed. Valerie Eliot (New York: Harcourt Brace Jovanovich, 1971), 8.

winter no longer contents him, he suffers from the knowledge of the Missing All.

For those on earth, the touchstone of reality is an infinite relational capacity—which means that reality can never be apprehended, only approached, imagined. Not to imagine it, however, is to be as the dead. The Dantean echoes in the sighing, undone crowd place the City as sister to the City of Desolation in canto 3 of the *Inferno,* a scene of "people . . . defeated by their pain." Here, too, the inhabitants are sundered from "THE PRIMAL LOVE" because of their "great refusal" of the knowledge of good and evil, their repudiation of "the good of the intellect." Here, too, roam wretched dejects from the scheme of salvation/damnation.[80]

In *Knowledge and Experience,* Eliot reasons that "so far as an object is an object it will have relations which . . . constitute it, but which ultimately transform and absorb it. The poorer an object is in relations, the less it is object." The City is unreal (Unreal) in this sense, in its virtual bankruptcy of relations that could transform and absorb it. "We do not know reality in substance," Eliot says, "we know it in relation."[81] An object, after all, is "a point of attention," and what is there to attend to in the routinized, mechanized City, where the crowd moves together like an automaton. What the city represents is a cancellation of relationship: of space ("the brown fog"); of time ("where Saint Mary Woolnoth kept the hours / With a dead sound on the final stroke of nine"), and of Primal Love ("And each man fixed his eyes before his feet").

The Lonely Crowd

Having lost a definitional scheme of the spirit, a metaphysical horizon—missing even what Elias Canetti calls "the 'feeling' space" of a true crowd[82]—this London "crowd" is inexorably atomized after the Bradleyan principle that "my experience falls within my own circle, a circle closed on the outside" (in words Eliot quotes in a note to part 5). It flows in a spectral quiet broken only by sighs and fatal bells and the jagged, desperate shout of the protagonist—he at least is real enough to feel pain. Where the true crowd builds to a "discharge" (Canetti), this one flows up and down and goes round in a ring, mechanically and perpetually propelled. It has just enough density to pour ("A

80. See *The Divine Comedy of Dante Alighieri, Inferno,* trans. Allen Mandelbaum (Berkeley: University of California Press, 1980), 20, 22.

81. Eliot, *Knowledge and Experience,* 94–97.

82. Elias Canetti, *Crowds and Power,* trans. Carol Stewart (New York: The Seabury Press, 1978), 35.

crowd flowed over London Bridge"), for a blasphemous substitution of itself for the Jordans of the Spirit, but no far-off goal. In truth, it is matter for a "dull canal" (part 3).

Because of the merciless period after "feet," this crowd seems to begin moving up the hill with a reluctant jerk. The tension between the consequently unflowing "feet" and "Flowed" spells a movement weirdly compelled, as does the antigravitational "Flowed up." The figure "A crowd flowed over London Bridge" mimics the significantly unrecognized natural flow of the river below—as if taking the side of bridges, of human society and furthering artifice, in the ancient enmity between bridges and rivers. But this flow, in actuality a death-flow, the spineless flow of the undone, lacks all joy of freeing motion, as signaled by the stiff sound of "A crowd flowed," a stiffness only lightly relieved by the flowing over of long o in "flowed over."

"The river," notes Canetti, "is only a limited crowd symbol . . . the symbol of a movement which is still under control, before the discharge"—that is, the moment when all who belong to the crowd get rid of their differences and feel equal. It is the symbol of "the *slow* crowd," and this last is "characterized by the remoteness of its goal."[83] In fact, the City crowd has, as noted, lost even its remote goal, and this it is the office of Saint Mary Woolnoth to mark—appropriately, with a dead sound of the bell stroke that (the ninth in the ninth hour) is "final" in declaring the death of the present moment. The church, as "a conscious slowing down of crowd events," is designed to defer the glorious "discharge" till time coincides with everlastingness. But the crowd, which belongs wholly to history and repetition (as do the bells themselves), passes by the church and proceeds down the fittingly named King William Street.

In part 5, the protagonist's own far-off goal will be God, an entity that obviates the need for a crowd. The protagonist will not turn to the Church, but will repudiate mass gatherings of human beings altogether—shudderingly so in his hyperbolic vision of "hooded hordes swarming / Over endless plains," a crowd beyond even a mock-flow, "stumbling" as it does "in a cracked earth / Ringed by the flat horizon only." The protagonist would not be touched by anything human and abject—and the crowd is a mass, shouldering phenomenon of touching and being touched. But he will delight to picture his spirit as a boat that, afloat on a vast flow, responds "Gaily, when invited, beating obedient / To controlling hands," hands that touch only where the body fails to reach.

83. Ibid., 84, 39.

Corpse-Body

A corpse is an implosion of the crowd phenomenon within a single body. A corpse that "sprouts" is one that, by discharging itself outward, directing its self-destructive manyness back into the scheme of generation, reenters life, that is, wheels once again toward death. The image of a sprouting corpse—a corpse "planted" in a garden—gothicizes the image evoked by the epithet "the hyacinth girl"; both consign the human being to the natural cycle alone—are, respectively, the nightmare and the erotic dream of the pagan love of generation.

When speaking of this corpse, the protagonist betrays—or mocks up—a terrific anxiety. He pretends to *want* the sprouting, but he protests too much; we detect a punishing irony. What is the good of rising, and sinking, and rising again, going up the hill and down, in a mad, libidinous, profitless cycle? The protagonist has already been alive for so long, so many times: "You who were with me in the ships at Mylae!"[84] As it was in the beginning: he and Stetson are still the drones of a competitive economy. Tellurian repetition has a stranglehold on the speaker, and his address to Stetson—that overfamiliar fellow man—has the abrupt ring of an accusation: You! Who were with me at Mylae! You who actually *planted* a corpse! You on the Wheel!

For the protagonist, as for Stephen Dedalus in *Ulysses,* history is a nightmare from which he is (already, if hardly known to himself) trying to wake: in his case, into the true present of the Absolute. If Eliot does not credit a notion of historical cycles as readily as other modernists do (as Pound, Yeats, Joyce, Woolf, and Lawrence do), the reason is his utter metaphysical resistance to the very element of time.

In *The Symbolism of Evil,* Paul Ricoeur describes the "myth of situation" that resulted from the Orphic reform of Dionysianism (a reform that became in turn the "ancient discourse" behind Platonic philosophy). In this myth, the soul is discovered (and for the first time) in and through pure opposition to the body, which is also for the first time posited as an entity, and dubbed *soma,* "jail." Condemned to the flesh for some unnamed fault, the soul is further stained by its jail, by desire and passion, so that its sentence is extended, it must endure still more agonies of abjection, of endurance of the natural cycle.[85] This

84. It may be the same "historical sense" that led Pound to the discovery that "all times are contemporaneous" that momentarily leads the protagonist to the feeling (the hallucination?) that he has persisted through many periods: though he takes to this idea and later will transform himself, for the duration of a number of lines, into the ages-old Tiresias.

85. Paul Ricoeur, *The Symbolism of Evil,* trans. Emerson Buchanan (Boston: Beacon Press, 1969), 283.

image and conviction of the body as a jail (which Plato cites in *Cratylus*) is alluded to in part 5 of *The Waste Land*: "I have heard the key / Turn in the door once and turn once only." Eliot's poem is a proto-Orphic protest against the punitive Wheel of Generation. (It is proto-Buddhist by the same token.) By this point in part 1, the protagonist is nearly hysterical with the emptiness of bodily life, nearly nauseated with its mad impulse to sprout again and again out of the same bed of death. The syntax of "That corpse you planted" bespeaks a brutal preoccupation. Must the protagonist shout out word of this evidently nefarious deed, for everyone in the street to hear? What complicity he must feel in it. How joined with his old partner in murder and creation.

Why this need for virtual public confession? Is it the Primal Father who lies in the garden, killed yet restored to a still-phallic life in a nonthreatening vegetal form, thus easing conscience a little (a very little)? Once allies in an ancient war, are Stetson and the protagonist also the original Brothers who conspired against the Unbearable Father? Does their ontogenetic backfiring go that far? Or have they murdered, instead, the Primal Mother, the principle of germination itself, the indifferent feminine power of reproduction—a power the soul must murder but which the Oedipal son must honor and protect ("Oh keep the Dog far hence . . . / Or with his nails he'll dig it up again!"). The burial of the dead seems in this instance an attempt to annihilate, in indiscriminate, condensed form, both phallic terrorization and female fertility—but the hysteria they evoke is countered by an equally strong hysteria of guilty denial of any wrongdoing: the corpse was, after all, "planted," and so has been allowed, after all, to sprout, in token satisfaction of both phallic and generative roles and impulses. Besides, if the protagonist himself is still ambivalent about wanting to be alive (as opposed, not to being "undone"—for that is what "life" amounts to—but to being "Neither / Living nor dead," being one with the One Alive); if he is ambivalent about denying the senses, living without women, beyond the phallus, beyond speech, then he may identify with the corpse, suffocating with it blindly under the soil, struggling to reenter the light and air, hysterical to flee sproutingly from the fate of becoming a handful of dust.

In any case, the protagonist's fantasy of an economically planted, burgeoning corpse makes a nightmare not only of economy but of the primitive human tendency to identify with nature. Frazer notes that "rude man . . . fails to distinguish the impulses and processes in himself from the methods which nature adopts to ensure the reproduction of plants and animals."[86] But to carry this to the point of displacing

86. Sir James George Frazer, *The Golden Bough: A Study in Magic and Religion* (New York: Macmillan, 1960), 160.

the human with the vegetal, converting the first into the second, proves a total, claustrophobic exclusion of the "soul" from the *soma,* apparently leaving it nowhere at all, snuffing it, blithely ruling it out of what alone is recognized as possessing "being"—effecting a sudden, eons-collapsing regression. The ritual sacrifice of fertility gods was not only meant to ensure the revival of vegetation, it was followed by the resurrection of those same gods; but so far as those gods do indeed represent the principle of generation (merely that), how much travesty of such sacrifices can there be in the sprouting corpse of "The Burial of the Dead"? The corpse is precisely not "buried," and this is in the spirit of pagan refusal of death.

Economics connects the City, Mylae, and planting a corpse. The multiplication and pullulation of matter—coins, cells, lives—is the common madness. What makes the waste land waste is the hysterical inability simply to let matter go to waste, the avoidance of the flesh-shedding asceticism of the East. Matter must be in motion, made current; it must rise, its economy flourish. The "archaic separation" from the maternal body that psychoanalysis sees as underlying anxiety over anal castoffs must not be reenacted, still less accepted. That moment when, unable to see, speak, think, or desire a woman, the protagonist became a symbolic corpse—that moment of No to the Mother, and indeed of No to the Father (for both the body and its protective systems of symbolicity were transcended)—that moment can be recovered only if death is accepted and *as a result* discovered to be the nothing it is.

The protagonist's apparent fear of loss of control over cast-off bodily stuff (the corpse having, in his little Gothic fantasy, an aspect of manure) is fear of the wrong death; the death the protagonist should fear is the one he dully takes part in as he flows with the crowd through the City. He mistakes or pretends to mistake the sprouting for an important sign of life, a salvational sign, in the City of Desolation. It must be pretends: in point of fact, his macabre anxiety that the sprouting may be prevented can only induce, just as it can only reflect, horror.[87] Continued (human) life at *that* cost is indeed a travesty, one that exposes the vanity of life itself, and in both senses. *He* knows that; and, he says, so do you, hypocrite reader, my brother, my likeness. You, too, feel the rampant modern hysteria, you too have had enough of nature, generation, history, flux, flesh.

87. The expression "friend to men" carries the sick suggestion that dogs, natural diggers-up of buried bones, may want to be close to men, even when the latter have become corpses. This raging adherence of physical life to physical life—man to garden, corpse to germination, dog to man—is, so the shrill tone implies, unbearable to contemplate.

What the protagonist's own hysteria is preparing is a conversion. "Hysteric conversion," remarks Kristeva, "is the symptom of an ego that, overtaxed by a 'bad object,' turns away from it, cleanses itself of it, and vomits it," relinquishing abjection even if and because it is eminently productive of culture (Kristeva cites Freud on the incest prohibition as what generates law, writing, property, and so on).[88] The protagonist's conversion will come with the abjection-tormented cry, "O Lord thou pluckest me out" (part 3). Here, by contrast, his hysteria merely flails at Stetson and himself and the reader; is the soul's self-wounding; its wild grief at having traffic with a corpse-body, with what is so abjectly "other," so virulently vital, that, released from human constraints, it adopts an independent line of flight straight into the vegetative, and sprouts (whereas—or so intimated the authoritative voice in paragraph 2—it is the *soul* that should sprout).

So at this point, terribly divided against himself, the protagonist half wants to die, like the Sibyl, and half to live on in any form, at whatever cost to his "soul" (of which, as yet, he has apparently had both very little, and all-changing, news). He is not yet ready to say, Let the dead bury the dead; he is still a denizen, albeit an explosively restive one, of the Unreal City.

Mimesis (Tone)

This fourth verse paragraph begins in a neutral "allegorical" style, a style adapted for "telling": "Unreal City / Under the brown fog of a winter dawn." But a change from diegesis to mimesis comes with the openly intensive "so" in "so many" at the end of line three: "A crowd flowed over London Bridge, so many." (Madame Sosostris had used "so" in "One must be so careful these days"—a contrastingly bombastic use.) As if riveted to the scene of an accident, the fourth line then repeats the expression "so many," leading up to it with stunned monosyllables: "I had not thought death had undone so many." So it is that out of the miasmic "Unreal City" a real "spirit" emerges, and begins confiding. (And so it was for Dante, except that, unlike Dante, the protagonist is participant as well as witness; he conducts a tour of this hell, and he is this hell. He it is who confides.)

The tone now fluctuates, edged with hysteria (which is always a crowd). The line "Sighs, short and infrequent, were exhaled" has something of Dante's shocked "objective" notation. But "Flowed up the hill and down King William Street" echoes the ups and downs (of

88. Kristeva, *Powers of Horror*, 45, 56–61.

both pictured content and stress) in nursery rhymes: after "Flowed up the hill," the reader half expects "and then back down again." The still half-wonderful repetitive character of life in nursery rhymes is thus both resavored and savaged by its jaundiced superposition on the daily round of an adult workforce. Not surprisingly, the tone soon turns sardonic: "With a dead sound on the final stroke of nine"—a line that, together with "And each man fixed his eyes before his feet," keeps up the listless, flowless rhythm of "I had not thought death had undone so many." "Final stroke" sounds medically dire. The cheerful echo of "hill" in "William," in the one line with a lilt to it, is counterbalanced by the double-locking double echo of "*kept* the *hours*" in "With a *dead sound*," a murder *by* sound, effected partly by the closing together in stressed words of the flat *e* and the sourly circling *ou*. (Similarly, the alliteration of "fixed . . . feet" in "And each man fixed his eyes before his feet" fetters the feet, just as the play of *e*'s across the line rivets the eye.)

Then, as noted, a monologic hysteria breaks out, merely disguised as dialogue (the protagonist cannot really expect an answer to such an outburst)—a hysteria that takes also a historical form: the speaker and Stetson are suddenly temporally multiplied, schizophrenic wanderers through the ages, each a many disguised as a one. The questions fired at Stetson are brittle, anxious, ironic: something (it seems to be his, and the speaker's own, attachment to life) is not being forgiven. That appositive "You who were with me in the ships at Mylae!" is hurtled like a spear into the dead heartwood of the past. Three anxious end-to-end questions are framed by two pained pairs of exclamations. But despite this appearance of symmetry, the tone seems about to split under its own pressure, and the syntax all but does splinter in "You! hypocrite lecteur!—mon semblable,—mon frère!" (much as this line is borrowed from Baudelaire's sonnet "To the Reader"). The passage thus shades precipitously toward the bad-nerves dialogue of the woman in part 2, "A Game of Chess."

Do we begin to know the protagonist better as a result of this longest of his monologues in one voice (if one voice can be said to encompass the tonal range from dead or neutral to febrile)? No doubt he was less histrionic, more "himself," while speaking about his experience on returning from the Hyacinth garden, not to mention his lines on the shower of rain and the Hofgarten. On the other hand, everything he says reveals him, he is everything that can be revealed (like many a modernist hero). In part 1, he comes further and further into voice, till voice itself grows shrill and he is breathing into the face of the reader his unbearable anxiety.

Mimesis (Syntax)

Throughout part 1, the syntax has been finely responsive to its tonal and conceptual burden, and largely for that reason continuously varied.

If, nonetheless, the poem opens with two sentences very similar in shape (down to their collusion with the line breaks), it is to confirm the speaker's die-hard conservatism:

April is the cruellest month, breeding	Winter kept us warm, covering
Lilacs out of the dead land, mixing	Earth in forgetful snow, feeding
Memory and desire. . . .	A little life with dried tubers.

Even so, the second sentence is properly shorter than the first: it says that comfort is distanced, and was anyway small. Elsewhere, too, the writing enacts (whether protectively or complainingly) the secular rule of repetition. Much of this takes the form of verbal doubling. "Marie, / Marie," for instance, carries its own mountain echo. "Your shadow . . . your shadow" is self-shadowing. "So many . . . so many" openly despairs of counting, seems itself undone.

Verbal and clausal repetition combine in the passage beginning "And I will show you something different" and ending "I will show you fear in a handful of dust"—a structure that, mockingly sheltering "Your shadow at morning striding behind you" and "your shadow at evening, rising to meet you," finally buries them in that terminal line of shoveling monosyllables. Here, as in the heavy recurrence of "this red rock," the repetition has the monolithic character of fate: is imposing, inexorable. By contrast, "Your arms full, and your hair wet" recognizes a weaker, if still weighty, power to gather in, a female magnetism.

In Madame Sosostris's monologue (again by contrast) the "Here is" catalog is brisk and, despite the repeated pointing, varied. The Madame would not waste words, her time has a price on it. Her one piece of elaboration ("The lady of situations") might be spoken in a sardonic undertone, as a wicked little gift to herself. Otherwise, her reading is marked by a rhythm of acceleration, the demonstrative "here" coming at ever quicker intervals, until, with the substitution "this card," a puzzled, pondering retardation is introduced, a coil formed by "which": "and this card, / Which is blank, is something he carries on his back, / Which I am forbidden to see." She inclines to rapping monosyllables ("here the Wheel," "I do not find / The Hanged Man," and so on). She is exact; she throws her predictions into the protagonist's future like weighted darts. He leaves. Now for his life.

In his address to the "Unreal City," syntax itself becomes de-realized. Here Eliot, with Pound's nudging, boldly adjusts word arrangement to theme (but this is in fact the rule in *The Waste Land*). Syntax refuses to claim, to hold in possession, the Unreal City. The latter is left to float, a specter; and the interrupted syntax suggests on the speaker's part a want of self-possession. Altogether different is the grammatical interruption in "Sighs, short and infrequent, were exhaled." With its formal tuck this sighing pattern, a new one in the poem, seems cut from some archaic literary cloth—is wonderingly sympathetic with the semantic content yet at the same time chronicle-efficient.

The fragment begining "Flowed up the hill" treats everything that follows "A crowd flowed over London Bridge" as an interruption. The fragment bestirs itself to allow the crowd some flow, even if an initially strenuous uphill flow. But after this jerky resumption of movement, the movement consists of little but jerks: "and stopped him, crying: 'Stetson!'"; the "You who" line; the horrifiedly pointing "That corpse you planted" line; the short-rhythmed questions; the neurasthenically knobby interruption "that's friend to men" after "Oh keep the Dog far hence"; and the "You!" even more abrupt than the one that pins Stetson to a bloody history, and in which the reader is surprised to find himself more central than Stetson. This "You!" itself introduces a jerky series of phrases that define the "you" as the always false other-subject, semblance of one's own spurious subjecthood. "Hypocrite" and "semblable" confirm this nuance, even as "mon frère" applies (too late) the balm of brotherhood to the sting of accusation.

He Do the Police . . .

This might be as fair a place as any to take the pulse of the notion of a single and unifying protagonist in *The Waste Land*.

Again, the argument is that this notion has not been sufficiently entertained and tested in earlier commentary on Eliot. Stanley Sultan's few pages on the subject in *Ulysses, The Waste Land, and Modernism* form—as will be more fully noted—the one substantial, and neglected, exception.

As has perhaps been demonstrated, part 1 presents no obstacles to reading the poem in this light. On the contrary, the hypothesis of a single speaker and performer adds shadow, depth, drama, and direction to everything in the movement. It discovers a poem of far more seriousness, profundity, and complexity than Edward Said (among others) regards it as being: namely, "a collection of voices repeat-

ing and varying and mimicking one another and literature generally."[89]

Certainly the original working title, "He Do the Police in Different
Voices," implies the presence of a single speaker in the poem who is
gifted at "taking off" the voices of others—just as the foundling
named Sloppy in Dickens's *Our Mutual Friend* is, according to the
doubtless biased and doting Betty Higden, "a beautiful reader of a
newspaper. He do the police in different voices."[90] This speaker has a
flair for tones of criminality, sensationalism, and outrage—the whole
gamut of abjection and judgment; or so the title implies. He shows a
relish for such tones, he is virtuosic at rendering them. The working
title was thus itself a harsh judgment on the protagonist (whom it
travesties). All speech is abjection? The very impulse to perform voice
is suspect? A complicity in the fascination of crime—say, murder? To
create and to murder are near akin? These severe intimations are of a
piece with the *contemptus mundi* of the poem.

The hypothesis of an all-centering, autobiographical protagonist-
narrator is not only consistent with the working title; it explains the
confident surfacing, in the latter part of the poem, of an unmistakable
religious pilgrim. Unless this pilgrim can be shown to develop (to inch,
scramble, flee) out of a waste land that is, or was, himself, the poem
splits apart into two unequal sections, a long one constituted by what
Lyndall Gordon calls "the Voices of Society" and a shorter one on a
lone pilgrim to elsewhere.[91] Neither Gordon nor A. D. Moody—each
so admirable on *The Waste Land*—connects what they concur in regarding as a pilgrim with what they might agree to call the Voices of
Society. But there is no difficulty in the way of positing the former as
the "doer" of the latter—as one of the social voices, yet *he who surpasses them* in being able to do and place them in an ironic relation to
other voices, including his own.

Gordon's valuable suggestion that the poem belongs in the religio-
literary category of "the exemplary life" is in fact better served by this
more unifying reading. "In the lives Eliot invokes," Gordon comments, "—Dante, Christ, Augustine, the grail knight, Ezekiel—there
is always a dark period of trial, whether in a desert, a slough of des-
pond, or a hell, followed by initiation, conversion, or the divine light
itself."[92] The protagonist is not merely one among others in hell (and

89. Edward W. Said, *Beginnings: Intention and Method* (New York: Basic Books,
1975), 10.

90. Charles Dickens, *Our Mutual Friend*, bk. 1, chap. 16.

91. Gordon, *Eliot's Early Years*, 106–7.

92. Ibid., 110.

the "conversation" between him and Stetson, who were alive and comparatively heroic together so long ago, only makes sense in a dimension of hell); hell is not merely others; the protagonist *is* hell, and it is out of this hell, at once his own and collective, that, through conversion, he must climb toward the divine light. If he does the voices of others, it is because in the first instance his ears are whores to them; he dramatizes, thus, his own abjection. He is not merely one of the denizens of the waste land; he is their sum, he is sin upon sin, even sinner upon sinner—or so his self-multiplying and self-shading ventriloquism suggests. Not that he does the voices altogether helplessly; on the contrary, he gathers them in his fist like a rattlesnake's severed coils and shakes them so as to disturb his own and his readers' war-dulled, jazz-dulled, machine-dulled ears. But, in any case, he demonstrates thus—he confesses—his own hellish entanglements with secularism and the flesh. The first three parts of the poem present the equation *the others = me,* if in a way that proves the equation a little false (it involves a sick self-belittlement). The rest of the poem clarifies the actual opposition of *others/me* that endows the first three parts with insidious drama.

And so, like Stanley Sultan, I find in the poem (and everywhere within it), a protagonist-narrator who, in Sultan's words,

recounts dramatically the voices he hears in the world and within himself, also: reflects ("April is the cruellest month"); quotes himself ("I . . . stopped him, crying: 'Stetson!'"); reports his responses to characters whom he has quoted ("—Yet when we came back, late, from the Hyacinth garden . . ."); narrates—with exposition, in the manner of narrators ("Madame Sosostris, famous clairvoyante, / Had a bad cold"); quotes from poems and popular songs; reports snatches of poems and songs he has been moved to repeat to himself; meditates; and so on.

Further, this "erudite, reflective, suffering young male protagonist . . . is [himself] a poet ["Sweet Thames run softly till I end my song"] . . . (the poem which is his narrative is his own poem)."[93] Sultan thus seconds Robert Langbaum's opinion that "the poem is essentially a monodrama":

We have to distinguish [Langbaum writes] the scenes in which the protagonist himself plays a part—the recollection of the Hyacinth garden, the visit to Madame Sosostris, the meeting with Stetson, the scene with the rich Belladonna—from the scene in the pub and at the typist's. We can either consider that the protagonist overhears the first and imagines the second, or

93. Stanley Sultan, *Ulysses, The Waste Land, and Modernism: A Jubilee Study* (Port Washington, N.Y.: Kennikat Press, 1977), 62–71.

that at these points the poet's consciousness takes leave of the protagonist to portray parallel instances. I prefer the first line of interpretation because it yields a more consistent structure on the model of romantic monodrama.[94]

Contributing to the collection *Eliot in His Time* (1973), Langbaum argued that, F. O. Matthiessen, Cleanth Brooks, and George Williamson having already reversed the earlier trend and begun to "find progression, unity, and positive meaning through the built-in analogy with the Grail and the vegetation myths," the logical next step was to explore the thesis of a single, continuous protagonist. Sultan, writing a few years later, agreed that *The Waste Land* "cannot be discussed with true authority" until the issue of its protagonist is arbitrated. Most subsequent commentators on *The Waste Land* have, however, shown the same disposition as earlier ones to leave this question dismissively out of focus.

Langbaum, concerned with "archetypalization" in the poem, finds in it a "buried life" that manifests itself "through the unconscious memory of characters from the past." If this means the protagonist's memory, I suggest that the relation to the past is, on the contrary, conscious, playful, ironic, at times even deliberately bathetic; in any case, always theatrical. The poem, that is to say, registers a crisis of speech itself, in which all speech is relativized, ironized, consciously inadequate before the impossible standards of an inaccessible (and to most an inadmissible) Absolute. What emerges from this acutely suffered *specular* relation to language is speech as performance; what rises to the occasion is a showman's instinct. In the protagonist, an incipient hysteria, a wish to throw himself across everything written and spoken, to claim all language as ready money, however counterfeit, to revel masochistically in its comedy, is at once supported and reined in by the exhibitionism, malice, ingenuity, and fun of a virtuoso of language and dramatic stance, of staged accents. The protagonist is on the one hand as serious as a church and on the other perfectly consistent with the Eliot who, so gossip said, showed up at dinner parties at the time with green powder on his face and a touch of lipstick on his mouth.

To speak at all is to engage in theater. Derrida describes expression (ex-pression) as "exteriorization." To speak is to place oneself at a distance from oneself in "pure auto-affection." Indeed, merely to be

94. Langbaum, "New Modes of Characterization in *The Waste Land*," 95–128. Langbaum incorporated this essay in a longer treatment of Eliot's poetry in his book *The Mysteries of Identity: A Theme in Modern Literature* (New York: Oxford University Press, 1977).

conscious is to do this, since "no consciousness is possible without the voice." Consciousness is "irreducible openness in the inside," not "the inwardness of an inside that is closed in upon itself." It is, in other words, "the eye and the world within speech. *Phenomenological reduction is a scene, a theater stage.*"[95]

The protagonist both suffers from and exploits this essential theatricality of voice. His nature is a poet's nature, at once powerfully secretive and helplessly "open"—empathetic, susceptible, yours for the asking. The protagonist is, in a phrase Delmore Schwartz applies to Eliot himself, a "sibylline listener." He listens in on others with the mercilessness of one who fails to hear "the silence" in their speech yet with the full dramatic sympathy of his empathic nature, too—with a tenth of that capacity for sympathy which also, at its fullest and subtlest stretch, enables him to detect the ethereal presence of an attendant "hooded" figure (part 5), or look into the heart of light.

Eliot's prose poem "Hysteria" was about just such a protohysterical, protosalvational empathy. "As she laughed, I was aware of becoming involved in her laughter and being part of it . . . I was drawn in by short gasps, inhaled by each momentary recovery, lost finally in the dark caverns of her throat, bruised by the ripple of unseen muscles."[96] Laughter is hysteria, empathy with voice is hysteria-in-the-making, acting is controlled hysteria. The protagonist "acts" the voices of others as if he had little choice in the matter, and even his "own" voice is, to him, theater, the voice of Hieronymo as he plots a Babel of other voices, plots the crash of Babel itself.

Almost helplessly many, almost incapacitated by his capacity for openness, the protagonist will nonetheless find in this susceptibility to otherness and outsidedness (a susceptibility that, largely "sympathy," makes them inward, his) his *virtú* and virtue, his identification with what is pure and utter: so Other that sympathy with it minimalizes his abjection, which becomes no more than a clot of sound that he must cough up, a phlegm of speech. By imbuing his protagonist with his own auditory and vocal genius of participation in the abjectness of his times and in approaches to the Absolute (for "the silence" must be heard, and speech must edge it), Eliot made his poem a barometer sensitive both to the foggy immediate air and to the atmospheric pres-

---

95. Jacques Derrida, *Speech and Phenomena and Other Essays on Husserl's Theory of Signs*, trans. David B. Allison (Evanston: Northwestern University Press, 1973), 32, 79, 86. Speech, moreover, is awareness of mortality: "The appearing of the *I* to itself in the *I am* is . . . originally a relation with its own possible disappearance. Therefore *I am* originally means *I am mortal*" (54).

96. Eliot, *Complete Poems and Plays 1909–1950*, 19.

sure high and far off, the "thunder of spring over distant mountains" (part 5). A group or medley of voices cannot attend to a charged, remote silence; for that a single protagonist was necessary, one who could both "do" the group and find in himself the anguish and strength to leave it, repressing the fatal impulse (as Moody puts it) "towards a renewal of human love" and seeking, instead, the Love Omnipotent.[97]

97. Moody, *Thomas Stearns Eliot: Poet,* 111.

A GAME OF CHESS

The Chair She Sat In

The Chair she sat in, like a burnished throne,
Glowed on the marble, where the glass
Held up by standards wrought with fruited vines
From which a golden Cupidon peeped out
(Another hid his eyes behind his wing)
Doubled the flames of sevenbranched candelabra
Reflecting light upon the table as
The glitter of her jewels rose to meet it,
From satin cases poured in rich profusion;
In vials of ivory and coloured glass
Unstoppered, lurked her strange synthetic perfumes,
Unguent, powdered, or liquid—troubled, confused
And drowned the sense in odours; stirred by the air
That freshened from the window, these ascended
In fattening the prolonged candle-flames,
Flung their smoke into the laquearia,
Stirring the pattern on the coffered ceiling.
Huge sea-wood fed with copper
Burned green and orange, framed by the coloured stone,
In which sad light a carvèd dolphin swam.
Above the antique mantel was displayed
As though a window gave upon the sylvan scene
The change of Philomel, by the barbarous king
So rudely forced; yet there the nightingale
Filled all the desert with inviolable voice
And still she cried, and still the world pursues,
"Jug Jug" to dirty ears.
And other withered stumps of time
Were told upon the walls; staring forms
Leaned out, leaning, hushing the room enclosed.
Footsteps shuffled on the stair.
Under the firelight, under the brush, her hair
Spread out in fiery points
Glowed into words, then would be savagely still.

"My nerves are bad to-night. Yes, bad. Stay with me.
"Speak to me. Why do you never speak? Speak.
"What are you thinking of? What thinking? What?
"I never know what you are thinking. Think."

I think we are in rats' alley
Where the dead men lost their bones.

"What is that noise?"
         The wind under the door.
"What is that noise now? What is the wind doing?"
        Nothing again nothing.
             "Do
"You know nothing? Do you see nothing? Do you remember
"Nothing?"
  I remember
Those are pearls that were his eyes.
"Are you alive, or not? Is there nothing in your head?"
                  But

O O O O that Shakespeherian Rag—
It's so elegant
So intelligent
"What shall I do now? What shall I do?"
"I shall rush out as I am, and walk the street
"With my hair down, so. What shall we do to-morrow?
"What shall we ever do?"
    The hot water at ten.
And if it rains, a closed car at four.
And we shall play a game of chess,
Pressing lidless eyes and waiting for a knock upon the door.

And Still the World Pursues

The protagonist devotes this extended verse paragraph to a disclosure of his married life. Having just shown himself among people walking round in a ring, after Madame Sosostris's prediction, he now shows himself in the company of the woman foretold by the card Belladonna, the Lady of the Rocks, the lady of situations. The City was the City of Desolation, which is in hell, and the protagonist's wife proves to be (as Lyndall Gordon notes) at least a weak demon, a victim-demon, at once pathetic and caustic.

Yes, despite the resounding Nay of the noumenal silence, the protagonist has evidently married, and married, of all women (yet in a sense she is all women), the hyacinth girl, the epitome of female narcissism. To understand his own "situation," it is not at all necessary that we establish the common identity of the two female figures—the one so fresh, the other so flammable—but in point of fact, the narrator takes some pains to plant clues leading to this conclusion. One of these, the statement, "I remember / The hyacinth garden," was cancelled from the original draft. This had preceded the line "Those are pearls that were his eyes."[1] Thus had this Phoenician Sailor elliptically traced news of his rich and strange destiny back to his suddenly blinded seeing of—and into—the heart of light. Still, several clues survive. Chief among these is the way part of the dialogue is spun out of the earlier passage: the paragraph itself remembers the hyacinth garden. The following charts the echoes:

I could not / Speak	Why do you never speak?
And my eyes failed	Do you see nothing?
I was neither / Living nor dead	Are you alive, or not?
And I knew nothing	Do / You know nothing?

To link the woman further to the earlier scene, Eliot places all the lexical and conceptual echoes among *her* words (in a verbal sleight). We find too the recurrence of a rapt narcissism, but now horribly starved for attention, demonic with demand for it. In a telling reversal hair, no longer artlessly dewy with drops of spring rain, is furiously brushed—with, in both senses, a vain attempt at a luring self-beautification—into fiery points. *Wehe,* is it she who once seemed so natural, the personification of spring flowers, who now clouds her dressing room with the cloying smoke of strange synthetic perfumes, in which the "sense" of the protagonist, that fragile sailor among women, "drowns"?

As with the fortune-teller's signposting of parts of the poem, this evident return of the earlier couple, this before (which was already, in one sense, an after) and after, is a compaction, a formal and moral economy, that Eliot (reinforced by the scissoring Pound) would have valued. If it is not a familiar idea in the commentary on the poem, perhaps the reason is a reluctance among many critics to relinquish the hyacinth girl as a radiant ideal of female youth and beauty: the eternal feminine, the always-to-be-desired female other. It was this ideal, however, that the protagonist himself was forced to experience as a mirage.

Eliot did not wait until his essay on Baudelaire (1930) to indicate, in prose, his sympathy with a mystical deconstruction of ordinary, romantic human emotions. In a review in the *Athenaeum* (May 30, 1919), he said of Stendhal and Flaubert that their understanding of "the awful separation between potential passion and any actualization possible in life" is "mysticism of a kind." In particular, they understood—and presumably the poet himself by this point well understood—"the indestructible barriers between one human being and

---

1. T. S. Eliot, *The Waste Land: A Facsimile and Transcript of the Original Drafts Including the Annotations of Ezra Pound*, ed. Valerie Eliot (New York: Harcourt Brace Jovanovich, 1971), 13.

another." "A Game of Chess" seems intended to be, like their work, a breaking down of the lumps of emotion that coagulate on the surface of existence and look like "important simple feelings"—a disintegration of them into something equally simple but "terrible and unknown." In the same review, Eliot said of some of Stendhal's scenes, his phrases too, that they "read like cutting one's own throat; they are a terrible humiliation to read, in the understanding of human feelings and human illusions of feeling that they force upon the reader."[2] "The Game of Chess" inflicts the same sort of humiliation, its two panels hinging remorselessly on one and the same negation of romantic and (where marriage is concerned) humanistic illusionism. Both show marriage as *Oed' und leer*—just what the protagonist had earlier intuited it would be.

Kristeva, speaking of death- and father-banished narrators—Beckett and other "militant bachelors of the early twentieth century"—says that, "rather than avoid the sexual act, they . . . assume it but only as an impossible relationship whose participants are condemned to a perpetual banishment that confines them within autoeroticism." This is effectively the case with the first married couple in "A Game of Chess," where the woman's frustrated self-strokings angrily substitute for caresses from her husband, and where the latter—for the moment cruelly and coldly contracting even his considerable capacity for voyeurism—diddles his own consciousness with literary phrases. "Against the modifying *whole* of the father's Death," adds Kristeva, "one chooses banishment toward the *part* constituting a fallen object or an object *of* love. . . . How trivial, this object of love—transposition of love for the Other."[3] The protagonist's marriage is the sign not only of sensual weakness but of this transposition. And by his judgmental, protective silence he punishes his wife—that synthetic woman—for her triviality as measured against the Loving Heart of the Other, the Silence. As an autoerotic she-demon, as a merely sensory enchantress, she cannot serve as a conduit to the Absolute—that fleshless, odorless, zero degree of what is overpainted even by such banished terms as Death and the Father.

Anxiety (Male)

The atmosphere in the "enclosed" room is one of all but unbearable anxiety. In a minimal definition, anxiety is a reaction to situations of

2. T. S. Eliot, "Beyle and Balzac," *Athenaeum* 4643 (30 May 1919):393.

3. Julia Kristeva, *Desire in Language*, ed. Leon S. Roudiez, trans. Alice Jardine, Thomas Gora and Leon S. Roudiez (New York: Columbia University Press, 1980), 150–51.

danger. What is the danger here? First, on the husband's part, a fear of being suffocated by objects and their hell-smoke. These objects (like the synthetic woman herself, their priestess, their *type*) are, on the one hand, intolerable substitutes for the (mythical) perfect and always absent mother. But since the latter is herself intolerable in her nightmare aspect of castrating Female Fate (an aspect that, as will be indicated, the synthetic wife incarnates), the objects are also unbearable as what would stop the soul's flight from the Archaic Mother into the transobjectal, never sexual Absolute. The common physical symptoms of anxiety include difficulty in breathing—a symptom that Freud traces to the birth trauma. When the protagonist suffered an anxiety attack in identifying himself covertly with a corpse "planted" in a "bed" that deprived it of breath, he imagined the corpse shaking off this terrible suffocation and sending up shoots into the air. In the Websterian plea that this struggle be allowed to continue, an anxiety-quelling regularity of beat begins to assert itself in the verse: "Oh *keep* the *Dog* far *hence,* that's *friend* to *men,* / Or *with* his *nails* he'll *dig* it *up* again!" *En* re-echoes tensely in "hence," "friend," and "men," in quick succession, then at long last relaxes in "again." The verse itself is being asked to have a heart. In "The Game of Chess," by a kind of reversal, the air that "freshens" from the window actually serves to fatten and prolong the candle flames, so that they fling their smoke through the perfume-laden air and stir, without animating, the pattern "on the coffered ceiling." Through conceptual similitude if not by a slip of the ear (coffered, coffin), we are back in an imaginary deathbed, a corpse-space, stirred yet finding it hard to breathe.

Anxiety, so Freud elaborates in *The Problem of Anxiety,* is a scuttling apprehension of danger to "the economy of self-preservation," and if birth is the first "gross disturbance in the economy of . . . narcissistic libido," separation from the mother (as when she leaves the room) is a common later one. So, too, is the threat of castration, of "separation from the genital," the "high narcissistic value" of which "may be referable to the fact that the possession of [the penis] contains a guaranty of reunion with the mother (or mother substitute) in the act of coitus."[4] In this view, separation from the genital *would* be separation from the mother. But the "castrated" mother, in league with the Father's No, may herself appear to be the agent of castration, and so it is here with the mother substitute. Ensconced in the "room enclosed," a claustrophobic womb image, the synthetic woman (the false moth-

4. Sigmund Freud, *The Problem of Anxiety,* trans. Henry Alden Bunker (New York: W. W. Norton, 1936), 78.

er), in a development from the hyacinth girl's armful of picked flowers, has surrounded herself with cut and carved things. Here, where female "vials" are insidiously "Unstoppered," sea-wood has been chopped or broken into pieces and is being turned to ashes. What swims (and does not swim) in the stone that frames the fire is "a carvèd dolphin," sad in the "sad light" of the sea-wood's denatured ("fed with copper") flames—the "grave" accent in "carvèd" suggesting a cruel, indelible cut. The very ceiling (despite its elevated position) is carved. The representations of primal, sylvan life in the room are "withered stumps" or else (unnaturally rigid) "lean out." (The imagery, linking both a sea creature and trees to the penis, becomes elsewhere in the poem—in "fishing" and "roots that clutch"—a reversal of castration logic.) The precious contents of the female satin cases have been spilled out, and glitter brittlely under mock-erections of the fat and prolonged candle flames, which are applauded, autoerotically, by the doubling "glass." So, then, does this mother woman refuse to have the penis near her, unless it has first been cut, carved like an ivory man into something precious and safely manipulable? Does she force on male sexuality a masturbatory glitter? (In Thomas Middleton's play *Women Beware Women*, as Eliot's note puts us on the trail to realizing, a young woman is seduced in one room while a chess game, played in an adjoining room, parallels the erotic moves. In a substitute for sexual intercourse, the husband and his synthetic wife will—so the former reflects—"play a game of chess, / Pressing," in another castration image, "lidless eyes.")

Besides being a suffocating mother woman, then, this representative of paternal wrath also deals out rigidity: not the absent but the petrified penis, a bitter mockery of its functional, organic counterpart. Lady of the Rocks, she is, in effect, a Medusa, causing everything around her to lose its sap, to petrify. In her chair (or royal "Chair") like a "burnished throne" she sits before a mirror held up by metallic "fruited vines" among which flirt (even the one who, in mock Oedipal self-castration, hides his eyes) golden Cupidons. But if indeed the protagonist is doomed to be blinded around her, stiffly unresponsive, let it be *his* choice of lithic conditions. Let his whole form be as still and oblivious to woman as a statue, as it was near the Hyacinth garden. Let his eyes be blinded, if blinded they must be, into sea-blessed pearls. Would his wife flame upon his sight, exacting attention? Let her flame upon a motionless indifferent dolphin as it dreams upon the deep, sad as the loss of response might be, even for him.

But again the protagonist is at this time all too conscious of her power to enforce in him (by what sorcery?) an involuntary brittleness.

The anxiety this woman evokes is finally the fear of death itself, death as a punishment for the crime of being phallic. Fear of castration, writes Freud, develops into dread of conscience: what "the ego apprehends as a danger and . . . responds [to] with the signal of anxiety" is—at the pole furthest from the birth trauma—"the anger, the punishment, of the superego, the loss of its love." "The final transformation undergone by this fear of the superego," Freud adds, "[appears] to me to consist of death-(life-) anxiety, fear felt for the projection of the superego upon the powers of destiny."[5] For the protagonist, these powers are signaled by the "Chair . . . like a burnished throne," by the *lurking* synthetic perfumes, by the "change" wrought by "the barbarous king" in a sylvan scene, by forms that stare and lean out from the walls, "hushing the room enclosed," and by "Footsteps [shuffling] on the stair." Climactically, while playing chess (the object of which is not to lose one's king) and pressing lidless eyes, the protagonist will await "a knock upon the door." Psychoanalytically, this fear of vengeful castration connects up with the cult of the vegetation spirit. In *Totem and Taboo,* Freud recalls that youthful gods of vegetation enjoyed the favors of maternal deities—a symbolization of early man's agricultural bonding with mother earth—but were punished for it with a short life or with castration produced by some agent of the father's wrath—as when the boar fatally gores Adonis's too beautiful "thigh."[6]

The similar violence wreaked upon Philomel, the cutting out of her tongue by Tereus to keep her from telling of his phallic violence, led, not to still another repetition of natural life, as with the vegetation gods, but to what the protagonist represents—beautifully—as a powerfully carrying, richly and purely spreading—in short, desert-filling—"inviolable voice." Here arises a variant on "Those are pearls that were his eyes"—the equivalent with regard to sound, and hence a justification for poetry (an idealization of it, whether a wishful one or not). Each instances a transformation of an organic "part" into an incorruptible and precious product (work). How miss the intimation that the changed Philomel is the type of the artist, a figure of the poet as woman (his penis "nothing") yet supremely powerful at the level of symbolicity (of inviolable voice)? Here the protagonist finds, for the moment, his chief defense against the barbarous power of the female-dominated Chair of destiny, the scissors of the Fates. If it is a crime to peep out at the mother's naked beauty, then let one's eyes be like those

5. Ibid., 79.
6. Sigmund Freud, *Totem and Taboo,* trans. A. A. Brill (New York: Random House, 1946), 196–97.

of the poet, which, as such, see not, but represent visual appearance only through the chaste (in Eliot, the very chaste) remove of words. And if it is wrong to eat the mother, to tongue her, to prick her with one's organs, then let the same give way to the piercing and measured cries that, impalpable, laying no flesh against hers, nonetheless ravish her ears.

Anxiety (Female)

The sort of anxiety that the woman displays is, in part, what Freud calls "that state of helplessness of the ego in the face of excessive tension arising from ungratified need . . . the excess of unutilized libido."[7] It is precisely this state of helplessness, this excess, that the protagonist is least fit to alleviate, owing to his own double anxiety: in the first place, of castration danger and, in the second, of the danger of metaphysical claustrophobia, a condition caused by a demonic hegemony of objects.

To relieve *her* anxiety, the woman must attempt to establish her justification, her absoluteness as a living object. Representative of the natural cycle as she is, she must see to it that her husband, her lover, feels referred to, serves her as a Magna Mater. Her infinite variety must never stale, never cloy the appetite she feeds. She will fascinate, she *must* fascinate. A would-be queen of the sensory realm, her room perfumed like the purple sails of Cleopatra's gilt ("burning") barge, surrounded as Cleopatra was by "pretty dimpled boys," even if hers are golden Cupidons, she presides over, and tries to make herself a paragon among, sensory objects. But all to no avail, for her Antony seems to see nothing (nothing is all that he sees).

Whence her desperation. Nature having failed her as an "innocent" resource (it had already begun to do so near the Hyacinth garden), she becomes a sorceress—as predicted by her card, Belladonna—of "strange and synthetic" aids to allurement.[8] To substitute for that atmosphere of illusion in which alone things live and have a future, to replace the radiance of erotic love, she fills her room with the crushed essences of aromatic plants and with bewitching flames and flamey heat. She sets herself up, not amid a garden, but amid minerals that glow, mirroring a flame of admiration, just as *she* longs to do. In short, she becomes even more theatrically self-presenting than she was

---

7. Freud, *The Problem of Anxiety*, 81.

8. The name of a plant that is also called "deadly nightshade," "belladonna" derives from the Italian words *belladonna*, "lit. fair lady (so called because it was believed to have been used by women to dilate the pupils of the eyes and to create an artificial pallor)" (*The Random House Dictionary of the English Language*).

as a naïvely romantic girl. She stages not merely her beauty but her own self-beautification, as if to ensure that the protagonist perceives her beauty as what she means it to be, an end in itself, the proper object of a cult. Artfully, she places her hair "Under the firelight, under the brush"—unaware that to the protagonist the state of being "under" is oppressive and terrifying ("Under the brown fog"). Watching herself brushing her hair in the mirror, sparks snapping at the tips of her hair, she is what she intends: theater.

But as failed theater, theater without applause, a series of desperately overdone performances, she feels ready to do something extreme—extremely theatrical—such as "rush out as I am, and walk the street / With my hair down, so." (Her flair is for the melodramatic—she lacks the protagonist's cool histrionic instinct.) Yes, she will storm her husband's air of indifference, make the very silence around the two of them a harpy, drown his "sense." Unhappy Narcissus, she is unable to drown in the merciless pool of her glass; vacant pool, she cannot get her husband to drown in her. And little does she know that, all the while, in his own mind, he drowns her by plunging her into depths of historical comparison—with Dido, Cleopatra, Philomel—that she cannot sustain. What he cannot forgive in her is, in part, her essential exclusion of culture, her presumption in believing that her natural or artificially assisted beauty is a greater phenomenon than the refined aestheticism of myth and epic and drama—that it should command the eyes and ears and mind, indeed the whole soul, of a man. His elaborate mock-heroic parallel of her with Cleopatra is two-edged, implying first of all that she is nothing nearly so grand as Cleopatra and, second, that even if she were she would be grand only because she was (finally) real theater, an object of genuine fascination because one touched by the inviolable wand of art. Art, at least, stills the appetites to the point where the senses can (as later in the description of Christopher Wren's interior of the church of St. Magnus Martyr) form a seam with the soul.

The Waste Land is not in its highest reaches the appeal for culture that these remarks might make it seem. But germane to it, and particularly to the passage in question, is the following comment on the artist's love of ideal perfection, a statement made by the harsh-mouthed hero of Wyndham Lewis's novel *Tarr* (1918):

With most people, who are not artists, all the finer part of their vitality goes into sex if it goes anywhere: during their courtship they become third-rate poets, all their instincts of drama come out freshly with their wives. The artist is he in whom this emotionality normally absorbed by sex is so strong that it claims a newer and more exclusive field of deployment. Its first creation is *the Artist* himself. . . . Now for a bang-up first-rate poet nothing short of a queen or a chimera is adequate, the power he's been born with exacts perfection . . . one by one his powers are turned away from the usual objects of a man's personal poetry or passion and so removed from the immediate world.[9]

Yes, for the protagonist, Art above Woman. But eventually—though here he wavers, if only by virtue of approaching the noumenal through the phenomenology of his poem—the Absolute above Art.

Drowning among Objects (Diegesis/Mimesis)

Even when the protagonist is not looking directly at his wife, he sees her everywhere in the room. A mere "she" in the first line, she is subsequently reduced, in the next thirty-three lines, to a pronominal agency of possession ("her jewels," "her strange synthetic perfumes," "her hair"). Yet she is not so much displaced by her possessions as expressed by them, a powerful equivalence existing between the two: "Like the fiery glow and pervading odors," as Elena Hristova notes in an unpublished paper, "she too is effusive, fervent, filled with desire to conquer what is around her." In describing the room, the protagonist presents his wife: the fraudulent claim of the object-world for devoted attention and attendance.

In *this* room, this cloying conspiracy against ascetic withdrawal, how resort to the defence of chaste description? The protagonist instinctively devotes himself, instead, to an elaborate description that, outwardly subservient, subtly subverts the (presumptuously) imposing aspect of the room. This it does by insinuating a metaphysical critique of objects as being, despite appearances, insubstantially nonabsolute—melting moments of attention. This room under its own objectal smoke is as unreal as the City under the brown fog of a winter dawn. "We find that we are certain of everything—relatively," Eliot writes in the conclusion to *Knowledge and Experience*, "and of nothing,—positively. The virtue of metaphysical analysis is in the destructibility of everything, since analysis gives us something equally real, and for some purposes more real, than that which is analysed. . . . The analysis of the object, from this point of view, reveals the fact that in asking what the object is we merely turn in a circle." The object, as such, is merely the "*moment of objectivity*," the "point of *attention*"; for "the objecthood of an object . . . is the fact that we intend it as an object: it is the attending that makes the object." (Yet "we may say with equal truth that if there were no object we could not attend.")

9. Wyndham Lewis, *Tarr* (Middlesex: Penguin Modern Classics, 1982), 20.

Eliot concludes that "an object is real . . . in proportion to its relations outside of its objectivity."[10] The peculiarity of the synthetic
woman's room—as the protagonist, no doubt maliciously, perceives
it—is its merely synthetic "reality" as a complex of objects whose
relations outside their own objectivity are simply circular relations
with one another (as with, again, their priestess, the woman herself).
They serve, so to speak, one another's vanity, just as they serve hers,
and vanity itself is a famine—is nothing. With its underworld flickers,
its bloatedly fat flames of a moment, its rock and shadow, the passage
inscribes a variant on Plato's Cave of the Unreal.

Everything on which the narrator's eyes alight—in a presumption
of finding a solid base for the *"moment of objectivity"*—is bewilderingly referred, or refers itself, to something outside its own
physical confines. Begging attention from other things, it seeks reflection, but the maddening quality of reflection is to give itself up again,
in an elusive, unreal bid for conclusion. For the senses and mind, there
is no resting place, only a series of instant evictions, a game of touch
and run, a nausea of slitherings. Everything in the room flickers with a
restiveness like that of the woman herself. The "where" and "when"
of each object is uncertain, just as the woman is of her place as the
protagonist's mate ("My nerves are bad to-night. Yes, bad. Stay with
me"); of her reality before his eyes, memory, and mind.

Although the first preposition is a deceptively restful "in," it is almost immediately followed by a more openly relative and exposed
preposition, "on": "The Chair she sat in, like a burnished throne, /
Glowed on the marble." The Chair is, through this prepositional shift,
displaced by its own reflection, etherealized as a point of attention—
literally and figuratively cast down, desubstanced. Nor is it certain
where its ghostly form glows. Where is "the marble"? On the floor,
one thinks, deceived by the palatial capital ("Chair") and simile ("like
a burnished throne"). But, no, the marble is "where" (here another
positional sidestep) "the glass / Held up by standards wrought with
fruited vines"—to stop there (and the verse itself keeps us waiting for
a predication for this "glass"). The marble is thus evidently—if almost
floatingly, so far as the description is concerned—on the dressing table
where . . . where the glass (not immediately identifiable as a mirror)
somehow also is. Well, at least the description is concerned to say
how: "where the glass / Held up by by standards wrought with fruited
vines"—at which point a charming aside about the vines: "From

10. T. S. Eliot, *Knowledge and Experience in the Philosophy of F. H. Bradley* (London: Faber and Faber, 1964), 157–61.

which a golden Cupidon peeped out"—and then an aside within the aside: "(Another hid his eyes behind his wing)." By this point we begin to gain a sense of where the glass is—it is on standards, which in turn are probably on "the marble"—but the syntax itself has become almost as diffuse as the glow of the Chair on the marble. No sooner, then, is the glass mentioned than our attention is redirected to what holds it up—the description again moving off from what it first all but failed to establish as an object. The Cupidons, at least, are described without distrust or haste, and if one of them is tucked into a parenthesis, this position mimes its histrionic pose of abashed modesty. But from what is the syntax itself, even while peeping, hiding its eyes? Why does it wince or pass like a hot potato from object to object? Why does it linger only among images of Oedipal voyeurism and shame?

Just when the glass is all but forgotten in the intricate description of its stand, we are asked to recall it, so as to picture—not the glass, exactly—but what it pictures: its doubling of the flames of the seven-branched candelabra. The flames only appear to be in the glass; at the same time, as the doubles of real flames, they are in some sense a real if fugitive part of the mirror. Which ought we to focus on, the real or the real-but-unreal flames? The impetus of the syntax decides: neither. Instead, we are referred once again to a substanceless glow on the (presumably marble-topped) table: "where the glass . . . / Doubled the flames of sevenbranched candelabra / Reflecting light upon the table." Yet the table, like the glass, is a blind point of attention (so is each of the Cupidons). The syntax, as if restlessly seeking something more lovingly corroborative (less like nonseeing mineral eyes)—yes, the starved spirit of the woman herself seems to be in it—at once scrambles on from it "Reflecting light upon the table as / The glitter of her jewels rose to meet it." So, from reflection to reflection, if to a more intense and adoring one ("rose to meet it"). Light *met,* as the wife would be met by her husband's eyes—as the narrator-husband flinchingly knows. Four quasi-distinct levels of light, then—above the candelabra, on the table, in the jewels, and in a meeting above them—yet all the same light, divided and multiplied as if for its own self-enhancement: narcissistically intensified to form, not a gentle *heart* of light, but an eye-hitting compaction of it. But, really, the visual imagination appears all too dazzled here, in a blinding of logic. The glitter of the jewels would seem to rise, yes, and would seem to "meet" the light descending from the candelabra. But it would only be this light reflected. In any case, the antecedent for the pronoun "it" is, inconsistently, the light the syntax previously situated as "upon the table" ("Reflecting light upon the table"). The syntax itself seems dazzled, and this effect is repeated in the final phrase before the temporary pause and shoring of the semicolon: "From satin cases poured in rich profusion." Having directed us up from the jewels, the syntax now pulls us back down to the satin cases. Does the glitter itself rise from these cases, as the syntax blurredly implies? Are the jewels still in the cases, or have they been poured out in rich profusion? Or both at once, in a frozen pour, as of (say) necklaces lying partly in and partly out? Or, instead, as in a freeze-frame shot of the action of pouring? So, then, some of the smoke in the room seems to have entered the syntax. Why doesn't this matter to the person forming these strange, synthetic phrases and clauses of description? Does the protagonist not perhaps secretly enjoy this cobweb of a description that seems to pursue itself with its own broom, this nausea of ambiguity that confirms the worst he has ever thought about the vanity and unreality of the physical world?

Relentlessly, after the semicolon, he gives us more of the same. Again the description proves a mare's nest of unreliability (unreadability). After the destabilizing prepositions following the first "in"— "on," "up," "with," "From," "out," "behind," "upon," "to," "From,"—and the bewildering "in" in "poured in rich profusion," we find another "In," this one apparently straightforward: "In vials of ivory and coloured glass / Unstoppered, lurked her strange synthetic perfumes." This "in" seems justified and illustrated by "lurked," not least through the inverted word order that gives extra force to the word. Yet, as if in a hysterical avoidance of the paranoia-bolstering "In" and "lurked"—especially in their combination with "vials," a word evoking "vile" as well as poisons (belladonna, deadly nightshade); as if fleeing the "enclosed" female space of the vials, the syntax performs its own parallel to the woman's later threat of breaking out of the anxiety that confines her: it snaps the law of logical self-consistency and next declares that the perfumes have escaped the vials (which are, after all, "Unstoppered"), and in such profusion as to trouble, confuse, and drown "the sense in odours." Now, though the perfumes may be at once in the vials and at large in the room in the form of odors, in a self-dispersal equivalent to that of the doubled flames or the flame-light met by the glittering jewel-light, the frightened "lurked" is biased in favor of "In," and so (tellingly) fails to prepare for what follows—the sinister, unstoppable escape of the sense-drowning odors. The narrator, wanting the perfumes to be neither in nor out, blots his syntax. The latter, after seeming already overcome by the allotropic abundance of the forms of the perfume ("Unguent, powdered, or liquid"), helplessly echoes the same mesmerizing triad in "troubled, confused / And drowned." Indeed, stumbling to the occasion immediately after a feebly interruptive dash, it ignores the fact that the subject of the three verbs, "perfumes," has remained stubbornly, and troublingly, and confusingly, attached to the earlier and contradictory verb, "lurked." A virtual, nonsensical simultaneity of two moments of objectivity occurs, echoing the spatial and temporal confusion of the jewels that were in, yet had been poured from, or were pouring from, the satin cases. Objects, it appears, are difficult to "place," because successive moments of "objectivity" become slurred together in them, or because it is their very nature to project themselves (in the first instance, into the senses, into us), as if in a bid to take over and subdue the passivities, the emptiness, around them. So, the protagonist seems to feel, would the woman take over and subject *him,* as a Siren of the Rocks (gilt chair, marble, glass, wrought standards, jewels) whose fatal seduction lies, not in song, but in the suffocating lyricism of the concentrated essence of "natural" life (of Hyacinth gardens).

Yet another confusing doubling of syntactic moments immediately follows: "stirred by the air / That freshened from the window, these ascended / In fattening the prolonged candle-flames, / Flung their smoke into the laquearia." The odors ascend, being stirred by the air that freshens from the window—but is it not the candle flames themselves that, fed by the ascending odors, fling their smoke into the laquearia, and not, as the syntax seems to maintain, the odors? In a sense, to the protagonist it is all one (just as the unguent, powdered, and liquid perfumes were all, in a sense, one). There is in his slipped syntax a weary disenchantment as well as a frightened confusion. Again, objects flatter and prolong one another (reflecting mirrors do so, and shiny table tops, and jewels, and flame-feeding odors), and in this scene it is above all the *flames as of hell* that are thus attended. Perhaps, then, it hardly matters what action or "place" is assigned to each—they conspire together for their own mutual expansion and glorification ("stirred by the air . . . these ascended . . . / Stirring the pattern on the coffered ceiling"), so as to extinguish what is other to their realm: the "sense" of life, the soul.

Hence, at last, the outright paranoid impression that from the walls "staring forms / Leaned out, leaning, hushing the room enclosed." These "forms"—the more horrifying for being unspecified, amorphous to the imagination—seem to bestir themselves against the occupants of the room (at least the narrator). In this world, to "stir" is to look for trouble, to be stirred is to be troubled. Dynamism is an evil.

The movement of description to the enclosing walls—made via the

open-sea-remembering wood aflame in the stone fireplace—soon
alights on a seeming window to a *true* refreshment (as opposed to the
evilly functioning window through which the flame-fattening air
freshens):

> Above the antique mantel was displayed
> As though a window gave upon the sylvan scene
> The change of Philomel, by the barbarous king
> So rudely forced; yet there the nightingale
> Filled all the desert with inviolable voice
> And still she cried, and still the world pursues,
> "Jug Jug" to dirty ears.

But as the sour development of this passage indicates (and as is con-
firmed by the follow-up: "And other withered stumps of time / Were
told upon the walls") the moment of the imaginative transcendence of
objectivity is short-lived; art being, perhaps even at best, a fragile and
temporary surpassing of the barbarous, the rudely forceful, stirrings,
pursuit, dirty ears—the waste land "desert." Even here the evilly dynamic element of time "troubles" the sense, so that conceptually discrete moments of time and action are conflated together. First "The
change of Philomel" with her subsequent triumph over her pain (such
as that triumph was): "yet there the nightingale / Filled all the desert
with inviolable voice." Is "there" sylvan or desert? It appears to be
one, and not, with the scene displayed above the mantel. Evidently,
then, the artistic depiction of the "change" has the power to expand (in a
benign parallel to the fattened and prolonged and reflected candle
flames) and compel the imagination to other and comparable concep-
tions—extensions of the actually depicted one (the "art" of Keats's
Grecian urn). "And still she cried" stretches the second imagining further, through centuries of time—indeed, down to a raw, demythicized
present ("and still the world pursues"): the present that cannot take in
the protagonist; the present immune to an aesthetic magic of
"change" as to a sea-change; a present irredeemably abject. Description, riding the treacherous dynamism of generative syntax, thus first
gives way to an excited and purifying imagination, then to a sardonic,
caricaturing use of fancy ("and still the world pursues, / 'Jug Jug' to
dirty ears"), then degenerates into compulsive, hallucinating paranoia
("staring forms / Leaned out"). Only the magical or divine or, at the
least, aesthetic transformation of objects administers to and appeases
the soul. Only the moment of untroubled imagination redeems the
writhing succession of the moments of objectivity. But "moment" is
all it is. Time itself must be transcended—entirely, utterly—if "Shan-

tih shantih shantih," the peace that passes the reach of the senses—indeed, of the restless, dynamic psyche as well—is to be attained. Art can do much, but is sadly based in abjection, in the violence and dynamism of the drives. Even the "static" display of the dynamic "change" of Philomel—that emblem of the soaringly aesthetic uses of suffering—fails to stop, for more than an instant, the impression of the appetitive stirring, fattening, doubling, lurking, flinging, smoking, burning, and leaning at work in the room—that is, the undying worm of consciousness (of time, of pursuit) in the narrator himself: the same mischievous worm that had wriggled throughout his ironic exercise in description, beginning with his opening gambit, "The Chair she sat in," with its capital so rudely forc'd.

Dialogue (Hers)

Speech in this passage sparks from out the woman's electrically eloquent hair:

> Under the firelight, under the brush, her hair
> Spread out in fiery points
> Glowed into words, then would be savagely still.

According to Jessie Weston, in the ancient Festival of the Weeping Women, women sacrificed their hair to the god in need of renewal. By sharp contrast, this woman's hair focuses her viciously barren self-concerns and is significantly the generative source of her "words," those products of narcissistic and frictional self-attendance. Speech belongs to what has refused sacrifice, the realm of female "fertility," in which even a clairvoyante appears more justified than not in pronouncing: "I do not find / The Hanged Man."

Enraged into words in a ferocious parody of the Renaissance ideal of the perfect female body that thinks, or of thought undivorced from sensory perception ("many men," Eliot wrote in a review of *The Education of Henry Adams*, "will admit that . . . their keenest sensuous experience has been 'as if the body thought' "),[11] this woman finds in dialogue the opportunity to be "herself." How long she has been trapped behind the glass of her husband's airless, nauseated description of the room! And speech does bring her forward, but as less a heroine than a harridan of anxiety. The unattractive pathos she exudes forms a complicated instance of Eliot's guilt-checked yet guilt-compelled humanity—a compassion as of one looking back from the platform of a receding train, a train one has voluntarily, in fact desperately, taken.

11. "A Sceptical Patrician," *Athenaeum* 4647 (23 May 1919):362.

Such compassion was already implicit in the small but surprisingly finished portrait of that perennial green apple, Marie, and it will seem almost palpable, if dry, in the solos sung by the three Thames-daughters. Here it takes the form of allowing us to perceive this woman's hopeless confinement inside a limited number of wildly repeated, unlovely words.

Out of the ornate, ambiguously voluptuous style of the long narrative passage, aging forward about three centuries, bursts and twangs her jazz-age cacophony, her savagely denuded, rhythmically broken English. Instead of the false *sostenuto* of the descriptive passage, a jabbing *pizzicato* of phrase. The paragraph as a whole suffers from a historical split and leap, a heteroglossic schizophrenia. It turns and shrinks from Baroque to Bauhaus, from Shakespeare to Shakespeherian rag, from Greek myth (with what George Steiner calls its "narrative coherence [and] lyric and plastic comeliness" even while treating of "the uncanny and the daemonic")[12] to the percussive *Sacre du printemps* that Eliot reviewed in his "London Letter" in *Dial* in September 1921, admiring its music for having caught "the scream of the motor horn, the rattle of machinery, the grind of wheels, the beating of iron and steel, . . . and the other barbaric cries of modern life."[13] His own Rites of Marriage is brutally dynamic, swift, starkly and intensely expressive, painful, pessimistic: lines as already blackened and wire-bare as "My nerves are bad to-night. Yes, bad. Stay with me" would, one imagines, stubbornly remain standing after a holocaust had melted down worlds of more beautiful, more merciful lines. The woman's words are all contemporaneous; bloomless; buzzless; stripped: "nerves," "bad," "Stay," "speak," "think," "noise," "nothing," "do," "rush"—they keep flashing out of her, each a spark of rancor and dissatisfaction. Her diction is as public as the street she threatens to dash into like an object obscenely on display (her pathetic imagining of a daring transformation). Couched in nervously reiterated and badgering questions that give them whip and sting, they strike the ear like words that could never again be beautiful: they belong now to torture, they have been abandoned by hope. Her lines tend to break into jagged rhythmical units of two or three fragments of increasingly limited sustainment, in a creeping discouragement of the initial speech impulse: "My nerves are bad to-night. Yes, bad. Stay with me"; "What are you thinking of? What thinking? What?" She makes gouging use of repeated monosyllables—"bad,"

12. George Steiner, *Antigones* (New York: Oxford University Press, 1984), 125.
13. "London Letter," *Dial* 61, no. 4 (September 1921), 453.

"me," "Speak," "What," "you," "do" "—as of "nothing." And how soon "thinking" snaps into a vicious, mock command, "Think." Something like the ragtime paradigm "O O O O" rules her rhythm so that everything she utters snaps without buoyancy, is spasmic. A dactyllic clutching and rasping motif—stay with me, speak to me, what are you, what is that—recurs like an uncontrollable tic. Then, too, she does haggish things with iambs, leaving them hardly distinguishable from the twitches of nervous prose: "My *nerves* are *bad* to-*night*"; "I *nev*er *know* what *you* are *think*ing. *Think.*"

Raw, free of the softening and humanizing effects of history, their immediate anxiety unrelieved by the tending-elsewhere of allusion, by orienting comparisons across the centuries, the woman's words scratch to take hold of an elusive (indeed impossible) immediate moment of objectivity, so as to keep her from drowning in nothingness. At the same time gun-shy before moments of objectivity, she finds herself both reaching for and rejecting the truth, and bewildered that her speech keeps coming up empty. Even when she is not asking questions she is still asking them—"I never know what you are thinking"—or answering unstated ones: "Stay with me." For her, reality is what is always in question. Hence her need to surround herself with (supposedly unequivocal) objects and her hunger to know her husband's mind as an object—to scrutinize it, make it yield up its *what* ("What are you thinking of? . . . What shall we do tomorrow"?). "The only way in which we can handle reality intellectually," Eliot wrote in his thesis, "is to turn it into objects, and the justification of this operation is that the world we live in has been built in this way." But for the woman, every question that would get at the what or why of things seems to go off with a pop, leaving charred shreds, not an answer, destroying the answer by the force with which it explodes. She would be healthier if she were more disillusioned—if she had a hard practical knowledge of the limits of her husband, of the morrow, of the wind; but her questions suggest a hysterical, a ridiculous, hope of a surprising and nightmare-ending answer, even if their machine-gun rapidity would frighten off anything gentle. She cannot have read as far in *Knowledge and Experience* as Eliot's statement: "The object of attention . . . has not certain definite limits: its 'that' and its 'what' exhibit a degree of looseness in practice. . . . We never can say, actually, to exactly what we are attending."[14] Or if she did so, she was not attending.

Not that she really expects any answers—at least not from her husband. Much as she might like to hear his voice, to get a response (never

14. Eliot, *Knowledge and Experience*, 161.

mind his precise answers), would it ease her anxiety, which seems, like his, to involve a dread of the unknown (that excluded area of the unseen, the unfathomable, that each fears)? Yet, if the protagonist refuses dialogue with her, it is in part because her dialogue refuses to be dialogic: its questions are bludgeons. Perverse with anger, past even wanting "communication," what she means to communicate is precisely her bitter feeling of being left out, of being the uninformed, the excluded—exile to him as he (and she along with him) is exile to something unknown. If she cannot appeal to his capacity for sensory enchantment or romantic illusion or marital fellowship, or even his pity, she will appeal to his guilt. Her nerves are bad. Yes, despite any doubts he might harbor, they are bad. She anticipates his doubt and trounces it. She will have her way. He owes it to her. Then her questions develop into a strafing. Finally they modulate into a whine of genuine distress and are almost genuine questions: "What shall I do now? What shall I do? . . . What shall we do tomorrow? / What shall we ever do?" No priestess of objects after all, she does not even find herself pacified by them. Everything she comes near seems repelled by her very approach. Objects are not only uncertain in the present; they give no clue at all to the future. She might as well be looking at a blank card. What should she do? Should she turn *herself* into even more of an object, rushing just as she is, with her hair down, into the street, making startled eyes know (or would they know?) exactly to what they were attending?

Dialogue (His)

Ironically, the husband does respond to her words, but to and for himself, and to and for us. It is as if the mute isolation he suffered as a sudden fatality outside the Hyacinth garden had bred in him a disposition to keep mum, and not only out of misanthropy (his new, unconscious bias toward the not conscious), but out of a conviction of the futility of speech (at least of discourse without reference to the Divine). By now assuming the void of human relations, the protagonist does not accept his wife's gambit and take a part in *her* theater; but, unable to still his inner voice, and aware of its essential theatricality, he indulges in autotheater, performing not so much with as against his wife, as the silent partner in a duet of which only he hears both parts. If he is thus more dreadfully ironic than she is, it is because he *does* see something (he sees everything), and because he does remember something (the iconic image of pearls that were eyes), and because he does know something (even if it is that which cannot be known): and all this separates him from her, indeed from humanity: a body of which he forms an edge, an edge that rejects the body yet remains of it, attached. Far deeper than his wife's, his self-disaffection is proportionally nearer to enlightenment. Indeed, he has all but reached the limit of nothingness (yes, nothing is what he sees), and already has knowledge (if only he has not misplaced it) that there is fullness upon fullness on the other side. If he were really to speak his mind, what would his wife make of it? (Prufrock rehearsed this impossibility.) No, evidently he must stay where he is, at the border between abjection and purity, nothing and the All, cultivating self-hurting meannesses of sardonic irony, until the ingathering bright bolt falls.

Meanwhile, in other words, theater, and of an arch kind. "Think."

> I think we are in rats' alley
> Where the dead men lost their bones.

By distinction from his wife's theater of rhythm (repetition, syncopation, abbreviation), of (ostensible) dialogic address, and of dramatized anxiety, his is a theater of smart trope (the urban rats' alley) and allusion (to the valley of the dead men's bones in Ezekiel and the miracle whereby the Breath of the Lord came as a mighty wind and shook the bones into new life). A theater, too, of sepulchral murmur, where almost every word (and almost each is a poor femur of a monosyllable) could arguably take a deadened stress: "I think we are in rat's alley / Where the dead men lost their bones." Then, with "The wind under the door," a theater of metrically matched but ironically undelivered response. This answer weds the question "What is noise?" to compose a traditional pentameter, even as the absence of quotation marks tells of a separation if not a divorce. And here, again, a theater of allusion: for Grover Smith justifiably hears an echo of Webster's *The Devil's Law Case*: "Is the wind in that doore still?"[15] The protagonist in fact continues with allusions to *The Tempest* ("Those are pearls") and *Women Beware Women* ("And we shall play a game of chess"). His discourse, in contrast to his wife's, bears historical awareness within it, his diction has on it the knowing bloom of centuries (a bloom like a powdery luster on inedible berries). Even his quotation from a hit ragtime song of the 1912 *Ziegfeld Follies* amounts to an ironic comment on its history-emptying use of the name of Shakespeare.[16] With its "captivating" rhythm, the song represents

15. Grover Smith, *T. S. Eliot's Poetry and Plays: A Study in Sources and Meaning* (Chicago: University of Chicago Press, 1974), 81.

16. The editors of *The Norton Anthology of Modern Poetry* credit Bruce R. McElderry with identifying the ragtime song. See *The Norton Anthology of Modern Poetry*, ed. Richard Ellmann and Robert O'Clair (New York: W. W. Norton, 1973), 463.

what Milan Kundera calls "a certain *primordial state of music,* a state prior to its history, [a state that] reflects the inherent idiocy of human life"—it is "life itself proclaiming its jubilant 'Here I am!'"[17] The "Here I am!" of life is, for the protagonist, precisely where value is not. History (allusion) represents a small increment of value over its idiocy; imagination (tropes) another tiny increment. But far greater is the transformative energy of the Divine—the Breath of Life, the strange and rich principle of sea-change.

The presence in the passage of such intimations as these last suggests that here the protagonist performs what is in part a theater of hope, even of faith. And this represents a continuation of his momentous (and no less theatrical) self-address as the Son of man in whom desire had failed. If his posturing, his all-but-pouting, theater gets in the way of his salvation—that quasi-theatrical state of (in words from "Little Gidding") "Knowing myself yet being someone other"—it also rehearses hope even as it shows signs of what Eliot found and praised in Baudelaire, the strength to suffer. Where the Breath of the Lord is concerned, the hope is also there in the disappointed answer to the question "What is the wind doing?": "Nothing again nothing." The answer despairs of a prior expectation so sincerely that it neglects punctuation (in fact, the approach to the Absolute in the poem may be roughly gauged by the diminishing use of punctuation—this last a system that belongs to the profane world of distinctions). Unbreathing, the answer is the very deadness of negated anticipation (nothing *again*). "Again nothing" is not the same thing as "nothing"; it is more nearly a *not yet.*[18] And where water and sea-change are concerned, the hope is there, by implication, even in the protagonist's weary (already Tiresian) foreknowledge of his weekend marital routine (counterpart to his weekday routine in the City): "The hot water at ten. / And if it rains, a closed car at four." There will be water to cleanse or comfort the body (Eliot's wife Vivien wrote the word "bottle" after "hot water" on the original draft),[19] and a "civilized" fending off of any rain (as when ducking out of the rain shower in Munich)—and that is all. What else could be expected where a carved dolphin, all of stone, swims in the sad, chemically colored light of burning sea-wood? Where only the satin

---

17. Milan Kundera, *The Book of Laughter and Forgetting,* trans. Michael Henry Heim, (Ontario: Penguin Books, 1981), 180.

18. Compare Jesus' words: "Marvel not that I said unto thee, Ye must be born again. The wind bloweth where it listeth, and thou hearest the sound thereof, but canst not tell whence it cometh, and whither it goeth; so is every one that is born of the spirit" (John 3:7–8).

19. Eliot, *The Waste Land: A Facsimile,* 12.

cases pour? In effect, the protagonist is still isolated in a place of "dry stone no sound of water." The memory "Those are pearls that were his eyes" implies how very much more could be expected from water. When Jesus was accused by a Pharisee of entering the temple without having taken a bath, he answered (according to the *Oxyrhynchus Papyri*, document number 840): "you have cleansed that *outer skin*, the skin that whores and flute players also anoint, bathe, cleanse, and adorn in order to arouse men's lust, whereas *inside they are filled with scorpions* and all kinds of wickedness. As for me (and my disciples), who *did not bathe*, according to you, we did bathe in the *running . . . waters* that come from the Father."[20] If only the protagonist could lay hold of some such riposte to "hot water at ten"! He seems to be longing for one, but his sentence fragments, his listless, brief, empty-seeming, bored catalog bow to the negative—the material and cautious limits of his present urban and secular relation to the delicious fluidity of the sacred. (Not till wind and water fly at him together, in a damp gust bringing rain, will he feel the first refreshment of salvation.)

As for the protagonist's suffering, his counterpointing despair, Eliot believed that such suffering, that *acedia* implies a possible, positive state of beatitude. If serious (under whatever veneer of theater), it is "fortunate" suffering. The protagonist will display more than the "strength merely to *suffer*"; strength is essential to salvation and related to his negative integrity—his constant perception of the nothingness of life. (It was doubtless this last that led Eliot to conclude that Kurtz's last words in *Heart of Darkness*, Conrad's lament for the illusory idealism of the "light"—those ending " 'The horror! the horror!' "—would prove a "somewhat elucidative" epigraph to his poem.)[21] Moody admirably relates to the protagonist's suffering a phrase of Baudelaire's that Eliot was to quote in the *Criterion* in 1924: "*an oasis of horror in a desert of Ennui.*"[22] Peculiarly, the protagonist's macabre talk of rats' alley and dead men's bones and pressing lidless eyes and waiting for a knock upon the door is nearer to godliness than his wife's desperate attempts to bring cheer into their marriage. His moroseness is at least a sign of "the unsuccessful struggle towards the spiritual life."

The protagonist brings the first movement of "A Game of Chess" to conclusion—a flinching, "waiting" one—in the trochaic, endlessly

20. See Julia Kristeva, *Powers of Horror: An Essay on Abjection*, trans. Leon S. Roudiez (New York: Columbia University Press, 1982), 116.

21. Eliot, *The Waste Land: A Facsimile*, 13.

22. A. D. Moody, *Thomas Stearns Eliot: Poet* (Cambridge: Cambridge University Press, 1979), 84. And see *Criterion* 3, no. 10 (January 1925):163.

waiting, fifteen-syllable line "Pressing lidless eyes and waiting for a knock upon the door." Here the rhythmic wince and fall bring back and indeed drive deeper than ever the protagonist's fear of *this* life as nothing but castration and death—nothing but nothing. Earlier, by contrast, the trochaic meter in "Those are pearls that were his eyes" had intimated the redemptive powers of the deep otherness of God, a transfiguration of castration into glorification. Trochaic rhythm thus signs an extirpation of "life" that can be either purely dreadful or entirely purifying. Why does the protagonist play with his wife a game he cannot win? Instead, he must break the board. He will understand that soon.

Hurry Up Please Its Time

When Lil's husband got demobbed, I said—
I didn't mince my words, I said to her myself,
Hurry up please its time
Now Albert's coming back, make yourself a bit smart.
He'll want to know what you done with that money he gave you
To get yourself some teeth. He did, I was there.
You have them all out, Lil, and get a nice set,
He said, I swear, I can't bear to look at you.
And no more can't I, I said, and think of poor Albert,
He's been in the army four years, he wants a good time,
And if you don't give it him, there's others will, I said,
Oh is there, she said. Something o' that, I said.
Then I'll know who to thank, she said, and give me a straight look.
Hurry up please its time
If you don't like it you can get on with it, I said.
Others can pick and choose if you can't.
But if Albert makes off, it won't be for lack of telling.
You ought to be ashamed, I said, to look so antique.
(And her only thirty-one.)
I can't help it, she said, pulling a long face,
It's them pills I took, to bring it off, she said
(She's had five already, and nearly died of young George.)
The chemist said it would be all right, but I've never been the same.
You *are* a proper fool, I said.
Well, if Albert won't leave you alone, there it is, I said,
What you get married for if you don't want children?
Hurry up please its time
Well, that Sunday Albert was home, they had a hot gammon,
And they asked me into dinner, to get the beauty of it hot—
Hurry up please its time
Hurry up please its time

Goonight Bill. Goonight Lou. Goonight May. Goonight.
Ta ta. Goonight. Goonight.
Good night, ladies, good night, sweet ladies, good night, good night.

What You Get Married For

This second and closing section of "A Game of Chess" focuses, like
the first, on marriage as *Oed' und leer*. Here, again, we find a "separation between potential passion and any actualization possible in life,"
if not an "awful" one; for "discontent with the inevitable inadequacy
of actual living to the passionate capacity," while strong enough here
to lead to friction and malaise, is proportionally limited by what seems
a reduced "passionate capacity."[23] It is only the protagonist—sounding his own exigency through the wholly capitalized, ever more insis-
tent "HURRY UP PLEASE ITS TIME"—who seems at all intent on working through lumps of mistakenly important feelings to the simple,
terrible, and unknown "mysticism" that—radical to experience yet
passing understanding—is alone adequate to passion. If this section
reads less like Eliot cutting his own throat; if it was in some ways
perhaps less humiliating for the poet to compose, in that there is far
less transfusion here of his own personality, and none of his own "story," still it *is* meant to read as a humbling "understanding of human
feelings and human illusions." The two panels of "A Game of Chess"
hinge on this humiliation as a diptych exposing the "inevitable inadequacy" of marital relations to the passionate capacity—relations all
too cankered with abject humanity.

If these characters seem unconscious of what Eliot called "the indestructible barriers between one human being and another," they are
protected by their own tough crudity. In contrast to the protagonist
and his wife, as portrayed in the first panel, they enjoy a life-sustaining
vulgarity. Not that the section quite gives back in this way what it
takes away in its air of an overheard exposé of abjection. There may
be a measure of envy in the suggestion of the undiscourageable hard-
ihood of such people (as if Eliot were exclaiming under his breath,
"How do they do it?"). No threat here to run into the street, no telling
of the bone-beads of nihilism; instead the lively narrative of a verbal
joust followed by a little dinner party featuring a hot gammon. But
this panel deplores no less than the first one does the scandal of human
relations, particularly the sexual relations of a man and a woman.
Indeed, is that horror not multiplied when the sexual appetite leads to
birth, repeating the horror all over again? The evil of generation, after

23. Eliot, "Beyle and Balzac," 393.

all, is that it generates. That it keeps the motion—the evil, restless motion—going.

The line "What you get married for if you don't want children?"—an inspired line contributed by Vivien—would mercilessly condemn poor Lil, already drained as the mother of five children, to still another corporeal increase of life, one that would lead to Lil's further exhaustion and prevent the crime of abortion, but would not exhaust the true crime, birth itself. Bodily degradation or abjection—represented only figuratively in the first panel, with its flammable hair, its perfumes conspiring to combat, disguise, and deny the natural female odors of which the original draft of part 3 and the poem "Whispers of Immortality" complain—bodily degradation is Lil's cross (a mock and unworthy one): her teeth are bad, she's run down, she looks antique, no man would want her, and her reproductive organs may be messed up. She represents the "lower fertility" on its shabby and put-upon side, its side of senseless overproduction, its side of squalid decay. She personifies what Bakhtin calls "the lower stratum of the body, the life of the belly and the reproductive organs"—with the mouth-end included for good measure, through her wretched teeth and narrative connection with appetite (the "beauty" of a hot gammon). Ingestion, copulation, conception, pregnancy, birth, abortion, poor self-hygiene: a somewhat mixed story but, in all, she is generation as what digs (as Bakhtin says degradation does) "a bodily grave for a new birth"—someone else's. Where carnival places all this under an aggressively, unapologetically vulgar aspect of fruitfulness ("the fruitful earth . . . [that] is always conceiving"), in *The Waste Land* it remains, simply, unredeemed degradation—no better than the "planting" of the corpse, which illustrates still another definition of "degrade": "To degrade is to bury, to sow, and to kill simultaneously, in order to bring forth something more."[24] Here the lower bodily stratum is always outside the One, and unable to believe or rejoice in the *natural* eternity of the bodily stratum itself— "the eternal incomplete unfinished nature of being."

Where in the first panel *culture* was shown in decay, with the synthetic woman its nervously crumbling touchstone, physical health itself suffers in the second one. Before, a woman's nerves were bad; here the "fruitful" body itself appears rotten. In the main, Lil's weakness is not a want of culture (though in her case more wealth and culture might equate with fewer children and better health); rather, her weakness lies in possessing a female body that appears to be like nothing so

24. Mikhail Bakhtin, *Rabelais and His World*, trans. Hélène Iswolsky (Bloomington: Indiana University Press, 1984), 21.

much as an autonomous machine of reproduction in the form of a beast of burden. She is the mother woman completely deglamorized—for the protagonist, a minor exorcism, a bit of cure by repulsion.

Lil! Brutally scissored and shortened from "Lily," the very name seems a rescission of the ideal of natural grace and beauty. Deadly nightshade, pale lily—no presence here, nor will there be any in the parts to come, of a woman who, like a hyacinth or the lilac, flauntingly and seductively puts by winter.

I Didn't Mince My Words (Diegesis, Mimesis)

This new monologuist—a talented gossip[25]—is almost swaggeringly full and sure of herself. She gives language a bad name because she aligns it so plainly with egoism, aggression, phobia. She speaks because her ego preens and bristles and needs words to puff itself up—as well, perhaps, as to give some of the salt of "life" to her tongue. Where the protagonist *implies,* this woman *says.* The first practices a form of modesty; the second pummels. The antitype of the fine artist—Henry James, Conrad, Eliot himself—the woman lays her opinions down like trump cards, and they all carry the smudge of her imprint, tell of her superiority to the abjection they put down. Ostensibly speaking of her friend Lil, she manages, all the same, to refer to herself no less than five times in two lines: "When Lil's husband got demobbed, *I* said— / *I* didn't mince *my* words, *I* said to her *myself.*" She gives not only language but *saying* a bad name. Where Conrad, in Eliot's formulation, "has no ideas, but [instead] a point of view, a 'world,' " this woman has yet to refine ideas into a sensibility.[26] Instead of transmuting observations into a state of mind (as Eliot praised the metaphysical poets for doing), thus *extinguishing personality,*[27] she delivers drubbings that are somehow made up of herself: "think of poor Albert, . . . You *are* a proper fool. . . . You ought to be ashamed. . . . What you get married for . . .": in her own mind she is a heroine of aggressive frankness, of corrective gusto. The role she glibly assigns to Lil is that of submission to, passivity before, her female destiny. (Underlying the coarse energy of her language is a cynicism toward marriage every bit as extreme as the protagonist's own—marriage for her evidently having no other purpose than the perpetuation of the species.) Yet how peacefully would she herself submit to this yoke? While she shoves Lil back into the marital jaws—those of making herself

25. "Eliot said this passage was 'pure Ellen Kellond.' " See Eliot, *The Waste Land: A Facsimile,* 127.

26. "A Sceptical Patrician," *Athenaeum* 4647 (23 May 1919):362.

27. T. S. Eliot, *Selected Essays* (London: Faber and Faber, 1958), 290.

nice for her husband and of bearing children—what is she herself doing besides downing pints, and gossiping, and threatening to be the other woman? Mostly she talks, and, however decadent her language, uses language to fight against decay (as is the nature of language). Her saying is a *saying against*—against rotten teeth, looking antique, making oneself infertile. For this monologuist, diegesis is a form of power over life—more, is the power *in* life: to be in a position to tell *about* is in effect to be able to tell *off*. Telling in itself keeps away the germs of abjection.

She herself utters nine *I said*'s; there are also three *she said*'s; one *he said;* and "the chemist said." A plethora of sayings. Yet what does all this saying come to? "The chemist said it would be alright, but I've never been the same." "Get a nice set, / He said"; but none was purchased. The monologuist's battery of pronouncements seems to have had no effect at all upon Lil. The spirited exchange between the two amounts to little more than an amateur agonistic entertainment: dialogue as theater. Albert comes home and they all get together to sink their teeth into a hot gammon.

More minced than she realizes, this narrator's words are polite in the tired cynical way familiar in clichés: vulgarly euphemistic in "make yourself a bit smart," "wants a good time," "Something o' that," "I'll know who to thank," "you can get on with it," "a proper fool," "so antique," "won't leave you alone," "there it is." Here, only looks are straight ("and give me a straight look"). Telling ("it won't be for lack of telling") turns out to be a kind of hinting—though no doubt the point gets across. The language is full not so much of fists as of padded gloves, and the reason for this is its want of lucidity—lucidity of the kind that supports an allegorical style, the kind that knows the value of (the) silence. What is important is not so much speaking the King's English—of knowing the range of resonance in "antique" or "beauty," of getting grammar right—as attaining all the way to a (Dantean) disillusionment with, as against a slipshod cynicism toward, the practical limits of life.

Yet certainly with this monologuist language itself is defiled—its clean and proper mouth afflicted as if by cavitied, broken, and missing teeth. This woman's language is a verbal counterpart to the bodily lower stratum—degraded, anonymous, belonging to no one and to anyone within the lower segment of the class and cultural system.

Appropriately, one of her first words is "demobbed," militaristic jargon—the only direct reference in the poem to the Great War. The word "mob" itself comes from the Latin *mobile vulgus,* "movable crowd": to be demobilized is in effect to be demobbed, released from a collective and nationalistic body devoted to an aggressive drive, a government-sponsored crowd. As for the narrator's grammar, although it would be easy to make too much of its solecisms—surrendering to an English teacher's vice—a prose writer and poet as fastidious as Eliot was may be supposed to have heard the identity-smearing conflict between "is" and "others" in "there's others will," to have heard the dead-center grammatical undoing of the word "done" in the long line: "He'll want to know what you done with that money he gave you," or to have noted the double negative in "And no more can't I," all with ears that registered, however subliminally, the evidence of abjection and confusion and unreality aswim in these misconstructions, these words that are all too down to earth. If he perhaps enjoyed at the same time the opportunity to slum in them, their strong pungency of the folk, their agonistic salt—being, as he was, a word and tone animal, as well as a metaphysical mind—nonetheless, to an Eliot, besmirchments of diction and grammar could only be acts of inattention to a proper linguistic cleanliness, one next to godliness, to "the silence": a language use concerned, however futilely in the "here below," with boundaries, purities, distinctions, with marshaling a whole arsenal against the degrading fallings-together, incestuous beddings, decompositions, that make up abjection. Incomplete linguistic toilet training, disregard of the paternal authority that founds grammar, oral fixation—all this is loosely implicit in the narrator's cynical and sensual pub discourse, all of it epitomized by the awful infantilism of "Goo" in "Goonight." The subsequent correction of the expression into the cleanly separated "Good night" is made, of course, in honor of a (clean and proper) quotation from Ophelia, a clean and proper lady (though Hamlet deeply suspected otherwise), sweet and chaste and preserved in that character by making a sudden and clean farewell.

The Protagonist as Arranger

Somewhat like the paracharacter in *Ulysses* that David Hayman has dubbed the arranger, Eliot's protagonist is given to making unpredictable and unsignaled interpolations of his own.[28] In the case of "HURRY UP PLEASE ITS TIME," the reasons are multiple. To begin with, the refrain testifies to his unusual power of—or liability to—empathy (hence mimesis). Repeating or overhearing the woman's monologue, he so enters into its implied ambience that, virtually *clear-hearing* (on the analogy of being clairvoyant), his ears ring with the traditional

28. David Hayman, Ulysses: *The Mechanics of Meaning* (Madison: University of Wisconsin Press, 1982), 84.

closing call of an English pub, and, moreover, hear it in a true-to-life accelerating rhythm of recurrence. Speech-obsessed though the monologuist is—she reports dialogue with apparent fanatical exactitude, but does not indulge in description—she yet understandably omits the motif of the closing call. Speech-obsessed as the protagonist is, he instinctively moves to include it.

The more so because it must remind him of the necessity of remembering his Creator now, in the days of his youth, before desire for the supercosmic fails altogether. The half-polite, half-peremptory call—a plea, a typographically thundered reminder—cajoles and urges him to his goal.

THE FIRE SERMON

THE RIVER'S TENT IS BROKEN

The river's tent is broken: the last fingers of leaf
Clutch and sink into the wet bank. The wind
Crosses the brown land, unheard. The nymphs are departed.
Sweet Thames, run softly, till I end my song.
The river bears no empty bottles, sandwich papers,
Silk handkerchiefs, cardboard boxes, cigarette ends
Or other testimony of summer nights. The nymphs are departed.
And their friends, the loitering heirs of city directors;
Departed, have left no addresses.
By the waters of Leman I sat down and wept . . .
Sweet Thames, run softly till I end my song,
Sweet Thames, run softly, for I speak not loud or long.
But at my back in a cold blast I hear
The rattle of the bones, and chuckle spread from ear to ear.

A rat crept softly through the vegetation
Dragging its slimy belly on the bank
While I was fishing in the dull canal
On a winter evening round behind the gashouse
Musing upon the king my brother's wreck
And on the king my father's death before him.
White bodies naked on the low damp ground
And bones cast in a little low dry garret,
Rattled by the rat's foot only, year to year.
But at my back from time to time I hear
The sound of horns and motors, which shall bring
Sweeney to Mrs. Porter in the spring.
O the moon shone bright on Mrs. Porter
And on her daughter
They wash their feet in soda water
Et, O ces voix d'enfants, chantant dans la coupole!

Twit twit twit
Jug jug jug jug jug jug
So rudely forc'd.
Tereu

After Spenser (Heteroglossia)

If the subject of part 2 is, in Grover Smith's words, "sex without love, specifically within marriage," the subject of part 3 is "the same horror

107

outside it."[1] The two parts together, indeed the first three parts, form a survey of the waste land. The protagonist acts as a prosecutor who, in an unusual move, conducts the jury to the scene of the crime. At the same time, he himself is one of the criminals. And so, he implies, is each member of the jury.

What, then, is the crime? It is the impure life of the senses.

The senses defile what they touch because a selfish greed of appetite is what drives them. The body is the opposite of giving; it is always a rage of self-reference. Even in its decay (as "Gerontion" emphasized) it milks its decrepitude for pleasures. The opening of part 3 tells how it is: "the last fingers of leaf / Clutch and sink into the wet bank." There is stubborn desperation and a refusal to relent in the line break— though the internal off-rhyme of "sink" and "bank" seals the doom of these "fingers." The opposite of the clutching of heroic roots where the sun beats, this clutching is at once febrile and feeble. It typifies the sensory activity of the waste land, in which, as culture itself becomes like a heap of leaves under the bare tree of an exhausted history, in- stinct has turned weak and unhealthy, the body of *being* is old. (Nietzsche: "Historical culture is indeed a kind of inborn grey- headedness.")[2]

Was there not a time, even in England, when the drives and the senses were appeased and refreshed by a synthesis of pagan and Chris- tian ideas, art purified and sweetened by it? When the imagination could delight in "A flocke of [virginal] *Nymphes* . . . / All lovely Daughters of the Flood," and think of equally virginal brides as not "begot of any earthly Seede, / But rather Angels or of Angels breede," and not neglect "the holy priest" and the saints? Spenser's "Prothala- mion" and "Epithalamion" suggest just such a seamless cultural tent, part gorgeous pagan greens and blues, part pearly sacred altar cloth. The latter combines "Nymphes [that] the silver scaly trouts doe tend full well" with "lawes of wedlock" and "sacred rites." Yes, then Nature itself was so sympathetic to wedlock that a poet could bid the Thames to quiet its flow while he performed his wedding song and expect a sweet compliance.

Without the admixture of "the sacred Altare" and "blessed Saints," romantic love collapses in disillusion, its tent broken. The pagan tent alone (the natural, sensory, and romantic fabric of life—

1. Grover Smith, *T. S. Eliot's Poetry and Plays: A Study in Sources and Meaning* (Chicago: University of Chicago Press, 1974), 79.

2. Friedrich Nietzsche, "On the Use and Disadvantages of History for Life," in *Untimely Meditations,* trans. R. J. Hollingdale (Cambridge: Cambridge University Press, 1983), 101.

romantic now, mythic formerly) cannot compare in strength and majesty to Jerusalem, the tabernacle that shall never be taken down, nor the stakes removed, nor the cords broken, situated where the Lord is "a place of broad rivers and streams . . . and the inhabitants shall not say, I am sick" (Isaiah 33:20–24). But only the wind and the protagonist remember the high dream of such a tent—the wind that crosses the brown land unheard by all save the speaker.

The latter ironically compares himself to Spenser as he catalogs the unholy loves along the banks of the machine-age Thames—through irony skirting self-pity. He mixes the lovely refrain from Spenser's song of the Brides ("two Swannes of goodly hewe" that "come softly swimming downe along the Lee," floating on "the Christal Flood," till welcomed at the appointed place by "Two gentle Knights of lovely face and feature") with the "brown" of his own spirit and age, the banks no longer "rutty" and "paynted all with variable flowers," the river without a "glyster fayre," and "the nymphs . . . departed." *He* can but speak, and not loud nor long, the principle of lyricism itself having sunk, the naïve, glad "I" having turned into a sour and frustrate voyeur.

No, choked by the memory of the river bearing "empty bottles, sandwich papers, / Silk handkerchiefs, cardboard boxes, cigarette ends," and "other testimony of summer nights," he *cannot* sing, and it is with rue that he offers "Silk handkerchiefs, cardboard boxes, cigarette ends" as an English line. He may try to make amends with the mostly iambic "Or *other testimony* of *summer nights*," but even this line is the plainest speech (leaving aside a subtle distinction) compared to the emphatically introduced iambs in "Sweet Thames, flow softly till I end my song."

Why, then, is he loitering along these banks and among unsavory memories of polluted love and a polluted river? For the same reason that he can only "speak," he is a cultural stray (and still more a stray from the Absolute), and might as well be at the bank of the river (that exemplum of necessitated flow and direction) as anywhere tormenting (punishing, appeasing). He is once a stray in that, as a modern man, he has, in Nietzsche's words, nothing whatever of his own:

Knowledge . . . now no longer acts as an agent for transforming the outside world but remains concealed within a chaotic inner world which modern man describes with a curious pride as his uniquely characteristic "subjectivity." . . . Our modern culture is not a living thing: it is . . . not a real culture at all but only a kind of knowledge of culture. . . . [The Greeks] during the period of their greatest strength kept a tenacious hold on their unhistorical sense, [whereas] we moderns have nothing whatever of our own; only by replenishing and cramming ourselves with the ages, customs, arts, philosophies, religions, discoveries of others do we become anything worthy of notice, that is to say, walking encyclopaedias, which is what an ancient Greek transported into our own time would perhaps take us for.[3]

Nietzsche adds (the text is "On the uses and disadvantages of history for life") that our means for overcoming what presses upon us "in too great abundance [is] to embrace it as lightly as possible so as quickly to expel it again and have done with it." From this comes the barbarism of straying, which is both the knowledgeable protagonist's predicament and, no less, his means of keeping afloat.

The speaker's cultural straying along the bank of the historical Thames parallels the psychological straying of the abject son of woman. Instead of sounding himself as to his "being," writes Kristeva, the subject born (as every subject is) out of abjection (a vomiting of the mother), sounds himself concerning his place:

"*Where* am I?" instead of "*Who* am I?" For the space that engrosses the deject, the excluded, is never *one*. . . . A deviser of territories, languages, works, the *deject* never stops demarcating his universe whose fluid confines . . . constantly question his solidity and impel him to start afresh. A tireless builder, the deject is in short a *stray*. He is on a journey . . . the end of which keeps receding.[4]

Psychological straying generates cultural straying and eventually the strayer's culture, encyclopedism. History proves an escalating process of "bogus cultivatedness" (Nietzsche), the instinct for life faltering as the historical sense hauls in and deposits load on load of accumulated rubbish.

Like the voided containers cast by lovers into the summer Thames, the stray, however much in motion, is ruled by afterness. On his way to nothing, he can turn his meandering into triumph only by making it over into a journey to the Beginning—the purity that resembles nothingness, lacking, as it does, territories, languages, works, but which dissolves the question "Where am I?" in the emotion of a powerful everywhereness. Mysticism is the radical cure for both historical encyclopedism and the primary, abjecting exclusion (vomiting) of the mother.

Meanwhile the pretreatment of a cultivated disgust: the protagonist contemplates a pollution that is no longer even present. The river may bear no empty bottles, or the like, but the river-sentence does, and after you have reflected on each item in the series, you've no strength

3. Ibid., 78–79.
4. Julia Kristeva, *Powers of Horror: An Essay on Abjection,* trans. Leon S. Roudiez (New York: Columbia University Press, 1982), 8.

left to think of the river cleansed of garbagey clutter, and no recol-
lectable motive for doing so. Once that polluted, polluted forever.

A bitter perversity governs the writing (the same bitterness that began to appear in the last paragraph of part 1). Feeling confined to
abjection, the protagonist retaliates by charging humanity with having
let purity down (as if humanity were ever anything but this betrayal).
To call the London women "nymphs" is to imply, unfairly, that they
could or should be nymphs but are not. The women have departed not
only from the banks but, more gravely, from the pagan "innocence"
of nymphhood. Not rivery but merely river-bordering, they were seduced by the antipastoral heirs of city directors. They are *after* my-
thology and the pastoral, forcing the protagonist, as "poet," to be
after Spenser. Strays, they have departed, and the heirs, too, but not to
the same destinations. They are no more faithful to one another than
the leaves are to the tree. The hymens of the women are as broken as
the river's canopy of foliage. The clutching is over, save for what the
fingers of leaves mockingly remember.

The syntax knows their sort, knows it well. "And their friends, the
loitering heirs of city directors" lacks a verb, trailing after the one in
"The nymphs are departed" like a stray dog sniffing after another dog.
"Departed, have left no addresses" doesn't even trouble to repeat the
subject: the indefiniteness as to whether the nymphs or their "friends"
is meant, or both, is dismissively contemptuous toward all. Something
loiters in the sentence structure itself, and something departs.

The syntactic erosion contributes to the atmosphere of shabby decay. So does the loitering of the line "And their friends, the loitering
heirs of city directors" around its many *r*'s, and again in the additional
slack in "loitering." A more diffuse effect is the feeble clutching of
the thin, flat, dead sound *en* (or *in*), with the variants *em, ym,* and
am. This sound is scattered like so many rotting leaves through the
first eight lines, appearing now to the left and now, driftingly, to the
right:

                    tent
                                        wind
                                      nymphs
            Thames   end
                  empty
                                                ends
                                              nymphs
                  friends

Then, too, numerous *b*'s and *p*'s ("broken," "bank," "departed,"
"papers" and so on) add their news of minor shatterings.

Verbal Poses

First posing as a belated and disillusioned Spenser, the speaker then echoes the Hebrews' lament for their exile by the waters of Babylon, the tent broken. Is he, too, in bondage? Yes, to and among the senses. With whatever irony at this point, the comparison exalts the protagonist's unhappiness into a religious longing for a metaphysical homeland. "Leman" (in "by the waters of Leman") is Rousseau's territory, and Rousseau the nominal fountainhead of romantic heresy. Further, as a peep at the compositional history of *The Waste Land*— Eliot finished writing the poem at Lausanne—it suggests that the metaphysical homesickness is the poet's own.

Banished as he is from the cyclical eternity of the mother's body, the protagonist is no less banished from the Father's sublime death, the purity on the reverse side of nothingness. (Again, the thought of each distracts him from the other.) To quote the Hebrews' lament is not the same as to merge beyond speech with Meaning; it is to indulge in meaning-echo, to pose. Can this longing be sincere if conveyed through a conscious impersonation? Yes, and no, if consciousness is inescapably theater, and all art, play.

Eliot even suggests elsewhere that such artful posing is a sign of life, as evidence of an excited "dramatic sense":

We are given plays of realism [he remarked in 1919] in which the parts are never allowed to be consciously dramatic, for fear, perhaps, of their appearing less real. But in actual life, or in those situations in our actual life which we enjoy consciously and keenly, we are, at times, aware of ourselves in this way, and these moments are of very great usefulness to dramatic verse.[5]

Articulated emotions are vital emotions. What, then, of the beatitude that cannot be expressed? Is there a dramatic mysticism? Eliot will fake or imitate one toward the close of the poem (particularly with the passage beginning "*Damyata:* The boat responded / Gaily"). Meanwhile, the protagonist finds that to "act" (if not entirely in the sense urged by his wife) is to be "alive" only in a theater of exile, and in the exile of theater itself.

A lost child of the "historical sense," overburdened and scattered from himself by historical knowledge, cynical with it, uprooted by it from the future, deprived (in Nietzsche's words) of "the mood of

5. See T. S. Eliot, "Whether Rostand Had Something about Him," *Athenaeum* 4656 (25 July 1919):665. Eliot thought versification itself "a definite concession to the desire for 'play,'" and urged that prose, too, "transmutes life in its own way by raising it to the condition of 'play.'" See "Prose and Verse," *Chapbook* 22 (April 1921):9.

pious illusion in which alone anything that wants to live can live," of
the "unconditional faith in right and perfection," the protagonist naturally speaks as ironically as he does allusively and, not yet fit for
piety, paces with conscious drama the boards of his temperament.[6]
Out of those who have also grieved over exile from the father's death,
who have wept, fasted, fished, prayed, praised, he creates noble company for himself, even identities for himself. If he can slip in and out of
Spenser, Hebrew exiles, Marvell, Ferdinand, and Prospero in the space
of a few lines, he may still be "in rats' alley / Where the dead men lost
their bones," but he is distracted and soothed by the middle and high
dreams of the dead. I would thus question Ronald Bush's view that
"one of the terrors of the speaker of *The Waste Land* is that he has
forfeited [imaginative, romantic, sensual] life to books, and is trapped
in ways of thinking and feeling acquired through convention."[7] I suggest that, on the contrary, books fuel the protagonist's lively and necessary "dramatic sense"; and, more important, they provide grateful
intimations of "inviolable voice." In any case, the Life the protagonist
already unconsciously seeks stands even farther from the life that can
be forfeited to books than from books themselves—from symbolicity
and abstraction and a direction of reference. Within the subuniversal
scheme of unreality, real life may equate with the dramatic sense and
its play with conventions (rather than with more sensual forms of
roused blood), but everything sensual is, by definition, unreal. Books
help the protagonist focus the absence of the transvital. They are re-
minders of the Missing All.

One of the assumptions of modernism is that every individual contains the blueprints of all the rest. "We have other lives," says wispy
Lucy Swithin in Virginia Woolf's *Between the Acts;* an exhibition of
the "dramatic sense" in a village pageant makes Lucy feel that she
"could have played . . . Cleopatra!"[8] So, too, the protagonist fishes in
himself and shortly brings up, among others, Spenser (the Poet) and
Ferdinand "Sitting on a bank, / Weeping again the King my father's
wrack" (the Lost Son)—a probable repertoire of roles, and at first
glance limited, but still enough to allow the protagonist to give a sudden twist to his mind and suddenly see himself as another (if still somehow "himself"). Yes, he once played prince of Naples, "was" him,
just as he once fought at Mylae. Hence his haunting memory "Those

6. Nietzsche, *Untimely Meditations*, 95.
7. Ronald Bush, *T. S. Eliot: A Study in Character and Style* (New York: Oxford
University Press, 1984), 59.
8. Virginia Woolf, *Between the Acts* (New York: Harcourt Brace Jovanovich,
1969), 70, 153.

are pearls that were his eyes." He belonged (and still belongs) to the world of *The Tempest,* a passing pagaent of unreality. He has always been bereft on a bank, hearing aerial news of his father's sublime death.

Now that he is at the bank of the Thames (or, in a sardonic change of locale, beside one of its dull canals), the identities that ripple down to him are water-accompanied, water-blessed, recalling his card, the drowned Phoenician Sailor and his well-starred reading of it as promising a sea change into something rich and strange. Spenser by the Thames, the Hebrews by the waters of Babylon, Ferdinand by the sea, even perhaps Parsifal, subject of Verlaine's line *"ces voix d'enfants, chantant dans la coupole,"* who is washed by holy water before he heals King Amfortas (in Wagner's *Parsifal*)—through identifications with each the physician-protagonist heals *himself* a little. On the other hand, his rapid, dissatisfied change of roles (all cast in the play of exile) suggests that, if *"every name in history is I,"* in Nietzsche's words,[9] there is also a *not me* that is mine, for me, despite me. So the protagonist is entitled to say of the others, and must say, "They're not me! *Something else* is me!" As *homo natura* or mercurial *homo historia* (the model of the "schizo" devised by Deleuze and Guattari), he is nothing, a phenomenal series of fabricated shapes and identities; only as *homo mystica* is he or could he be "himself," unique—only, paradoxically, by identifying himself with the All.

At this stage, the protagonist is still phobic enough to hesitate between playing the son (Ferdinand) or the father (Prospero, one of the figures evoked by the line "Musing upon the king my brother's wreck). More, he is still hysterical enough (as will appear) to be undecided between being a man or a woman (or both at once in a disjunctive synthesis). The Oedipal triangulation is—for him—wobbly, watery, as subject to shifts, repositionings, as the objects in the "enclosed room." Where is the Father who authoritatively proclaims differentiations: gender, system, space, language? Ironic self-awareness, bitter fruit of the historic sense, has killed him. In Nietzsche's words again, his culture is not "a real culture at all, but only a kind of knowledge of culture." What is more, "knowledge, its mightiest wingbeats notwithstanding, has not been able to soar aloft, a profound sense of helplessness remains."[10] Eventually, the protagonist will try to move beyond the dead fathers into the imageless Absolute. For the present,

9. Quoted in Gilles Deleuze and Félix Guattari, *Anti-Oedipus: Capitalism and Schizophrenia,* trans. Robert Hurley, Mark Seem, and Helen R. Lane (Minneapolis: University of Minnesota Press, 1983), 21.

10. Nietzsche, *Untimely Meditations,* 101.

and even later when he quotes Saint Augustine and the Buddha, he can only play fathers, just as fathers themselves can only play authority in a world where the one Authority cannot be played. So he looks to Ezekiel, Shakespeare, Dante, Augustine, and the rest, for a thread to follow out of the maze of the engulfing mother (earth, woman, time, the senses). Oedipal differentiations are at least useful as rungs of a ladder that must be climbed to the Imageless; but then the ladder must be kicked away, from nowhere, by no one. If "the name that haunts all history is simply the paternal name," as Deleuze and Guattari put it, if it is a flight from the archaic mother, then the protagonist must break out of history (as well as out of nature). History is, like the Christian Trinity, an obliteration "of the feminine image in favor of a phallic symbol." So the culture-making Oedipal triangle "displaces itself towards its own cause"—the Father's No—"and attempts to integreate it."[11] The Absolute, however, isn't phallic. The protagonist glimpsed it as a "heart." Also as a silence, *the* silence, beyond the presumptuous potencies of words.

Fishing Where the Rat Creeps

In the original draft of *The Waste Land,* as in the first edition, a typographical break precedes "A rat crept softly through the vegetation"—sensibly, since the line indicates a change of place and a lapse from present observation into memory, or possibly narrative fantasy (for it is unlikely that the protagonist literally fished in the dull canal). What he pictures is his ironic attempt to fish up something from and of the unknown, despite the dullest of conditions (urban, sensual, belated). To practice meditation on the Absolute within the ephemeral and unreal city is to find the spirit at half-pressure, at best. The location suggests that the protagonist's courage is still limited, his self-removal from the herd tentative. The gashouse is to "the heart of light" what the dull canal is to the calm sea ("The sea was calm"—part 5). These are metaphors of a still constricted, an ill-lit, passion for metamorphosis.

Yet in imagining himself fishing the protagonist is all but saying to himself: Somehow you have already begun to quest for the pre- and transtemporal. Passive though fishing might seem. Passive as ascetic contemplation might be. Yes, something in him is preparing to be drawn up like a futilely struggling phallic creature into the marbleizing heart of light.

If this impluse were stronger, the rat would not be so active, so slimy. Thoreau: "We are conscious of an animal in us, which awakens

---

11. Deleuze and Guattari, *Anti-Oedipus,* 75.

in proportion as our higher nature slumbers. It is reptile and sensual, and perhaps cannot be wholly expelled."[12] Indeed, the rat, not the fishing, dominates the sentence: "A rat crept softly through the vegetation / Dragging its slimy belly on the bank / While I was fishing." The fishing is thus made to seem beset, contradicted. The powerful antidote to the mud-slimed rat, namely the sea-washed fish, is present only potentially, in an enfolded, undelivered form, in "fishing." At the source of the protagonist's articulation is a nomination of what seems horribly ready to disregard articulations of forms, differentiations between the mineral and the organic, earth and water; something relentlessly and prolongingly dragging (or so the line break before "Dragging" suggests) its slimy belly on a miry bank, as if smearing together atoms of flesh and atoms of "dust." The rat figures abjection and its subversions of clean and proper bodies, distinct and secure identities. Reduced by a close-up to a creeping digestive system, it subsumes the horror implicit in the signs of oral appetite recalled from the summertime Thames. Food, notes Kristeva, is "a boundary between nature and culture, between the human and the nonhuman."[13] Belly to bank is not just animate to inanimate, but the animate at its most nature-ingesting and substance-reducing, an aggression against as well as a slithering companionship with inert, low, and anonymous matter. Unabashedly abject, the rat seems shockingly unafraid of a bad death, a death by smearing.

This rat suggests all the vitality that lies over against the soul, the organic *not self,* the sublinguistic and subsymbolic—the opposite of soaring. It represents, thus, in part, what is feared in the mother. By contrast, the fish is a totem animal, a substitute (chiefly) for the father. Inclined to be remote from us, alien, it incorporates the father's abstract power and death, his otherness in relation to human warmth and sensuality. Then, too, the fish maintains equilibrium, separateness, self-direction, within the maternally undifferentiated and archaic. Yet when drawn up into the air, it dies—the father, or law, language, abstraction, being but the sacrificial way to the Real. The hunger for the incommunicable, for what surpasses articulation, is strong in this image of fishing, this attempt to bait "the silence."

In the Grail legend itself, the fish is a gift from God, a more than material sustenance in a wilderness. Jessie Weston relates how the name Fisher King derived from a story told of Joseph of Arimathea, who was fabled to have brought the Holy Grail to England. Once

---

12. *The Portable Thoreau,* ed. Carl Bode (New York: Viking Press, 1947), 465.
13. Kristeva, *Powers of Horror,* 75.

when Joseph was traveling with companions in the wild, "some of the company fell into sin." God commanded one of the group, Brons, to catch a fish. This done, the fish and the Grail together provided a "mystic meal" of which only the sinless could partake. Thus were the righteous separated from the sinful. Brons was thenceforward known as "The Rich Fisher." By corruption, this became *Roi Pescheur*, or the Fisher King.[14] It seems reasonable, then, to assume that fishing in Eliot's poem figures a hunger for the Mystic Meal, for proof of purity, redemption from sin. And indeed, nothing contradicts this.

Yet how distracted by the sensual the protagonist is, how held back by his own fascinated disgust. Freeing itself from the past tense, forming a floating summary of the doomed sensuality of the waste land, the fragment

> White bodies naked on the low damp ground
> And bones cast in a little low dry garret,
> Rattled by the rat's foot only, year to year

is obsessively interjected. It is not so much a thought as an imagist equation for the fate that awaits the carelessly sensual, those indifferent to the clean and proper body ("naked on the low damp ground"), or the clean and proper self. Erotic white naked bodies, already difficult to distinguish, at a distance, from cast-up victims of drowning (the corpse-haunted Thames of Dickens's *Our Mutual Friend* seems just a wind-flip of a page away), become, in time, dry bones, still a "low" status, if ironically a little more elevated ("low garret"); bones "Rattled by the rat's foot only, year to year," not by the Breath of the Lord, as in the valley of the dead men's bones in Ezekiel. Attic rubbish.

The conviction that ossification is our lot reflects, as noted, the feeling of the prematurely wizened children of history that they live among the remains of the dead. Nietzsche speaks of "this dreadful ossification of our age, this restless rattling of the bones."[15] Life, or the unhistorical ("Insofar as it stands in the service of life, history stands in the service of an unhistorical power"),[16] is, or feels, savagely diminished to "White bodies naked on the low damp ground," a verbless construction that leaves them hovering already near to their further reduction to utterly passive bones.

To live so much among the dead, to rattle their bones, is to live like

14. Jessie Weston, *From Ritual to Romance* (Garden City: Doubleday, 1957), 116–17.

15. Nietzsche, *Untimely Meditations,* 109.

16. Ibid., 67.

a lower form of life among the rubbish of former accomplishment. A skulking bad conscience is implied by the casting (whether indifferent or secretive) of the bones in a garret. The "little low dry garret" suggests not only a Dostoyevskian hole-and-corner associated with crime and the fetor of death but an artist's bare scene of hopeless struggle against his knowledge of the arbitrary cultural achievements of the past. (Nietzsche: "every age is different, it does not matter what you are like").

This casting of life into a studious obscurity, the sense that it has been relegated to a cultural rubbish heap (save for the slimy animal instinct for survival), is counterposed by the casting of the fishing line into fertile depths. But at this point, they are still shallow and man-made depths.

Borrowings and Avant-gardism

It will be asked, How is imitation to be rendered healthy and vital? . . . it is at least interesting, if not profitable, to note that two very distinguishing characters of vital imitation are, its Frankness and its Audacity: its Frankness is especially singular; there is never any effort to conceal the degree of the sources of its borrowing. Raffaelle carries off a whole figure from Masaccio, or borrows an entire composition from Perugino, with as much tranquillity and simplicity of innocence as a young Spartan pickpocket. . . . There is at least a presumption, when we find this frank acceptance, that there is a sense within the mind of power capable of transforming and renewing whatever it adopts; and too conscious, too exalted, to fear the accusation of plagiarism,—too certain that it can prove, and has proved, its independence, to be afraid of expressing its homage to what it admires in the most open and indubitable way; and the necessary consequence of this sense of power is the other sign I have named—the Audacity of treatment when it finds treatment necessary, the unhesitating and sweeping sacrifice of precedent where precedent becomes inconvenient.

John Ruskin, *The Seven Lamps of Architecture*[17]

Feet and Back

Over the dejectedly verbless, inertly repetitive interlude of the white bodies and rattled bones, the protagonist again recalls and alters Marvell. First he had substituted gothic claptrap—rattling bones and a chuckle—for what the lover in Marvell's "To His Coy Mistress" says he hears at his back, namely, "Time's winged chariot hurrying near": this was to keep the meaning while giving it a grotesque inflection.

---

17. John Ruskin, *The Seven Lamps of Architecture* (New York: Noonday Press, 1961), 146.

(Michel Tournier, in *The Ogre,* comments: "a touch of the grotesque is the invariable signature of the Prince of Darkness," this last himself a figment created by purity, or "horror of life, hatred of man, morbid passion for the void.")[18] By using "chuckle" instead of "grin" in "chuckle spread from ear to ear" the protagonist had (of course in logical consistency with "I hear") opposed cynical laughter to "the silence," but the dark playfulness seemed really his own—he seemed to be caricaturing death, as if he were no longer entirely and utterly afraid of a handful of dust. The comically drawn out rhyme of "I hear . . . spread from ear to ear," where even the visual reflection of *ea* in "spread" adds its spreading light note of self-echoing design, raises in its own way the question: Is this the worst scare that death can produce? Now, in a full resumption of the present tense, the protagonist claims to hear at his back "from time to time . . . / The sound of horns and motors, which shall bring / Sweeney to Mrs. Porter in the spring." And here "at my back" has a different meaning: that of facing away (despite the receptive ears) from the travesty of copulation rites represented by Sweeney and Mrs. Porter "in the spring." In keeping with his self-image as one "fishing in the dull canal," the protagonist sees himself as already putting (in words from part 5) "the arid plain" behind him, if only in being (as if obeying an obscure thirst) at the riverbank, his back to the nearby mechanized sounds of death.

To place Mrs. Porter under the bright moon is to make her (first through her name) a comic fertility goddess: a source of generation ("And on her daughter") but an Earth Goddess marked by a low sign of liability to impurity and corruption: smelly feet. There is an incremental comic horror in the succession from the mock-lyric "O the moon shone bright on Mrs. Porter" to "And on her daughter" to "They wash their feet in soda water." To begin with, Mrs. Porter's marital status and surname are all wrong for the lyrical moonlight. And together, mother and daughter attest to the fearful power of woman to reproduce life, the maternal body as porter and portal (an impure capacity, according to Leviticus 12), the *repetition* of bodily being. As for their malodorous clay feet, these antigoddesses are, not clean and proper, but defiled just where their weight presses against earth. Now, it was Parsifal's feet that were bathed in a holy spring by the enchantress Kundry, in ritual preparation for healing Amfortas— an echo of the bathing of Christ's feet in the tears of a woman who

18. Michel Tournier, *The Ogre,* trans. Barbara Bray (New York: Pantheon, 1972), 75.

stood behind him and wiped them afterward with the hairs of her head. These cleansings recognize a proper boundary between the flesh (as metonym of the self) and the indiscriminate, inanimate earth. As Kristeva observes, "filth is not a quality in itself, but . . . applies only to what relates to a *boundary* and, more particularly, represents the object jettisoned out of that boundary, its other side, a margin."[19] In the scheme of Eliot's poem, men properly step across a boundary that women seem condemned to both violate and represent.

On the one hand, the protagonist would *see* the defilement, the white naked flesh against damp ground, and on the other he would turn his unseeing back on it, present toward it a monolithic wall of rejection or exclusion, the flesh at its hardest, its least feeling. What he would put as far as possible behind him is the abject realm of anality and its equivalents (decay, disease, abortion, wasted effort, a corpse, and so on). Excremental downfall has formed a motif in the poem from "And down we went" "stony rubbish," "A heap of broken images," and "a handful of dust"—even, as a vanishing, from "*Oed' und leer das Meer.*" The flow of the London crowd itself was excremental, a flow of those "undone." And the protagonist is to fear death by water. That the satin cases in "A Game of Chess" had been poured in rich profusion did not prevent the protagonist's syntax from trying to put the jewels and their glitter back inside. The vials were objectionably unstoppered, letting their contents leak out in a sweet miasma. The protagonist thought he was in rats' alley, among lost bones. And so on. Such images equate exile with excremental waste. To be unstoppered (sphincteral) is not to live forever, not to be metaphysical: the Gnostic master Valentinus claimed that Jesus "ate and drank, but did not defecate."[20] Menses, of course, belong to the same pattern of defilement and loss, and we are told that one version of the song about Mrs. Porter (which was popular with the Australian army during the First World War) specifies douching, not the washing of feet. (Compare "the good old hearty female stench" that Eliot in the first draft attributes to Fresca.)[21]

If feet (as synecdoches for the belly and loins and, more abstractly, the senses) are the site of filth, then elevation above the earth (the ground, the plain) signs a state of purification. So it is with the chil-

---

19. Kristeva, *Powers of Horror,* 69.

20. Quoted by Milan Kundera in *The Unbearable Lightness of Being,* trans. Michael Henry Heim (New York: Harper & Row, 1984), 246.

21. T. S. Eliot, *The Waste Land: A Facsimile and Transcript of the Original Drafts Including the Annotations of Ezra Pound,* ed. Valerie Eliot (New York: Harcourt Brace Jovanovich, 1971), 23.

dren who—in Verlaine's line—sing in the cupola (Wagner's libretto told of softest voices singing of highest healing's wonder).[22] Virtually still unborn in their dome, they seem safely distanced from the bestial floor, where the rat drags its slimy belly on the bank. Whose sons and daughters are they? They form a privileged group apart, trans-Oedipal but blessed by the eternity of childhood, of prepubescent innocence.

Modern Consciousness and Ritual

The lines "Twit twit twit / Jug jug jug jug jug jug"—low onomatopoeic renderings of the nightingale's sounds, via the Elizabethans—have an effect of mock ritual, being a "mindless" repetition of an animated machine (Descartes's *machina animata*). This is a near ritual of "naturalism" (which will later appear in a more benign form in the "water-dripping" line in part 5). The verbal repetition enacts all earthly repetition and suggests the sexual violence and consumption that compel it.

By contrast, true ritual will appear at the end of the poem as a self-closing close to the entire poem. The verbal repetition of "Shantih shantih shantih" closes discourse from, so to speak, above, at the edge of "the silence," and not from below, like the twitting cries of animal desire and the jug jug of brute satisfaction.

But for the most part, *The Waste Land* is far from being ritualistic. It is too much a strenuous casting off of the world for that, too much a poem *against*. Antiritualistically, the lines of the poem, with the exception of the later water-dripping song, embrace an extraordinary variety of materials and tones. We admire here what Eliot admired in Donne, a "recognition of the complexity of feeling and its rapid alterations and antitheses" and a continual "regrouping" of elements of feeling under a mood that was previously subordinate, as against "the substitution of one mood for a wholly different one." "The age," Eliot wrote in 1923, "objects to the simplification and separation of the mental faculties . . . we accept the belief that any state of mind is extremely complex, and chiefly composed of odds and ends in constant flux manipulated by desire and fear."[23]

Opposing the contemporary attitude toward life—which like that of the Elizabethans' was "one of anarchism, of dissolution, of decay"—the poet reproduced some of the Elizabethan "artistic greed-

22. Richard Wagner, *The Authentic Librettos of the Wagner Operas* (New York: Crown, 1938), 470.

23. T. S. Eliot, "John Donne," *Nation and Athenaeum* 33, no. 10 (9 June 1923):332.

iness," its "desire for every sort of effect together," its "unwillingness to accept any limitation and abide by it,"[24] even as he created a classic, in the sense illumined by his remark that "what is meant by a classical moment in literature is surely a moment of *stasis*, when the creative impulse finds a form which satisfies the best intellect of the time, a moment when a type is produced."[25] This seeming avarice of style, tone, mode, range of reference, was inevitable in a poem that however concretely, attempts to sum up history in order, for the most part, to write it off. The poem may seem to sacrifice perspective (many have thought so) to static and sensational spots of material (conforming, thus, to György Lukács's caricature of the perspectiveless ideology of modernism);[26] but in fact its perspective-fostering organization could hardly be more complete, and the more so for Pound's contributions to it.

Eliot's later long poems, "The Hollow Men," "Ash-Wednesday," and *Four Quartets,* complex as they also may be, are less concerned to show that "any state of mind is extremely complex." They display, by comparison, a liturgical and at moments conceptual flattening. Less dramatic, they aspire in varying degrees to the condition of ritual. Eliot's taste for ritual was in fact already well developed in 1923, when, writing on Donne, he identified his own age with complexity: "All art," he said in a piece on Marianne Moore, "emulates the condition of ritual. That is what it comes from and to what it must always return for nourishment."[27] Again, in the same year, in a piece called "The Beating of a Drum," he said that, though "the drama was originally ritual," consisting of "a set of repeated movement, . . . essentially a dance," "we have lost the drum."[28] *The Waste Land* came at the crossroads between Eliot's intense organizational avant-gardism (a concomitant of a strenuous engagement with complexity of mind)—his conviction that "the dogmatic slumbers of the last hundred years are broken, and the chaos must be faced . . . we cannot have any order but our own"[29]— and, on the other hand, his impulse to beat the ideational and ritualistic drum of submission and penitence.

24. T. S. Eliot, "Four Elizabethan Dramatists," *Criterion* 2, no. 6 (February 1924):122–23.

25. T. S. Eliot, "A Commentary," *Criterion* 2, no. 7 (April 1924):232.

26. See György Lukács, "The Ideology of Modernism," in *Realism in Our Time: Literature and the Class Struggle,* trans. John and Necke Mander (New York: Harper & Row, 1964), 17–46.

27. T. S. Eliot, "Marianne Moore," *Dial* 75, no. 6 (December 1923), 597.

28. T. S. Eliot, "The Beating of a Drum," *Nation and Athenaeum* 34, no. 1 (6 October 1923):12.

29. Ibid.

MR. EUGENIDES

Unreal City
Under the brown fog of a winter noon
Mr. Eugenides, the Smyrna merchant
Unshaven, with a pocket full of currants
C.i.f. London: documents at sight,
Asked me in demotic French
To luncheon at the Cannon Street Hotel
Followed by a weekend at the Metropole.

To Have It or Not to Have It

The phobic or clean and proper self is based on symbolic boundaries. As a moral purity, it also has its physical counterpart, a corporeality uncontaminated by foreign substances. Inviolable, hard, the masculine dream-body is a system of internal musterings and external armor, aggressive thrusts and exclusions. Phobic logic turns the male physique into a secondary phallus. Thus, a male who would open his body to another male would let in death, be fucked by death. (Death is always the other, *other*-power. The murderer—Stetson?—tries to coincide with this power. So does the male in the "manly state.")

Mr. Eugenides, the aggressor in the little scene narrated in these lines, proposes, so it would seem, to invade the physical boundaries of the protagonist—one who himself shrinks phobically from invading the female body. The names "Cannon" and "Metropole," although actual names of places that a Mr. Eugenides would be likely to recommend, are comically apt. And the comedy is fitting, for the phallic life is a farce, or so the protagonist is on his way to realizing. The phallus? The fetish of fetishes, the arch-fetish, a terrorizing symbol of desire as power. What it is impossible to "have," except fitfully, and in the anxious plane of mortality. What it is "death" to be without.

For the subject, states Jacques Lacan, "the position of the phallus is always veiled . . . it's a question of to have it or not to have it. But the radical position of the subject at the level of privation, of the subject as subject of desire, is not to be it. The subject is himself, so to speak, a negative object." The protagonist will puruse this logic to its end: that of ascetic self-evacuation. "At the level of castration," adds Lacan, "the subject appears in a blackout [*syncope*] of the signifier. It's something else when he appears at the level of the Other, in a state of submission to the law of one and all."[30] In *The Waste Land,* however,

---

30. Jacques Lacan, "Desire and the Interpretation of Desire in *Hamlet,*" in *Literature and Psychoanalysis: The Question of Reading: Otherwise,* ed. Shoshana Felman (Baltimore: The Johns Hopkins University Press, 1982), 48–49.

the "one and all" disappears in the glare of the One and All. The tribal "other," with its homosexual bond (that of both men and women in a "feminine position" with respect to the father's law) is a false idol, a scene continually threatened by the void at its "heart," and "Freud even says: as though the throne and the altar were in danger" (Philippe Sollers).[31] In later years, Eliot will endorse the (homosexual) community, but here his protagonist moves without social loyalty or pity toward the radical Otherness of the One.

Meanwhile, with regard to the "question of to have it or not to have it," the protagonist appears to be in a yes/no position that makes him unfit for women yet keeps him hovering near them. Not that he is any more fit for Mr. Eugenides. Shrinking from the abjectness of women as he does, he is not about to emulate the feminine position with respect to the father (the male counterpart of supposed penis envy). Neither could he desire a feminine man, though such a partner might protect him from the "nothing" of the maternal phallus.

The only resolution of this unsatisfactory choice between incestuous violation, on the one hand, and the abjection of being violated, on the other, is to get out of the phallic game. Does the phallus, in any case, amount to anything more than a symbol of castration (that of every man as well as of every woman)? Does Hamlet not say, "The body is with the king but the king is not with the body?" Lacan comments: "Replace the word 'king' with the word 'phallus' and you'll see that that's exactly the point—the body is bound up in this matter of the phallus—and how—but the phallus, on the contrary, is bound to nothing: it always slips through your fingers." Again: "the phallus, even the real phallus, is a *ghost*."[32] So this "king" is a thing "of nothing." "Poor man," remarks Sollers, "that's why he owes it to himself to die."[33]

"The Oedipus complex," Lacan notes, "goes into its decline insofar as the subject must mourn the phallus." Yet "the Oedipus complex must be terminated as completely as possible, for the consequence of this complex in both man and woman is the scar, the emotional stigma, of the castration complex."[34] Is not castration, then, both the cause and the cure of the complex, in an absurd circularity? If so, there is nothing but castration.

Hamlet-like as he is before the question of to have it or not to have it, the protagonist finds no erotic charge or charm in that sleazy phal-

31. Philippe Sollers, "Freud's Hand," Ibid., 331.
32. Lacan, "Desire and the Interpretation of Desire in *Hamlet*," ibid., 50–52.
33. Ibid., 332.
34. Ibid., 46–47.

lus, Mr. Eugenides (though the meter, as will be noted, suggests that he is at least flattered or amused by the proposition). Everything about the merchant (except possibly his forwardness) seems calculated to cement the protagonist's defenses. His name may mean "well born," but that association mocks his vulgarity (and some may see in it a reference to the ancient Phoenician traders and their traffic in now lost mysteries). His name also reflects the Greek work for "offspring, stock," *genos;* but neither could that association recommend him to a protagonist sick of all "breeding." Then, too, where a beard suggests a man's concern to keep himself whole and hidden behind a natural screen, "Unshaven" (virtually italicized by its placement and capital) suggests a lack of decent solicitude for a clean and proper self. Shaded face, shady character. And "a pocket full of currants"? The image is faintly anal, hints of animal droppings in a nest.

With their proximity to Mr. Eugenides' groin, the currants (small seedless raisins of the Levant) also suggest the "sterility" of homosexuality. Yet in this work heterosexuality is no less essentially sterile. Whether as the horror of generation or of incest or as specious romance or as a spasm of male vanity (as in the clerk soon to appear), sexuality has nothing whatever to recommend it.

Heteroglossia

Writing of Mr. Eugenides, Hugh Ross Williamson remarks: "the sudden impact of the jargon of commerce . . . defines the secondary symbolism of the character. In this crazy age of mammon-worshippers, there is no god but commerce, and the banker and the economist are his prophets. Its most typical representative is the merchant; his language its secret liturgy."[35] Certainly "C.i.f. London" has stood in as much need of annotation for many readers as has the Sanskrit in part 5 or even the lines in French, German, and Italian, not to mention the numerous literary allusions. "Carriage and insurance free to London," explains Eliot's note. Abbreviations not unlike the V's and *cf*'s peppering the notes themselves, in another secret liturgy, that of scholarship, documents not on sight. "C.i.f.," if nothing sinister, is something barbarous in verse: the masculine symbolic system in its most brutally efficient, body-free, odor-free form. The harmony between such symbolicity and the ego's puritanical need for mastery is clear: "it gave me a sense of pleasure and of power manipulating those curi-

35. Hugh Ross Williamson, *The Poetry of T. S. Eliot* (London: Hodder & Stoughton, 1932), 125.

ous little figures," Eliot said when referring to symbolic logic.[36] The *poetry* of *The Waste Land* hovers between "C.i.f." and the feminine and soothing, if not cathartic, satiation of the senses in sensory properties.

From the original draft, Eliot dropped the snobbish "abominable French" and adopted Pound's substitution, "demotic," which half replaces judgment with characterization.[37] Somewhere, then, in Izmir, Turkey or during economic forays into France, the merchant had consorted with French-speaking persons who were not of the class to read, say, Verlaine's "Parsifal." The one language the protagonist has in common with the merchant is the City language of documents, with their communication as direct and loveless as a weekend at the Metropole.

Mimesis

As an arch-economist of materials, passionate opponent of unredeemed waste, Eliot was concerned to make good Madame Sosostris's prophecy of a one-eyed merchant. Mr. Eugenides' singleness of vision, it happens, is also a species of economy, a living on the *qui vive* for both business and sensual opportunities. But what is a man advantaged, with this material economy, "if he gain the whole world, and lose himself, or be cast away?" (Luke 9:25).

At any rate, the narrative is paced to convey something of the character's hustle and bustle; with its hard manner and heartlessly hearty tone, it forms an oblique "showing." The breathless yet crammingly factual syntax of "Mr. Eugenides, the Smyrna merchant / Unshaven, with a pocket full of currants / C.i.f. London: documents at sight, / Asked me . . . " *is* the character.

If "Unreal City" is placed at the head of the paragraph like a name on a city gate, Mr. Eugenides, impervious and self-satisfied, takes no notice of it—unlike the spirits that loom into focus in the *Inferno*, he doesn't know that he's in hell. Never mind his association with business; he seems ripe for carnival, for comedy in the earliest sense of the word, as indicated by its Greek root, *komos,* "merry-making, revel." The verse rather enjoys his vulgar vitality, it rises to a curious near-gaiety at the end: "To *lunch*eon *at* the *Ca*nnon *Street* Hotel / *Fo*llowed by a *week*end *at* the *Metropole*." There is a little giddiness in the dip into slacks initiated by "Followed." Smartly recurring *ee*'s and *o*'s,

---

36. See Peter Ackroyd, *T. S. Eliot: A Life* (New York: Simon and Schuster, 1984), 59.

37. Eliot, *The Waste Land: A Facsimile,* 31, 43.

("Street Hotel / Followed . . . weekend . . . Metropole") and buoyant *l*'s, together with skipping stresses, add to the gay effect. Carnival
levity? Pan's pipe heard along a current tracing an ancient Mediterra-
nean route?

Map and Match

Mr. Eugenides is one in a series of examples in part 3 of the body's
inconsequent burning. Does he not belong to a more or less static
layout of instances? Part 3 is even more indifferent than part 2 to the
ordering of events into a total action—to emplotment. It simulates the
rhizomic structure to which modernism, on its Nietzschean, pluralistic
side, aspires. "A rhizome," as Deleuze and Guattari put it in *On the
Line,* "can be cracked and broken at any point; it starts off again"—
like an iris or a burrow—"following one or another of its lines, or
even other lines."[38] In the contrasting arborescent model, a root fixes
a point and thus an order that is created along a line of binary divisions. A rhizome, instead, decenters itself as it spreads, deterritorializing and reterritorializing its existence.

Like *Ulysses,* with its weak diachronic logic, its ambiguous plot, its
covert reterritorialization of the *Odyssey, The Waste Land,* with its
largely inferential plot, seems, on the face of it, rhizomic (decentered
both stylistically and structurally). "The Fire Sermon," specifically,
seems to map the London sexual topography—map it, not pho-
tograph it, so that its organization is open to numerous plottings, con-
nectable from any point to any point. A map (a rhizome) has multiple
entrances, reversible lines of direction. This holds true of part 3 until
its close, where, convulsed with disgust, the protagonist virtually sets a
match to the map (thus confirming that there *is* a plot). "The Fire
Sermon" ends in a rupture that prevents all further ruptures (rhizomic
activity); it marks a departure to a far-off goal (the antiroot of all).
This Territory Beyond Territory would be unmappable in itself. Here
the whole would not be peripheral to the parts, as in a rhizome, but
cocentral with each of them. Everything would connect with everything else, but instantly, without lines.

The arborescent paradigm—implicit in the title and in the momentous image of roots that clutch—has only a temporary importance
in the poem. It reflects the protagonist's sense of being directed away
from the cowering constricted place he occupies as one trying to huddle apart from abjection—his obscure shootings into new depths and

38. Gilles Deleuze and Félix Guattari, *On the Line,* trans. John Johnston (New
York: Semiotext(e), 1983), 17–18.

unguessable heights, his growth into elsewhere. Thus it shades into the rhizomic model of deterritorializing rupture (rapture).

Still, whether his appearance is rhizomic or not within part 3, Mr. Eugenides not only branches out of a tuber set by Madame Sosostris; he happens along after evidence of the protagonist's incest dread, his shrinking objection to Mrs. Porter (somebody's wife), "Jug jug" and the "rudely forced," to indicate that to the protagonist the sexual game is unplayable all round. Having established this, the protagonist is wearily ready, in a final self-punishment for his sexual fascinations and ambiguities, to impersonate a hermaphroditic Tiresias—one who has taken both the masculine and the feminine positions in the game; one who, now an old man with wrinkled dugs (indeed, effectively always so) is excused from the game but condemned to observe it, serving as its patron and as the most apathetic and patronizing of voyeurs.

At the Violet Hour

At the violet hour, when the eyes and back
Turn upward from the desk, when the human engine waits
Like a taxi throbbing waiting,
I Tiresias, though blind, throbbing between two lives,
Old man with wrinkled female breasts, can see
At the violet hour, the evening hour that strives
Homeward, and brings the sailor home from sea,
The typist home at teatime, clears her breakfast, lights
Her stove, and lays out food in tins.
Out of the window perilously spread
Her drying combinations touched by the sun's last rays,
On the divan are piled (at night her bed)
Stockings, slippers, camisoles, and stays.
I Tiresias, old man with wrinkled dugs
Perceived the scene, and foretold the rest—
I too awaited the expected guest.
He, the young man carbuncular, arrives,
A small house agent's clerk, with one bold stare,
One of the low on whom assurance sits
As a silk hat on a Bradford millionaire.
The time is now propitious, as he guesses,
The meal is ended, she is bored and tired,
Endeavours to engage her in caresses
Which still are unreproved, if undesired.
Flushed and decided, he assaults at once;
Exploring hands encounter no defence;
His vanity requires no response,
And makes a welcome of indifference.

(And I Tiresias have foresuffered all
Enacted on this same divan or bed;
I who have sat by Thebes below the wall
And walked among the lowest of the dead.)
Bestows one final patronising kiss,
And gropes his way, finding the stairs unlit . . .

She turns and looks a moment in the glass,
Hardly aware of her departed lover;
Her brain allows one half-formed thought to pass:
"Well now that's done: and I'm glad it's over."
When lovely woman stoops to folly and
Paces about her room again alone,
She smoothes her hair with automatic hand,
And puts a record on the gramophone.

I Tiresias

Understandably trying to honor Eliot's dictum that "what Tiresias *sees* . . . is the substance of the poem," many readers have struggled to posit Tiresias as the dominant consciousness of *The Waste Land*.[39] Thus Grover Smith: "The memories of Tiresias as the Fisher King contain no more important event than his failure with the hyacinth girl," etc.[40] A similar exaggeration of Tiresias' importance explains Claude Edmonde Magny's description of *The Waste Land* as an "epic of collective consciousness . . . unfolded in an All-knowing mind, *total* rather than omniscient."[41] But what Tiresias *sees* is the "substance," simply, of the protagonist's objection to life, not of the poem. Throb though he does between two lives, this Tiresias has apparently never throbbed between life and death, throbbed "with the agony of spiritual life."[42] And so, blindness for blindness, he sees less far into the heart of what cannot be seen than the protagonist already has. The latter has an ear like that of "the practised sailor," one that can distinguish "in the most boisterous storm . . . and at a surprising distance, the peculiar note of breakers on a reef . . . [the note] of the extremity and never of the mean" (in words from Eliot's "A Commentary" in the October 1924 issue of *Criterion*, where Eliot is already recommending "authority not democracy, . . . dogmatism not toler-

39. See Eliot's note to line 218.
40. Smith, *T. S. Eliot's Poetry and Plays*, 74.
41. Claude Edmonde Magny, "A Double Note on T. S. Eliot and James Joyce," in *T. S. Eliot,* compiled by Richard March and Tambimuttu (Chicago: Henry Regnery, 1949), 216.
42. T. S. Eliot, "A Prediction in Regard to Three English Authors, Writers Who, though Masters of Thought, Are Likewise Masters of Art," *Vanity Fair* 21, no. 6 (February 1924):98.

ance," extremity and never the mean).[43] By contrast, Tiresias is seedy from his exposure and overexposure to the commonplace, an expert witness of abjection. Tiresias is only one of the protagonist's farewell performances, the dross he must leave behind before he consciously cultivates a form of seeing "infinitely more disillusioned" than any suggested by Tiresias. Whereas Tiresias is half woman, the protagonist has it in him to renounce woman and follow the "father" into the impalpable, and this is his challenge and peril to life, which is reduced to being at best a thing of mother wit calling her children to her along a wilderness road.

The protagonist becomes Tiresias only for the sake of a skit in which everything sexual is automatic, degrading, and comic. If "Tiresias" foresees what will happen in this typist's room, the reason is that he is a compend of the relations between the sexes—their moldering annals. He knows they only repeat themselves within narrow and desolate limits. Like an empathic omniscient narrator (which is essentially what he represents, androgyny and all), he can read the typist's "one half-formed thought." Here, for a *good* laugh at sexuality, the protagonist portrays (for the first time in the poem) a sexual encounter; but what is shown is not *agos,* defilement, so much as ego and a nearly pathological apathy (abulia, an entrapping disillusionment). The scenario is Oedipal. Tiresias, who sat below the wall of Thebes, an unreal city under an Oedipal miasma; who has walked and still walks among the lowest of the dead, those ruled by the unreality of desire, like the clerk, and those who have come listlessly to the end of desire, like the typist—Tiresias as such trails a memory of extreme Oedipal suffering. Through him, the protagonist condemns the phallic upstart in himself (poor, frightened thing though this "son and lover" might be). The pseudo-Augustan style adopted during the course of the paragraph sounds the punishing if weak accents of the father. Its intent is to ridicule if not quash (for this bug is unkillable) the clerk of the "small" house agent whose vocation traffics, without piety, in the sale of houses, those dim symbols of feminine sanctity, care, and enclosure. (The legend that Hera blinded Tiresias for judging that women enjoy sex more than men do involves a related violation of the supposed purity of the mother woman—a sullying of her ideal image that cannot go unpunished.) The typist, too—the slovenly bad mother who would thus let herself be used, who can hardly "keep house"—is brought under the lash of the style. Tiresias looks upon both from the appalled standpoint of castration fear (to be blind and a her-

43. T. S. Eliot, "A Commentary," *Criterion* 3, no. 9 (October 1924):4.

maphrodite is a castration and a half). If through Tiresias the protagonist identifies more readily with the typist, following her home,
awaiting with her the expected guest, the reason is that his terribly
watchful superego denies and distances the pimply, horny adolescent
youth still roaming somewhere in himself, and still pretentiously phallic as "a silk hat." Besides, the typist is numb, and numbness this
Tiresias could almost welcome. She doesn't glorify the phallus that has
been "denied" her, nor does she suffer from the conviction that she
herself is "nothing"; she just *is* nothing (nothing to herself), a blank
page on which desire has been x-ed out.

In a rival version of the legend, Tiresias is blinded by Athena as
punishment for watching her bathe ("White bodies"). Certainly
Eliot's Tiresias is the type of the Oedipal peeper, a "seer" partly in the
voyeuristic sense, having grown old while waiting around to glimpse
the bathing mother, if not the unspeakable glory of the primal scene.
Eliot's Tiresias is the type of the Oedipal voyeur theatrically developed
into a sort of sour impresario of squalid sex scenes, brief fires of lust,
poker and ash. His single mastery is of language, and language,
Kristeva remarks, is "the gouged-out eye, the wound, the basic incom-
pleteness."[44]

Perilously Spread Combinations (Mimesis)

At moments, Tiresias seems to lack even this mastery: some of his
syntactical combinations are perilously spread. Indeed, instances of
perilous combinations of various descriptions prevail in these two
verse paragraphs (really one paragraph that has been spread). This
figure is in keeping with Tiresias' bisexuality and sagging longevity of
mind, which in turn focus the chance splits and perpetuities, the ten-
uous orders, of the waste land, abject region of heterogeneity, abrupt
disruptions, strayings, violated borders.

At first this Tiresias who is not Tiresias, this ancient-contemporary,
man-woman, doer-seer, adopts a formally elaborate but oddly slipping syntax that, as intimated, suits the immense spread of his experience and the probable strangeness and sleepiness of a mind that has
endured so long and seen and suffered so much. The opening lines of
the first paragraph hint (not only through the description of the mechanization of modern city workers, but through a disordered style) that
mechanical efficiency induces disruption where the human soul was
once thought to be. The manner tells of inner chaos, broken connections. "When the eyes and back / Turn upward from the desk" is

44. Kristeva, *Powers of Horror*, 89.

English only of a heartless, inorganic, "foreign," Tiresian kind. As a description of a typist rising from a desk, its efficiency is bizarre, avoiding laborious description but suggesting a perilous disconnection between the fore and aft, the eyes and back, of the same body. Both suggesting and, mechanically, denying it. The first in that, where the phrase "violet hour" beautifully sustains the definite article, "eyes" and "back" feel pointed at by it—freakishly isolated, the more so for being on opposite sides of the body, and emphasized. The second in that, grotesquely, eyes and back seem to turn in the same direction, in unison (By contrast, the protagonist himself will never appear more collected than when, his back firmly presented to the waste land, his eyes scan a white mountain road.) The implication is that mechanized labor decenters and partially dismantles the human organism, which is held together only by the main force and lie of a mechanical syntax (if not, pathetically, by a desire to pull oneself at least together enough to go home).

"When the human engine waits / Like a taxi throbbing waiting" is not English, either. Again Tiresias might be translating at sight from another, unpracticed tongue. With its "unnatural" falling, throbbing rhythm—"*When* the *hum*an *eng*ine *waits*," etc.—the clause is exact only impressionistically, in rendering the mechanized, horns-and-motor existence of the modern urban stray, whose heart is like a taxi, throbbing, waiting: a temporary conveyance with nothing to convey. (Conversely, the typist treats her kitchen, her divan, her "lover," everything, as if to her it is all no more than a taxi she has taken.) The redundancy of the writing enacts the inefficiency of a life in which apparent movement conceals (even from those in motion) a constant waiting. So like the first "when" clause, this one is at once clumsy and expressively right, formidably turned. Yes, this Tiresias perceives differently from anyone else in modern time, but what he perceives is precisely its modernness, its hapless difference from preceding ages: it is the antiquity of his intellect, his knowledge of "tradition," that makes it so avant-garde, so "original." Thus, this Tiresias may begin with an enchanting flourish borrowed from "tradition," "At the violet hour," a phrase he might have heard in the original Greek from Sappho's own lips. But by oddly placing it side by side with signs of mechanization he "sufficiently suggests," in Hugh Ross Williamson's words, "the extent to which the rhythm of nature has been broken."[45] Not that nature is a true norm; but its overcoming must lie in the direction of the transcendental, not the mechanical.

45. Williamson, *The Poetry of T. S. Eliot*, 125–26.

As the initial phrase brings out, Tiresias has a notion about "narrating." Indeed, who more aware than he of the scandalous connections between story and Oedipal anticipations, peepings, denudings, atonements? He begins like a novelist with the *when* of the episode he is about to relate, but then curiously prolongs this theme as if forgetful of his narrative destination, in the process bungling the syntax. His diegesis shakes like an aged hand, and so becomes mimesis. Why should this mind trailing chronicles and geographies of memory feel pressure to take a single direction and strive on? What is there that he (of all people) should take a breathless interest in? Things happen as they will, and as they have already happened; time future is contained in time past. He is fabulously old and experienced, his listeners must expect to be patient. He has sat beneath many walls, and been summoned to many courts.

His narrative is not only perilously spread through the two queer "when" clauses; it is delayed as well as furthered by the dodderingly informative lines "I Tiresias, though blind, throbbing between two lives, / Old man with wrinkled female breasts." The paradox of "though blind . . . can see" is muffled by the cotton wad of exposition that lies between its two poles. Half forgetfully and half nostalgically, Tiresias then returns the narrative sentence to its descriptive starting point, "At the violet hour," placing the phrase indeed in the same imposing initial position in a line. Is he missing the Greek homeland, doting on it in a sentence full of dotage? His second "At the violet hour" remembers the first one only dimly, as in a dream. Well, his language throbs more than reasons, seems half a self-communion that, while indifferent to the reader, creates an intimate effect, the twists and iterations charging the syntax with a nodding music.

What does he want to tell that happened at the violet hour? We must wait to find out; for, the syntax already perilously spread, he extends it further through still more subordination, as if an author too feeble and apathetic for the Oedipal violence of narrative, fit only for the leisurely bag-stuffings of description. He elaborates again on the violet hour, now personifying it and saying that it "strives / Homeward, and brings the sailor home from sea, / The typist home at tea-time." Strives homeward? Sappho had said of the violet hour of evening that it "[brings] in all that bright morning scattered";[46] Eliot's verb "strives" reflects the protagonist's sense of how hard it is to make an ending of all that secularism has scattered. In one sense overnarrating, overstuffing, Tiresias gratuitously brings in the sailor; yet this too

46. Ibid.

reflects something in the protagonist who "does" him, namely his growing preoccupation with an inhuman Otherness, and his remembrance of his card, the drowned Phoenician Sailor. Is it perhaps with regret that the protagonist, as Tiresias, sees the sailor brought in from the sea? Is the violet hour the hour when the light dies, royally bleeding? Still, the parallelism in "the sailor home from sea, / The typist home at teatime," including the pitilessly conjoining rhyme of "sea" and "tea," works mock-heroically against the typist, not the sailor. Whereas the latter had ventured forth for the day on a grandly impersonal body of water, the former merely put in a dehumanizing day at the office, and as to water, her use for it seems entirely domestic—for tea, for the washing of combinations.

But, again, what is it Tiresias would say, not about the violet hour, but about what happens then? If the violet hour sets a limbo between light and dark, this narrator seems in danger of never leaving it. Indeed, he breaks out only through an act of violence, splintering the sentence he had been absent-mindedly erecting so as to bend it and nail it in the right place. It appears now that what he had wanted to say was, in brief, "I Tiresias . . . can see / At the violet hour [that] brings . . . / The typist home at teatime, [the typist clear] her breakfast, [light] Her stove, and [lay] out food in tins." But by the time he has doddered to "The typist home at teatime," he has only enough presence of mind to exploit his erroneous impression that he has just named the subject of a major clause, "The typist," and conclude with a positively military smartness and snap: the spare and direct diachronic series "clears . . . lights . . . and lays out"—the misfitting present tense a sort of earnest that he's truly awake. Yes, to force himself to concentrate on another, the millionth, empty moment, he hits (none too soon) on the idea of imitating the efficient, alertly formal Augustan style, of which he had had some acquaintance just a century and a half back.

It is at this point that the verse begins to emulate the heroic quatrain as practiced by, among others, Dryden. For the first time in the paragraph, true and alternating rhymes now appear:

> Out of the window perilously spread
> Her drying combinations touched by the sun's last rays,
> On the divan are piled (at night her bed)
> Stockings, slippers, camisoles, and stays.

The protagonist, having decided to be on his guard in the presence (indeed, the bedroom) of this slovenly female, abruptly equips Tiresias with a style all aggression. Here, although disorder still marks the syntax, it has lost its ambiguity. We are no longer faced with a choice between regarding it as symptomatic of an aged and tired mind or as a stylistic deadpan that, with wall-eyed phrases and sentences, mocks the incoherence of the modern. Simply, it mocks. The severe "form" that frames the disorder—and not just of the semantic content but of the style—erases all doubt.

For instance, "Her drying combinations, touched by the sun's last rays, spread perilously out of the window" may be better English (better prose) than "Out of the window perilously spread / Her drying combinations touched by the sun's last rays," but only this last makes proper fun of the typist's killing freedom from peril. Sprawling like her sensibility, like her will, it first suggests that the window itself is perilously spread open—and that image almost *will* bear the suspense of "perilously"; but, no, only her daintily named "combinations" are perilously spread, with mock female alarm, an alarm mockingly nearly justified by the naughty touch of the sun's last rays, even if they are elderly rays that the passive voice renders doubly harmless. The combinations are made to suffer a thrill of fear, a horror of sullying that the typist herself is beyond feeling. The clause, as lineated, is full of what *cannot* be said about, or for, the situation: the window is *not* open "on the foam / Of perilous seas, in faery lands forlorn," as in Keats's "Ode to a Nightingale." The combinations (metonymic representatives of the typist herself) are not in any peril worth speaking of. The sentence at first does not even seem to be a sentence, the inverted word order and mystifying line break and the grammatical ambiguity of "spread" making it seem unfinished.

With mimed slovenliness, the syntax continues its indictment of the tpyist: "On the divan are piled (at night her bed) / Stockings, slippers, camisoles, and stays." Her bed is not piled at night on the divan, nor are the stockings, slippers, camisoles, and stays at night her bed, as this sleepy sentence may seem to state. The parenthesis, which is sloppy, suits the typist, so the wink of the writing implies. The perilous grammatical spread of the words "divan" and "her bed" enacts her disinclination for domestic order. (She perhaps endures too much meaningless discipline during the work day.) That "bed" is needed to rhyme with "spread" is only a secondary consideration, an accident of prosody that coincides with the scene-of-an-accident condition of the divan. The sibilant series "Stockings, slippers, camisoles, and stays" comes across as rustlingly and insidiously female. Bored and indifferent, the typist tosses these articles together and, sympathetically, their sounds slither together into an indiscriminate heap.

Automatic Hand (Mimesis)

Enter the "small house agent's clerk," his "one bold stare" a kind of erection, and the style, alerted, becomes even more military:

> He, the young man carbuncular, arrives,
> A small house agent's clerk, with one bold stare,
> One of the low on whom assurance sits
> As a silk hat on a Bradford millionaire.
> The time is now propitious, as he guesses,
> The meal is ended, she is bored and tired,
> Endeavours to engage her in caresses
> Which still are unreproved, if undesired.

Shaking off the passiveness of inversions ("Out of the window perilously spread / Her drying combinations"; "On the divan are piled," etc.) the manner catches something of the clerk's masculine go-to-itiveness. At the same time, the now more regular prosody keeps itself, phobically, at a formal distance from the clerk's hot, raw physical energy—washing its hands in advance, as it were, of his lack of breeding, his readiness to lunge. Syntax soon takes its revenge against him by erasing him as a pronominal subject before the ironically elegant "Endeavours"—as, later, before "Bestows" ("Bestows one final patronising kiss, / And gropes his way, finding the stairs unlit . . . "). In both instances, the presumption of an understood pronoun mimes the clerk's own presumptiveness, and the consequent capitalized prominence of the verb his propensity to swagger. His conceit prevents him from establishing any but a mechanical syntax with the typist, one that leaves out whatever he may be thought to be besides eruptive "action." Maliciously, the narrator dismembers him, accordingly, into a bold stare, an air of assurance, exploring hands, atomizing him until, forced to grope down an unlit stairway, he is dismissed as a piece of incoherence antithetical to the heart of light.

Bringing in a standard of organized sensibility that the clerk and typist cannot rise to, the prosody lowers this standard on them like a boom, so that they drop lower in esteem than they would if presented in a more forgiving manner. The four square quality of the verse boxes them up as if they were small specimens of life whose behavior is being scientifically observed (and indeed in the original draft they're called crawling bugs). The effect of the meter and even more of the rhyme is to stuff everything into a bag and pull the string tight, suffocating the contents by an external neatness. The anarchy inside is tidily dispatched, and "rightly so," says the manner. At the same time, however, the air of pastiche and the deliberate, insulting solecisms—such as "(at night her bed)" and the gaping pronominal turnabout in "she is bored and tired, / Endeavours to engage her"—feign a bored, indifferent, automatic hand in the writer, as if to say, "I Tiresias have foresuffered all / Enacted on this same divan or bed," and none of it is serious, for none of it is real.

The Latinate diction contributes to this Janus-faced manner, with its murmur "boring" and its contradictory eagerness for the kill. Words like "unreproved" and "undesired" have no real grip to them; they are formally distant, clinical, abstract. They correlate with boredom. On the other hand, in concealing offensive facts behind a screen of learning, they offer the fastidious sensibility of this Tiresias some protection. Further, they may be thought to mime the pretentious writing of little-educated Englishmen of the time, or so Hugh Kenner infers from Eliot's comment on how "an artisan who can talk the English language beautifully while about his work or in a public bar, may compose a letter painfully written in a dead language bearing some resemblance to a newspaper leader and decorated with words like 'maelstrom' and 'pandemonium.' "[47] Finally, the Latinate words prove aggressive in their imputation that anything less refined than they are must be almost too low for words. No one would be safe around a narrator who "employs" (that must be the word) "Endeavours," "engage," "encounter," and "Enacted" all in the span of eight lines, not to mention "unreproved," "undesired," "requires," "response," "indifference," and "foresuffered." Such language is antagonistic to life; it "requires" those who act to have their excuses ready.

Once the sharply objectionable clerk has departed, the tone becomes softer, the verse takes on an almost postcoital ease. Looking into "the glass," then smoothing her hair, the typist for a moment may remind us of another enemy of the Absolute, the woman combing her hair in "A Game of Chess," but her "automatic hand" places her still lower among the dead, as one of those who have entirely blocked out feeling (her brain *allows* one half-formed thought to *pass*). She has only enough nervous energy to pace (pace "again") about her room. Is anxiety about to break out, after all? No, "She smoothes her hair with automatic hand / And puts a record on the gramophone," proving as casual, withal, as the rhyme of "and" ("When lovely woman stoops to folly and / Paces") and "hand." Even vanity is dulled in her, she but "looks a moment in the glass'; she's past staging her beauty, cultivating it as a Female Otherness that can make a sailor forget the

47. Hugh Kenner, *The Invisible Poet: T. S. Eliot* (New York: Harcourt, Brace and World, 1959), 169.

Infinite. Instead, disillusioned but not enlightened, further along the path to nothingness than the fiery-haired woman but unaware of the *other* face of nothingness, that is, purity, she paces blindly about the margins of a truly spiritual life, bored out of her head (again, "Her brain allows one half-formed thought to pass"). Is she not contemptibly successful at repressing the experience of pain, of emptiness? No, the verse will waste no pity on her, she would not understand its relevance—she's that safe. Nonetheless, it takes leave of her almost equitably, resigning her to a limbo of mild mechanical throbs and habitual circlings as automatic and soothing as those of the gramophone.

So it is that the protagonist adopts for a while a measure, hence a sensibility, that allows him to "do" a voice of social assurance and authority (as earlier he had done a biblical one), dicing out every syllable with a placing moral intelligence. But, borrowed as it is from an earlier, socially more coherent age, this intelligence simply amounts, as said, to a "skit," a halfway house on the long trek to purity, and—compared to the austerities imposed by the latter, the word-chastising silence—a rather comfortable interlude. The protagonist may emulate Dryden, who, Eliot noted, "applies vocabulary, images, and ceremony which arouse epic associations of grandeur, to make an enemy helplessly ridiculous," but he has yet to dare the heights of grandeur himself, and meanwhile his Augustan discourse is not unlike the clerk's "one bold stare," just as histrionic and arrogant.[48] Through tired Tiresias, he applies judgment, performs it, not with throbbing agony of soul but with a relatively automatic hand. The metaphysical "soul" cannot be evoked, and can scarcely be involved, in the social, cultural and snobbish accents of the pastiche. The clerk may descend from his quick, insectival coupling with a scapegrace lack of ceremony or dignity; but the protagonist himself has still heroically to ascend.

This Music

"This muscic crept by me upon the waters"
And along the Strand, up Queen Victoria Street.
O City city, I can sometimes hear
Beside a public bar in Lower Thames Street,
The pleasant whining of a mandoline
And a clatter and a chatter from within
Where fishmen lounge at noon: where the walls
Of Magnus Martyr hold
Inexplicable splendour of Ionian white and gold.

---

48. T. S. Eliot, "John Dryden," in *Selected Essays* (London: Faber and Faber, 1958), 307.

Water Music

Here the mask of Tiresias is cast aside and that of Ferdinand put on, if only for the duration of a line and that an openly quoted one, a *patent* mask. The quotation marks are necessary, in fact, to leave unambiguous the fact that the protagonist has, under music's magic charm, become himself again, insofar as he is verbally discoverable as something other than Protagonist & Company. In any case, the quotation marks are useful in cordoning off the suggestion of the preternatural; nor could the protagonist have said, "This music crept by me upon the waters / And along the Strand," etc., minus the separating effect of the inverted commas, without having seemed callowly clever, performing a warp in time as if playing a musical saw, whereas the *appeal* of the scene that he is already in the process of describing is precisely its naturalness. From the Tiresias skit, the protagonist emerges once again as a City worker, only strolling as Eliot himself was fond of doing to Lower Thames Street during lunch hour. For the moment contented, his agony appeased, he feels no need of a mask. A brilliant quasi-cinematic dissolve from the gramophone record, via the quotation from *The Tempest,* to the "pleasant whining of a mandoline," a musical glissando, and, presto, he is himself again.

The line " 'This music crept by me upon the waters' " prepares us for an access to peace, if not wonder. In contrast to the creeping of the rat along the bank, this music, creeping *on the water,* speaks of a miraculous purification of flesh into what does not fade ("*Full fadom five thy father lies,*" sings Ariel; "*Of his bones are coral made; / Those are pearls that were his eyes: / Nothing of him that doth fade, / But doth suffer a sea-change / Into something rich and strange*"). Moreover, it allays the agony of separation from the father:

> Where should this music be?
>   i' th' air or th' earth?
> . . . sure, it waits upon
> Some god o' th' island. Sitting on a bank,
> Weeping again the King my father's wrack,
> This music crept by me upon the waters,
> Allaying both their fury and my passion
> With its sweet air: Thence I have followed it. . . .
>
>   (1.2.390–96)

This creeping awakens, not a shudder of abjection, but a primal religious shudder, hairs raised in response to the preternatural. To be sure, the music the protagonist actually hears is only the pleasant whining of a mandolin in Lower Thames Street; but in the ambience of the lounging fishmen (who sharply contrast with the lunging clerk), even such music conjoins with water to unclot and dissolve in the protagonist the meaner self-hoardings and tighter self-inquisitions. The first concatenation of water and music in the poem, the sailor's song from *Tristan und Isolde,* occurred in fatal, because romantic, circumstances. And the later association of the Thames with "my song" was, of course, one of dirty water with fallen speech. In exile from the homeland one does not sing—so the Hebrews hanged their harps upon the willows by the rivers of Babylon, for "How shall we sing the Lord's song in a strange land?" (Psalms 137:4). But the hand-produced music of the mandolin (in contrast to the gramophone music near the drying combinations) is free of the pathos of both exile and romance (or "situations"). Its context is one of equitable and easy human relations, a happy buzz of sociality, not passion. Further, as a near anachronism in the jazz age, the mandolin blends in where fishmen have (so Eliot said of them) "spat out time." It combines with the smell of fish and the sea to intimate eternity; music, notes Ned Rorem, is "the present prolonged."[49] Does the protagonist, then, like Ferdinand, receive musical news of the Missing King? What is the God he seeks, "the heart" of things, if not absolute freedom from past and future, the true eternal present?

O City City

Animated as he is by the mandoline music (which, in contrast to the gramophone, evokes a live animal sound), together with its harmonious context, the protagonist apostrophizes the City, truly apostrophizes it, for the first time. A poetic bargain is struck: "I'll animate you," he seems to say, "since you have animated me, at this spot, in this and like moments." The city (small "c") is the overbearing City become a communal moment of objectivity; the Unreal City become real, or at least not *Un*real.

Here the protagonist enjoys a détente with aspects of the "lower fertility" that—surprisingly—suddenly appear consonant with the "higher" one: the smell of the sea off the fishmen's stalls; the amalgamation that "fishmen" suggests between the human and the deep otherness of God; the happy noises of communal dining and lounging; perhaps above all a splendor of Ionian white and gold. Free of machines and documents, the scene relieves the protagonist of the pressure of contemporaneity; free of women, it puts him at ease with the

49. Ned Rorem, "Pictures and Places," in *Music from Inside Out* (New York: George Braziller, 1967), 16.

body, the senses. Hitherto, have his ears admitted pleasure in any sounds (save the unheard "inviolable voice" of Philomel)? Here they delight in a subdued music of sociality as well as a clamant instrument—noting without extreme prejudice "a clatter and a chatter from within," despite the absence of the Mystic Fish Meal, much as the substance for the latter is at hand. The writing itself is strong in the capacity known as "ear": pleasurably empathic, for instance, is the resonance in "The plea*sant whining* of a *mandoline*"; and in this last the iambs are (in Whitmanic phrase) easily strummed. Again, "And a clatter and a chatter from within," besides ending with a charmed echoing resonance, indeed a rhyme, strikes a merrily quickened music through its skipping slacks and staccato recurrences ("And a . . . -er and a . . . -er from with-") as well as through the onomatopoeic internal rhyme of its two strongest beats ("clat-" and "chat-"). The terms "clatter" and "chatter," like "pleasant whining," hold back from ennobling the sounds of the public bar, but prove acceptable by pleading "no contest" with "the silence," to which the protagonist (so his carefully limiting words suggests) secretly remains faithful. There is nothing of the Siren about them; they are innocent of deception and pretension, they can be enjoyed without great involvement, without fear.

And the protagonist's eyes, have they delighted in anything since the hyacinth girl? Here, in contrast to the "enclosed room," they thrill to walls that "hold," as treasure is held, "Inexplicable splendour of Ionian white and gold." The Wren interior of Magnus Martyr is less architecture than art, less art than miracle ("Inexplicable"). Its "white and gold"—dignified and straitened by the classical epithet "Ionian"—suggest, respectively, purity and incalculable riches. The first offsets the white of "White bodies," and the second the gold in "golden Cupidons." Both transcend the too-earthen brown of the befogged Unreal City.

Again the writing validates the explicit emotional evaluation (as with "pleasant whining"). The monosyllables and alliteration of "where the walls" correlate with a deliberately crafted architectural holding, as (fortuitously) do the dual, matched sounds of "Magnus Martyr." "Gold," already a symbol of preciousness that endures, is further shored up by its couplet rhyme with "hold." The retaining and sustaining pattern of rhymed, paired words recurs, obscured, in *splic* and *splen*. "Ionian" embraces the vowels of the two words it modifies, "white" and "gold." The constellation of the sounds in the last line is itself opulent, with "In-" reappearing in "splendour" and "Ionian," and the four major stresses falling on two pairs of vowels: "In-" and "splen," and "on" (in "Ionian") and "gold." Then, too, the rhythm is worshipfully breathless. The line "Of Magnus Martyr hold," with its six brief syllables and suspended verb, seems to wall in an adoration that, no longer able to restrain itself, pours forth in the following line fifteen syllables in rich profusion.

Remarkable, this allowance of naturalistic description in a poem so chastely, and with such anguish, metaphoric. Remarkable, too, this acknowledgment that art, even a visual art of material objects, can evoke the Inexplicable and rejoice more, much more, than the senses. Wren's interior, together with the conception of Philomel's inviolable voice, supports, even if it does not entirely justify, Eliot's project: that of creating a verbal "object" enshrining his devotion to the nonverbal, nonobjectal Silence.

Despite the poem's reputation, then, for furious displays of culture, the protagonist proves happiest (within history, within culture) where culture is least pretentious in its secular reaches, reserving its splendor for allusions to the "other world." This is the fullest significance of the small "c" in "city." Terry Eagleton is, I think, mistaken to argue that *The Waste Land* produces "an ideology of *cultural knowledge*." Eliot's relation to the culture of the past and present, including literary "tradition" and his own practice of its prosodic forms, is at best a matter of bricolage and at worst ruthless. His avant-gardism lies precisely in the implication—rising from beginning to end in his poem— that culture, even one's own latest and most brilliant contribution to it, is always the radically insufficient. Hence the error of Eagleton's view that

the reader who finds his or her access to the poem's "meaning" baulked by its inscrutable gesturing off-stage is already in possession of that "meaning" without knowing it. Cultures collapse, but Culture survives and its form is *The Waste Land*. . . . It is in this sense that the poem's signifying codes contradict their signifieds: for if history is indeed sterility then the work itself could not come into being, and if the work exists then it does so only as an implicit denial of its "content."[50]

The "gesturing" of the poem is all done onstage, and the stage is Culture. The poem indeed exists as an implicit denial of its "content," but the latter is not "the decay of Europe" but the futility of style, and the contradiction lies a stage further than Eagleton places it: not between "signifying codes" and "their signifieds" but between codes and the Unsignifiable.

50. Terry Eagleton, *Criticism and Ideology: A Study in Marxist Literary History* (London: Verso Edition, 1978), 148–49.

What eases the contradiction is the perhaps delusory hope that "song," or the musicality of structure and form, the emotionally "immediate," might succeed where language (where mere "speech") fails. Hence the importance to Eliot of a musical *social constellation* of things during lunch hour at the Billingsgate Fish Market. (One might fancy that he'd come back to just such a moment as this to start out on the path that led to *The Idea of a Christian Society* and *Four Quartets,* as against the path his protagonist takes, to the mountains of the Spirit, where persons and communities as such do not exist, but only the entirely Other.) Hence, even more, the importance of Wren's interior, a form that signifies nothing except, precisely, the spendor of the inexplicable.

THE RIVER SWEATS

The river sweats
Oil and tar
The barges drift
With the turning tide
Red sails
Wide
To leeward, swing on the heavy spar.
The barges wash
Drifting logs
Down Greenwich reach
Past the Isle of Dogs.
       Weialala leia
       Wallala leialala

Elizabeth and Leicester
Beating oars
The stern was formed
A gilded shell
Red and gold
The brisk swell
Rippled both shores
Southwest wind
Carried down stream
The peal of bells
White towers
       Weialala leia
       Wallala leialala

"Trams and dusty trees.
Highbury bore me. Richmond and Kew
Undid me. By Richmond I raised my knees
Supine on the floor of a narrow canoe."

"My feet are at Moorgate, and my heart
Under my feet. After the event
He wept. He promised 'a new start'.
I made no comment. What should I resent?"

"On Margate Sands.
I can connect
Nothing with nothing.
The broken fingernails of dirty hands.
My people humble people who expect
Nothing."
            la la

The Return of the Nymphs

This long section—which, ironically or casually, Eliot in a note treats
it as single, dubbing it "The Song of the (three) Thames-daughters"—
falls into two parts: (1) the protagonist's impersonation of river
nymphs and (2) his contrasting impressions of three modern London
women, all young, who live near the Thames. The nymphs sing two
trios, in brisk, staccato measure. The modern women speak, in turn,
their listless, lonely substitutes for song. The "(three) Thames-
daughters" are, in either guise, the protagonist's inventions. Himself a
"dramatic" creation, the protagonist generates out of his sense of his
own spirit and substance still other dramatic presences, and in this
fictitiousness discovers much of his humanity (in every sense the word
will bear).

His "Song" first mythifies, then demythifies, the daughters. To
start with, they are "natural" female deities such as the male imagination once delighted in contemplating. Yes, even Prufrock once delighted in them: "I have heard the mermaids singing, each to each."
The river nymphs, like the mermaids Prufrock has seen "riding seaward on the waves / Combing the white hair of the waves blown back
/ When the wind blows the water white and black," represent a perfect
equation between the life of the "human" body, or vitality in human
form, and natural, elemental energy—hence the abolition of pain and
suffering. (It is true that Wagner's Rhine-daughters, freely used as
models for Eliot's Thames-daughters, suffer; but, as part of a concealed sun myth, they lament the loss of their river's gleaming gold,
and not the pain of individuation.) Shallow, dazzling, such beings as
the mermaids display a flawless adaptation to existence, a paradisal
equivalence between their desires and the things within their reach;
between their abilities and the adventures they undertake. They are
born and live in a world made for them; unlike Prufrock, they are

never self-divided, forced to choose between the pleasures of the body and the bliss of the soul. How and of what would such creatures sing? Prufrock says he heard them, and the protagonist would hear them, too. Suppose they dwelled in the Thames, as embodiments of the river itself, but stilled and quickened into feminine form and voice. Again, how and of what would they sing?

They would sing of the river itself, so the trios imply. The river is their intelligence, theirs its stream of impressions. They are nothing other than its sensory genius. When the river is slack and soiled, they feel a little slack and soiled; when it is brisk, they are brisk. Not that, as nymphs, they are ever less than innocently vital.

Yes, as if refreshed by his visit to Lower Thames Street, the protagonist grants the daughters the heart to sing with gusto even of the dirty Thames, which they describe with more or less naïve naturalistic keeness—"more or less" because the protagonist cannot refrain from contributing, if not quite interjecting, a little of his own disillusionment with industrial London. "Sweats" marks this ambiguity. It tells, disappointedly, of pollution, but, really, all that the nymphs as such *say* is that, like an active body, the river sweats. They note and name the "Oil and tar," but in the same way that they drink in all appearances, nonjudgmentally, with primal appetite for sensory spectacle.

As to the "how" of their singing, they favor a two-beat measure, swift and choppy and capable of making each notation, however spare, appear vivid (capable, too, of suspensefully prolonging a single appropriate monosyllable, such as "Wide"). This decidedly fresh measure, new in a poem more prose-weary than tuneful, is adapted from Wagner's nymphs, who, whether rueing the theft of their gold or in bickering byplay with Siegfried, attack everything with the same verbal gusto, in the unvarying pulse of their single nature. In keeping, the Thames-daughters cannot speak unless to sing, or sing unless to chant in the most vibrant rhythms. Seizing on the protagonist's habit of protean self-evasion and self-extension as a pretext for creating one of the changes of style and pace necessary to a long poem (and, conversely, writing a long poem because of the protagonist's mercurial identity), Eliot sees to it that these heroines of the "lower vitality" stroke their way through language. Instinctive advocates of Appearance, and natively vigorous, they do not hold back. Omitting punctuation, as what would hinder their song and is anyway unnecessary, except where it clarifies rhythm, they transfuse their own vim into what they sing about. (Punctuation is culture; the nymphs are, virtually, nature.) Watery, they sing with the slipping impulsiveness of a river, whether the song be of the present Thames (much as it was evoked in Conrad's

Heart of Darkness, a title that might have given birth, through antithetical repulsion, to the phrase "the heart of light") or of the Thames
that Spenser bade run softly and on which Queen Elizabeth and
Leicester disported in a gilded shell. Again, they cannot distinguish the
two Thameses intellectually, only concretely, as sensory realities (for
them, nothing can appear Unreal). Unhampered by complicated historical or metaphysical judgments, wholly *song,* they express themselves in a rhythm as sustained and unsustained, as uncommitted yet
all out, as briskly flowing water.

Corporeal and industrial waste; loss of direction; going round in
cycles; stumps, Dogs—by this point in the poem such material must
seem familiar, but here, in the first trio, a pure verse intelligence, freed
of the protagonist's typical need to excoriate, takes command. For
instance, it places "barges" close upon "tar" not only tarringly but for
the pleasurable echo of it; enjoys the return of the *t* in "turning tide";
and portentously gives a whole line to "Red sails," as if dimly remembering the awesome, ambiguous accents on "red rock" and as if to
daub "Red" and "sails" into the verbal painting with an incisive, disturbing twist of the palette knife. After the wide-eyed isolation of the
word "Wide," a heavy, swinging feeling is wanted for the spar, where-
upon comes a greatly expanded line of nine syllables, plus a caesura to
enact the swing. Out at the extremity of its own imagined length, as of
that of the line, "spar" points back to "tar." In a verbal drift, the
earlier clause "the barges drift" becomes "The barges wash / Drifting
logs." These are matters on which the ear, with its empathic sense,
decides, and the nymphs are the *joy of empathy.*

Significantly, however, the verse *is* slightly different in the second
trio, and that because the objects of empathy are—if still sensory objects—qualitatively different, in fact resplendent. Whatever may be
judged of Elizabeth and Leicester based on information from other
texts, they are here merely (and for them freeingly) objects of the
Thames-daughters' sensory observations; and what the nymphs remember of the Elizabethan Thames (for they have shifted now to the
past tense) is at once a general and very exact impression of both
human and natural vigor. At that time, oars beat, sterns were formed,
the swell was brisk, and the river, in streaming plenitude, pouringly
alive throughout its breadth, ripplingly washed and connected both
shores. Bells pealed then from white towers, as against uttered final
strokes under brown fog, and the wind did something: it carried news
and joy of religion downstream. There was no drifting, then—no
straying. Purposeful and buoyant energy—energy to shape and to carry; energy of contact—marked the times. All this the nymphs re-

member, for they have always been part of the river—are indeed its memory.

The nymphs respond to *this* Thames—a splendor that, if not inexplicable, is still a splendor[51]—with verse both more firmly and more delicately formed for the ear than that through which they told of the sweating river, drifting barges, a swinging spar, drifting logs. They capture the naval prosody of beating oars, the elemental prosody of the brisk swell and southwest wind, with stress patterns that, shaking off the effect of brutal aimlessness, of rough swings, meld into a larger, more continually self-refreshing structure. Now avoiding verbal repetition with its suggestion of drift, they also avoid the blunt, almost accusatory accents of "The riv*er sweats* / *Oil* and *tar* / The *barg*es *drift*," etc. By comparison, "Elizabeth and Leicester," for instance, contains only civilly muffled, sibilantly pleasant stresses. As for "Beating oars," it is only so plosive, stirringly so, as it deserves to be. Then, too, the rhythm is ripplingly varied. Thus the iambs of "The stern was formed" may be matched in the next line, "A gilded shell," but the quickened, disyllabic middle of this last, together with its grammatical difference, dispels any effect of rote repetition. The first line is muscular, the second lingers enchanted over "gilded." A new rhythmic figure is then introduced by "The brisk swell," another by "Rippled both shores," a third by "Southwest wind," and still a fourth by "White towers." By contrast, in the first trio we find recurrences of two bald iambs ("The river sweats"; "The barges drift," etc.) and of a catelectic trochaic measure ("Oil and tar"; "Drifting logs"; "Past the Isle of Dogs"). Enliveningly, five of the lines in the second trio begin with words of more than one syllable, providing impetus for what follows, as against only one in the first ("Drifting logs").

In this second paragraph, rhyme is more agreeable, too. The present-day Thames repelled verbal harmony. "Sweat" remained outside rhyme, understandably uncourted by any other word. "Sails" and "reach" went unechoed, too. As for the rhyme for "tar" ("spar"), it was delayed five lines. "Logs" was made to rhyme with "Dogs"—not a rhyme one could care for. And if through sound "Wide" and "wash" relate to "Weialala," and do so even if the *w* is pronounced as a *v*, it is only from a "drifting" distance. By contrast, two triple rhymes (with one word aslant in each set) add musical harmony to the second trio: first "Oars," "formed," and "shores," then "shell," "swell," and "bells." A purring *r* sounds through "Leicester," "oars,"

51. What the lounging fishmen are to the Fisher King or, better, the knight who saves him, Elizabeth's gilded shell, with its *red* and gold, is to the "Inexplicable splendour of Ionian white and gold."

"formed," "shores," and "towers." "White" is placed near "Weialala," which seems almost to pour out of it. Each terminal word is curved toward close relation with another word or with several words.

Still, the exact repetition of the refrain, a reduction of the Rhine-daughters' wonderfully watery verbal ripple, consorts with the singleness, in all circumstances, of the nymphs' nature, the rough identity of the prosody of the two trios. Constituting in the original a supposed untranslatably deep lament, it emerges, in the new context, despite its watery collapses on itself, as a happily indifferent liquid babble—for how, in any case, should moving water be pierced by pain? (As for the "la la" that concludes the entire "Song" in listless or mocking echo, it is post-nymphic, a contemporary suburban woman's acerb poor-Ophelia routine.)

The Nymphs Are Departed

The turn to the second group of paragraphs—the three solos—is comparable to leaving behind the mermaids Prufrock sees riding seaward and joining the small-motioned "sea-girls"—funereally wreathed in sickly "seaweed red and brown"—among whom he says he lingers in stagnant depths. Only these *new* Thames-daughters are no longer dream-girls, not, at least, in their own jaundiced view. Rather, they are the sort of "human voices"—small but in their way real—in which a Prufrock drowns.

As mere women, real women, the Thames-daughters represent not the lower fertility but the pathos of lives either never made buoyant by hope, lives of an immemorial resignation to "nothing," or lives that have sunk or dwindled past the phase where romantic illusions are still entertained (with no high dream arriving to dispel the deserts of disillusion). These women not only seem too depressed to sing; they can scarcely speak in sentences—their words flag into fragments; the speech impulse grows discouraged in them, and soon ceases. Their lines may be longer than those of their mythic sisters, but they are virtually lines of prose. The excited, irregular pulse has died and the briskness that remains is curiously unhappy and flat, a witty yet bored efficiency. "The verse is low in tone," Eugenio Montale said of *The Waste Land,* "the tone of *récitatif,* . . . a knowing dismantling and reduction of the line already present in Whitman. . . . Starting from *récitatif,* Eliot often arrives at song, reaches a high tone from the lowest, most conversational tone possible. He is above all (let us say it) a poet-musician."[52] Yes, and *récitatif* takes on even a quasi-debilitated

52. Eugenio Montale, "Invitation to the Reading of T. S. Eliot," in *The Second Life of Art: Selected Essays,* trans. Jonathan Galassi (New York: Ecco Press, 1982), 181–82.

form in the daughters' solos. The "Song" drops precipitously, with them, from watery lyricism to dusty prosaicism, as language collapses into a weary realization of "the awful separation between potential passion and any actualization possible in life." Yeats might have cited these solos when he said that Eliot works "without apparent imagination." Of course the word "apparent" is important, here, even if "in describing [a] life that has lost heart [Eliot's] own art seems grey, cold, dry."[53] For the solos are, precisely, strong imaginings of humble and defeated personalities. They are the work of a "poet-musician" whose material for the moment is the quasi-prosaic syntax of despair.

Although parataxis marks trios and solos alike, periods are used in the latter to produce an unlovely bareness and inertness of language, consonant with a choking-off of illusion:

> Trams and dusty trees.
> Highbury bore me. Richmond and Kew
> Undid me. . . .
> . . . .
>   After the event
> He wept. He promised "a new start."
> I made no comment. What should I resent?
> . . . .
> On Margate Sands.
> . . . .
> The broken fingernails of dirty hands.

Trams and dusty trees *period*. Broken fingernails of dirty hands, period. Brute matter is not only ground into the flesh ("dirty hands"), but weighs heavily on the spirit. It forms a terminus of vision; the daughters can see beyond it to nothing else. Their loss of access to expectation leaves (again apparently) a total, helpless passivity. Where the singing nymphs intensify the world to the level of their own energy, here the syntax, on behalf of the environment, says *take that and that,* and the women do.

Yet if the solos appear to be discourse "undone," they are actually tightly formed, even wittily so, and, pondering this, and allowing for the protagonist's natural propensity to show his own hand while "doing" them, I think we must conclude that their very disillusionment has hardened them and made them thorny—that they can match the protagonist disillusion for disillusion, loveless wit for wit. Not entirely helpless or passive, after all, they are drily shrewd. The first speaker especially so. If her statement "Highbury bore me" seems to say that environment alone is generative, and if her words "Richmond

53. William Butler Yeats, "Introduction to the Oxford Book of Modern Verse," in *Selected Criticism*, ed. A. Norman Jeffares (London: Macmillan, 1964), 223.

and Kew / Undid me" suggest that environment alone destroys, what is notable about the whole statement, "Highbury bore me. Richmond and Kew / Undid me" is its pithy, pungent, unexpected antithesis, not to mention the clever use of "Undid" (which of course recalls the more serious "I had not thought death had undone so many"), or the tricky line break that springs it on us, or the suspicion of a pun in "bore." The writing suggests formidable reserves of acuity, and a sort of tail-lashing unforgivingness. Then, too, her next expression, "I raised my knees," may be supposed intelligently sardonic. What a way to introduce an anecdote about the experience of sex that sealed her disillusion. Well, a perfect way, really. The deceptive elevation that it ironically suggests is immediately, deliberately, and effectively quashed by the artfully suspended follow-up, "Supine." This speaker enjoys taking it out of a sentence, giving expectation a smart thump. She seems to know, besides, that "raised my knees" is all wrong in its possible suggestion of childbirth ("Highbury bore me"), when, really, all that happened was that she was "undone." She seems to know, too, that this profane raising of her knees was the often-warned-against opposite of a proper kneeling upon them. But it is not for her, at this point, to care. She, too, is mistress of the devastating line break: "My feet are at Moorgate, and my heart / Under my feet." So she subverts the popular romantic formula *but my heart is elsewhere*. "Under my feet" is unexpected, but what *could* be expected after the oddly self-atomizing "My feet are at Moorgate"—that fake-naïve confession of a feeling of self-dissociation? What this daughter says in her daunting way is that the whole of her is at Moorgate, that she treads on her dreams, such as they are, or were. "After the event," she adds, "He wept." "*The* event"? "The *event*"? Any way one turns the phrase, it seems ridiculous, consciously and mockingly inflated. This is wry, but the semibiblical "He wept" (recalling "Jesus wept"—John 11:35) is murderous. "He promised 'a new start' ": after the quotation marks, she has no need to add, "of course." She speaks here as a woman who knows men; and through her, and along with her, the protagonist speaks as one who guesses that there *can* be no promising "new start" except ouside the generative and romantic cycle.

This underlining of the speakers' cleverness serves to confirm Moody's finding that there is in these women "no illusion or evasion; no rationalizing and no sentimentalising."[54] It is the lucidity of their disillusionment that wins the protagonist's sympathy and respect.

54. A. D. Moody, *Thomas Stearns Eliot: Poet* (Cambridge: Cambridge University Press, 1979), 94.

Where the women in the poem are concerned, we find a progression from those who still possess some innocence and yearning—Marie, the hyacinth girl—to one who has lost innocence yet still yearns, to women without either innocence or illusion-licensed, illusion-empowered desire: the typist and the Thames-daughters in their guise as suburban women. But where the typist scarcely admits disillusionment into consciousness, the daughters are half-hardened and half-forlorn with it. Like the protagonist, they have worn through illusion, but without finding anything on the other side. Whereas his card is the drowned Phoenician sailor, they and those around them are removed from water ("dusty trees"; "the floor of a narrow canoe"; "My feet are at Moorgate"; "On Margate Sands"; "The broken fingernails of dirty hands"). But in a sense the protagonist recognizes them as sisters, does not patronize them, makes them as chillingly knowing as he is. To say that the first two solos are "as simple and natural as speech can be," as Moody does, may be to veil their aspect of complicated verbal machines—masterworks of muted bitterness, traps for innocence.

The first two solos form the surreptitious beginning of what remains a surreptitious, a broken and eroded, sonnet. The two quatrains unfold the same pattern: an initial indication of a hopelessly static condition, of a soul that has gone out, followed by a little narrative of the snuffing of whatever romantic flame it may once have suffered. This repetition establishes a standard story, as well as a capacity for cutting wit, that may be taken for granted in the sestet, which is thus freed for broader evocations, climactic generalizations. The development in the second solo, the value-involving, if rhetorical, question "What should I resent?" leads in the third to what must suffice instead of a credo, simply an admission of how it is. "On Margate Sands," this third daughter begins; again, on Margate Sands period. And so already we know that she "can connect / Nothing with nothing," her deceptive pause after "connect" notwithstanding. Seeming to let her eyes glaze over, to wax impressionistic, she adds, "The broken fingernails of dirty hands." But, at once metaphor and metonym of the waste land, this figure forms an evocatively exact imagist equation for the futility and abjection of striving amid the stony rubbish of a historical social organization in which the Divine Architecture and the Divine Fountain are no longer (not that they could ever be adequately) represented. It epitomizes much of the art of the poem, being metastatic, disconnected, theatrical, lucid, and plainly spoken, and an acknowledgment of dismemberment, of exile from some unarticulated wholeness. As iambic pentameter, the line is more simply aligned with poetic tradition than many of the others in the poem—yet untraditional in its stinging isolation as a fragment, and even its uncompromisingly "unpoetic" specifications.

The "sonnet" climaxes with its broadest generalization and central word: "My people humble people who expect / Nothing." "Nothing" rhymes, fittingly, with "nothing," as what cannot be identified or harmonized with anything except itself, its own total absence of possibility.

All told, the forty one lines of the "Song" witness and perform a catastrophe of sensibility. Here, feeling unshadowed by thought (and why should creatures of nature think?) gives way to thought on which feeling lies like dust. First doing females who are all nature, the protagonist then does women who have lost all "natural" feeling. He thereby suggests that women no longer serve men as a mythic bridge to nature. They can no longer be thought to enjoy a privileged instinctual and sensory relation to it; in them, too, the senses have fallen into ashes, the flame of eroticism having died. So it is that the protagonist extinguishes the last remnants of the desire for romance still flickering at random in his own being. He may move on now from the idolatries of fertility worship and human love, having exhausted all hope that lies in "faithful" mimesis, in circlings back to the mother. In the latter converge not only survival needs but the first mimetic yearnings. The mother, in the psychoanalytical view, "is the other subject, an object that guarantees my being as subject."[55] The protagonist's propensity to identify with, to "do," women has only betrayed his nostalgia to be a subject in a realm of still magical, still sympathetic, objects. D. W. Winnicott suggests that art itself, with its "play" objects, reflects this nostalgia.[56] However that may be, the protagonist will now turn to literary modes of representation that are, in the conventional sense of the word, less nostalgically "mimetic" than some he has already tried, in an effort to free himself, as subject, from delusive and seductive objects and so prepare himself for an assumption onto a plane of feeling where subjectivity and objectivity can no longer be distinguished.

To Carthage Then I Came

To Carthage then I came

Burning burning burning burning
O Lord Thou pluckest me out
O Lord Thou pluckest

burning

55. Kristeva, *Powers of Horror*, 32.
56. D. W. Winnicott, *Playing and Reality* (New York: Basic Books, 1971), chaps. 4 and 5.

Thou Pluckest

Up to this point, the protagonist has pretty successfully evaded his own agony. He has devoted himself, instead, to studying its evasion in others (Marie, the City crowd, and so on). Now he suffers its eruption, its flame, its power to release spirituality. From a dimension of himself he had neglected all this while yet couldn't put to sleep, or entirely starve, bursts a devout ejaculation—a showing, even to him, of the actual force of his soul. Coming from some very near place in his being, it breaks into and through all temporizations, surprising his self-theater, his comfortable self-dispersals and disguises. He had filled in the blanks of the calendar one by one with faces cut out of the pages of the temporal—and now here is something direct from himself, and known only from within as a faceless movement up and outward into consubstantiality with the Divine. Acknowledging his complicity with all he has seen, the "dirty" fingers of his voyeurism, he feels a contrition that establishes at once a freeing, vertical relation to the One, an experience of abrupt extrication from the maze of the historical, metonymic, horizontal realm of contingencies, including his own accidental "personality" and "story."

In Augustine's *Confessions*, "To Carthage then I came" marks the author's youthful sojourn in an Unreal City, where he experienced a "famine of that inward food, Thyself, My God," desiring, instead, to be "scraped by the touch of objects of sense" and to fall headlong into ensnaring love. In Carthage, he acknowledges, he "wandered with a stiff neck, withdrawing further from Thee, loving mine own ways, and not Thine; loving a vagrant liberty." He permitted "that same nature, of which He is Author," to be "polluted by perversity of lust." Yet, a fisher among readers, like the protagonist, Augustine was converted by a reading of Cicero's "Hortensius": "How did I burn then, my God, how did I burn to re-mount from earthly things to Thee. . . . For with Thee is wisdom." All this in book 3. And in book 10 Augustine declares, in a passage even more splendid than what the *Confessions* soon accustoms us to:

But I, my God and my Glory, do hence also sing a hymn to Thee, and do consecrate praise to Him who consecrateth me, because those beautiful patterns which through men's souls are conveyed into their cunning hands, come from that Beauty, which is above our souls, which my soul day and night sigheth after. But the framers and followers of the outward beauties derive thence the rule of judging of them, but not of using them. And He is there, though they perceive Him not, that so they might not wander, but keep their strength for Thee, and not scatter it abroad upon pleasurable wearinesses. And I, though I speak and see this, entangle my steps with these outward beauties; but Thou pluckest me out, O Lord, Thou pluckest me out; because Thy loving-kindness is before my eyes.[57]

Assuming knowledge of Augustine's story, and in any case dramatizing the abruptness of his conversion, the protagonist elides the former with an inward peremptoriness, cutting from "To Carthage then I came" via the reiterated "burning" (a one-word gist of the charges that the Buddha prefers against the senses in his "Fire Sermon"), a word that subsumes Augustine's indictment of Carthage as a "cauldron of unholy loves," to "O Lord Thou pluckest me out." His own story is elided and summed up in the process. He thus turns Augustine's diegesis into the acutest showing. Earlier in the poem, syntax had occasionally warped and slipped, but not till now has it suffered interruptions like gasps, twists that signify violent spins and that reduce sweeps of unnecessary narrative detail to an understood, swift, world-departing blur. Syntax itself is altogether consumed in the confessional, repentant, and anguished line "Burning burning burning burning." (The line calcines the elegant systems of repetition in Buddha's sermon—a sermon Eliot admired as a supreme specimen of the genre.)[58] The illusion of an immediate showing finds support in Augustine's ever-grateful present tense, his constant vigilance against his proclivity to sin: "I entangle my steps with these outward beauties, but Thou pluckest me out, O Lord." Further, this last, by a shift of "O Lord" to the beginning of the clause and line, is changed from statement to outcry. Then the breath-short "O Lord Thou pluckest" sententially plucks out consciousness of self as object, in a grammatical equivalent of nirvana. In a final curtailment, the single "burning" at the close, reversing the effect of the echoic "la la" at the end of the Thames-daughters' "Song," enacts a marked lightening of agony. Appearing four times in succession in a line, "burning" seemed an unremitting experience of what the Buddha described as the infatuations and hatreds of the senses. And if the largely latent image of the cauldron is considered—as what brings fire to bear upon water, or, in the symbolism of the poem, the senses on the soul—then the single "burning" indicates the lessening of the soul's torment as a result of having Loving-Kindness before its eyes, the strong fire-fighting activity of hope and faith. At the same time, this final "burning" signals that the protagonist's birth is not yet "exhausted," his "attachment" dis-

57. Saint Augustine, *The Confessions of Saint Augustine,* trans. Edward B. Pusey (New York: Washington Square Press, 1960, 204. The earlier quotations are from book 3.
58. See T. S. Eliot, "The Preacher as Artist," *Athenaeum* 4674 (28 November 1919):1252.

solved, in the Buddha's terms, so that he is no more for this world. He is still, after all, formed of flesh, and, with whatever alleviation, on fire.

Abridgements, then, as of instant speech and thought working epitomizingly on other texts, suggesting an experience too vertiginous and ecstatic for niceties of syntax, let alone of punctuation. So it is that, without any narrative gesture whatsoever, with rational discourse itself going up in flames, the protagonist's story advances to his election of asceticism. Emotionally flush with the "surface" of the text, he simply *is* his election. One now not with women or even with kings and princes, but with church fathers, priests of priests; one now not with lost sons but with fathers of wisdom, he feels lifted out of the feminine and demonic cauldron of sensuality and hence from the jaws of death: as violently plucked out as a fish is pawed from a stream, saved from its life of abject writhings. For him, no more nature, or as little as possible. Now he knows: the mother's flowery bosom is on fire, the father's frigid austere law comparatively a bower of bliss, and the Unnameable itself the true name of joy.

Speech and Writing; Quotation and Authenticity

So inveterate is his habit of speaking through others that, even in this moment of supreme "authenticity," the protagonist quotes and virtually becomes others. But now more than ever this habit is a form of humility and modesty; of submission to a "tradition" of ascetic wisdom; a matter, not of attitudinizing, of intensifying an empty life through theater, but of acknowledging the one perennial mode for salvation, the voluntary desiccation of the senses, so that the rain of otherness might be attracted, and fall.

This recourse to quotation (of Augustine) and paraphrase (of the Buddha) is less compromising to the protagonist than it might seem; for, the issue of any possible originality aside, speech can only function in any case to make him the already secondary, already artificially focused "subject" of the symbolicity of language. Of the Other, language, including the word "Lord," can never be more than an inauthentic, if well-intended, sign. That is why there is modesty, a specifically linguistic one not least of all, in representing one's own conversion through the (historically consecrated) words of those whose spirituality has scarcely been doubted.

Has the protagonist, then, escaped his own partly compelled, partly ironic and critical self-theater by finding himself suddenly cast into a new and ecstatic role by a superior dramatist (Loving-kindness)—a role beyond his meager powers of manipulation? It is in any case what this master illusionist (with no mean powers of manipulation) would have us feel, as he lets his self-narrative snap with a slap as of broken film, lost in a passionate final flickering, a blare of naked projected light.

To effect the illusion of authenticity, the passage must appear to be—despite its extracts from and allusions to famous texts—essentially oral, not written. The shattering of linearity, the stopped-breath self-abbreviations, the total absence of punctuation, make the passage seem oral, swift, contemporaneous, and intimate with the nerves. A conversion of writing, by intensity, into speech.

Yet not only is this moment nothing if not written; it is a double writing, writing as, and over the surface of, quotation. The illusion of speech, here, is theater (in the nonpejorative sense used throughout this study): the simulation (mimesis) of an actual or anyway imaginable intensity of conversion. Speech is favored because of its illusion of what Derrida calls "teleological essence"—that of the proximity of the signifier to the signified, even its "effacement in immediate presence."[59] Out of the abundance of the heart, says Matthew, the mouth speaketh (12:35). Yet if this illusion of "immediate presence" comes through even the illusion of speech-through-writing, the reason is that alphabetic writing is reactivated only through what, again, Eudora Welty calls the "reader's voice," which is not to be confused with the actual speaking voice of the reader: auditory as much as vocal, it is the (silent) hearing or phonetic of apprehension of script. If on the one hand writing, in Derrida's words, "exhausts life,"[60] if "all clergies . . . were constituted at the same time as writing and by the disposition of graphic power," writing appearing "as meaning and mastery (by idealization)," still writing remains inert until "animated . . . by the act of meaning . . . which transforms it into a spiritual flesh."[61] This "act of meaning" is the understanding achieved through the reader's voice. All writing is, then, effectively speech, insofar as it activates this intelligent voice—as Augustine's *Confessions* does. What the protagonist conspires to do is to make Augustine's spoken writing appear *spoken anew* and *by him*. His method: abbreviation and parataxis, and jazz- or cinema-age intercuttings with a ground bass of suffering (the repeated "burning"). The structural splintering of the passage, the extreme narrative condensation, effect a plu-

59. Jacques Derrida, *Speech and Phenomena and Other Essays on Husserl's Theory of Signs*, trans. David B. Allison (Evanston: Northwestern University Press, 1973), 80.
60. Jacques Derrida, *Of Grammatology*, trans. Gayatri Spivak (Baltimore: The Johns Hopkins University Press, 1976), 17.
61. Ibid., 92. Also *Speech and Phenomena*, 81.

ridimensionality that equates with "immediate experience," dispelling the flatly distancing "unicity" of writing. An instance of form attempting to get around the limitations of discourse. Of trying, indeed, to surprise and baffle momentarily even the reader's voice, so as to show, with its own structural spiritedness, where spirit needs to go.

Both the mind and the senses, the Buddha said, are on fire.[62] Poetry essays a pluridimensionality that would put out the fires of each with showers from the other. Narrative, or action, further subdues them, and structural disruption—their fate in *The Waste Land*—achieves this best of all. Although "words move . . . / Only in time," so Eliot was later to say in "Burnt Norton," they "reach / Into the silence. Only by the form, the pattern, / Can words or music reach / The stillness." This assurance, which is stated as a lovely idea in the later work, is, however, hard to come by in *The Waste Land,* with its complicated pattern and its own comparative obliquity to ideas. At the end of the "The Fire Sermon," the equivocal multiple outcry that is also speech and quotation, the spontaneity that is also allusion and writing, and writing twice-over, locates the tension and conflict in Eliot's relations to writing and speech, tradition and originality, the senses and the abstract, poetry and the silence. His instinct tells him that the greater the immediacy, the greater the proximity of the Absolute. What, though, of the *illusion* of immediacy? Is theater ever more than a self-delusion? Is art ever more than artful? There are questions to which a poet must turn a deaf ear if he is still to be a poet. Eliot's poem, one of the most theatrical imaginable, is theatrical precisely because, despite all the wax of "silence" that the poet may imagine stuffing into his ears, the sounds of life still reach him, and, first and last, as a heteroglossic babble, a relentless rehearsal, however redirected, of others' words. In response to that, he *must* be theatrical— at once more theatrical than others and under the constant threat of a blackout, heaven blazing into the head.

62. See "The Fire-Sermon," in Henry Clarke Warren, *Buddhism in Translations: Passages Selected from the Buddhist Sacred Books* (Cambridge, Mass: Harvard University Press, 1922), 352–53.

DEATH BY WATER

PHLEBAS THE PHOENICIAN

Phlebas the Phoenician, a fortnight dead,
Forgot the cry of gulls, and the deep sea swell
And the profit and loss.

A current under sea
Picked his bones in whispers. As he rose and fell
He passed the sages of his age and youth
Entering the whirlpool.

Gentile or Jew
O you who turn the wheel and look to windward,
Consider Phlebas, who was once handsome and tall as you.

Consider Phlebas (Diegesis)

Pound had attempted to save at least some of the story that originally
made up the main part of "Death by Water"—namely, a voyage
"From the Dry Salvages to the eastern banks"—by making multiple
deletions. Perceiving that at this time Eliot's style throve on terseness,
twists, ellipses, and died in explicitness, he slashed into Eliot's surprisingly discursive narrative. Inconsistently, he let stand the stilted "And
if Another knows, I know I know not, / Who only know that there is
no more noise now."[1] Eliot, however, dropped these lines, together
with the entire Pound-crossed passage; and so was lost a confirmation
of the primacy of silence and the Other in the protagonist's deepest
experience of reality.

The only passage that Pound found beyond improvement is what
now serves as the whole of part 4—the coolingly placed episode of
Phlebas the Phoenician's death by drowning. In writing this passage
and in entitling part 4 "Death by Water," Eliot had in mind—as
Pound perceived—Madame Sosostris's predication of the protagonist's card and the fate he should fear ("Fear death by water").
Must stay in, as Pound said—Phlebas being needed absolutely where

1. T. S. Eliot, *The Waste Land: A Facsimile and Transcript of the Original Drafts
Including the Annotations of Ezra Pound*, ed. Valerie Eliot (New York: Harcourt Brace
Jovanovich, 1971), 69.

he is. Absolutely? Eliot could have gone straight from "burning" to the opening line of part 5, "After the torchlight red on sweaty faces," with a jump-cut economy; from flame to flame; from a conversion experience to a lament for the absence of "the Hanged Man," a sacrificial god to ease the approach to the Absolute, to Another. The move would further have been justified in that the subsequent ascetic ordeal represented through the ascending of a mountain where there "is no water but only rock" is a variant of—a slow narrative trope for—"O Lord Thou pluckest me out." Indeed, the drowning of Phlebas interrupts this lucid continuity. But there would have been, withal, a problem: namely, that the voice "doing" the opening paragraph of part 5 is not that of the converted protagonist. The one doing "Death by Water" *is* his, but, again, coolingly, in an impersonal, diegetic mode, as one who, having converted to the "Lord" in time, may now bring a warning to others. Having thus reestablished himself as a protagonist-*narrator,* a master of changing personae, scenes, and styles, he finds himself justified in doing yet another voice, at the beginning of part 5, before settling into what is allegorically and, so to speak, irreducibly his own.

As Moody notes, "Death by Water" effects a gentle transition, "preparing the emotions for the next stage"—both the protagonist's and the reader's emotions.[2] Switching from "mimesis" of himself to diegesis about another, the protagonist fabricates a fable both of how to die to carnal pride and how to navigate the soul toward the Absolute. As in the "Son of man" passage, in effect he instructs himself in the third person. He projects an absolute knowledge and assurance. And thus he steadies himself, discovers or therapeutically feigns a new spiritual authority. Yes, in taking up Madame Sosostris's identification of his card and elaborating on it, he tells, omnisciently, of a meaningless reversion of existence into nonexistence, of a watery undoing of life—the fate that Madame Sosostris had cautioned against and that he now actively seeks to avoid. (Madame Sosostris, with her tarot pack, has thus served his appetite for telling stories; the two virtually collaborate in making a character and a fate out of "the drowned Phoenician Sailor." She supplies the portentous motif, he draws out the portentous meaning. Both are, in their varying ways, showpersons; both fictionalize or theatricalize experience.)

The therapeutic value of "Death by Water" lies in the first place in its cool *written* detachment after the burning speech at the close of

2. A. D. Moody, *Thomas Stearns Eliot: Poet* (Cambridge: Cambridge University Press, 1979), 96.

"The Fire Sermon." The two quatrains (for they are basically that, despite a split line in each), rhyming *abcb defe,* reintroduce, after the violent scattering of the end of part 3, the formal measure of verse. The narrational-instructional tone and momentum of "Phlebas the Phoenician, a fortnight dead, / Forgot the cry of gulls" is all detachment of performance, all deliberate intentionality, all spell-weaving. The very name, "Phlebas the Phoenician," introduces, after "burning," a liberating remoteness and fictionality. As for "a fortnight dead," no parenthesis has been so formally felt since "Sighs, short and infrequent, were exhaled." And the memento mori turn of the close— the ambiguous address (is it gentle? stern?) of "Gentile or Jew / O you who turn the wheel and look to windward") and the sobering direction ("Consider Phlebas, who was once handsome and tall as you")— sets the protagonist over against us, over against the page, over against Phlebas, as one who wields a taxing pen. The passage climaxes in a formally full-blown, an expansive cadence, a complete—and completely *written*—flourish. Composition at the level of clausal relations has come to the protagonist's crisis with a soothing ice pack, brought him a tale full of elemental distance, a tale shaped like a little dipper.

Recovering from the searing conversion cries at the end of "The Fire Sermon," the protagonist also plunges his burning senses into the fantasy of a prolonged, ambiguously soothing subaqueous exhaustion of his birth, annihilation of his attachments (even, of the bonding of his flesh to his bones). Phlebas, his one-eyed sensual part, his surrogate, travels back through the stages of his life, from the end to the beginning, unwinding and undoing all that he was. As a contemplative discipline, a rite of self-purification, the protagonist fantasizes a death that is *utter,* a complete reducing back of the natural and psychical creature into nothingness. The supernatural and the superhuman are, by definition, beyond nature and beyond the (human) psyche: in a sense that is more accessible through Buddhism or Hindusim than through anthropomorphizing Christianity, they, or *it,* is wholly *spiritual.* Phlebas represents all that is not wholly of the spirit in the human being, and so disappears entirely, down a female symbol, a narrowing spiral of increasingly rapid rotations, of delirious circlings, back into the nothingness of the elemental. With him disappears everything in himself of which the protagonist was ashamed, the beast-body of a Mr. Eugenides, with its acquisitive sailings, its concern with "profit and loss," its circulating "currents" of blood and appetite, its one-eyed pecker and anus, its flight from women, its liability to being picked over, in whispers, by the terrible mother, Nature. With him disappears the lower phallic fertility whose "sacrifice," in Erich Neu-

mann's words, "is the precondition of spirituality."[3] Everything spu-
riously "handsome and tall."

To crown his detachment, to ensure that all his telling is *telling*, and
to practice the therapy of *playing physician*, the protagonist, as intimated, draws a moral from his tale. What must one do to avoid Phlebas's end? Look, implies the protagonist, to how you navigate. If your
hands are on the wheel, if you pilot with a stiff neck your own small
craft of will, you thereby withdraw from the Other, loving a vagrant
liberty. You who turn the *wheel:* the Wheel that Madame Sosostris
saw in the cards is in the first instance the wheel of fortune ("profit
and loss"). In its greatest reaches it is the ultimately self-disintegrating,
all-turning whirl of the elements (so in "Gerontion," in a parallel with
Phlebas, "De Bailhace, Fresca, Mrs. Cammel [are] whirled / Beyond
the circuit of the shuddering Bear / In fractured atoms"). Only the
circumferenceless Reality of God chastens this whirl: *His* oceanic will,
not the upstart carnal will of man. To look to windward is to sail
against, not with, not from, the Breath of the Lord.

Thus, though one might have expected a section entitled "Death by
Water" to develop the dazzling motif "Those are pearls that were his
eyes," it extends and brings very near to consummation (the true consummation must wait until part 5) the more subdued, but more abun-
dant, motif of navigation, with its issue of self-direction versus submission to a superhuman will. This motif began, ironically, comically,
sadly, with Marie's "he took me out on a sled, / And I was frightened." It appeared again with exotic subtlety in the lines from *Tristan
und Isolde,* became all but explicit in "Fear death by water"; reap-
peared in allusive form in "The Chair she sat in, like a burnished
throne" and again in "drowned the sense in odours"; stirred in "What
is the wind doing?"; lay shut up in "closed car at four"; gleamed
around Ophelia; lurked in "Musing upon the king my brother's wreck
/ And on the king my father's death before him"; gained reprieve in
"the sailor home from sea"; winked in "perilously spread / Her drying
combinations"; was laid to rest again in "Where fishmen lounge at
noon"; darkened in "The barges drift / With the turning tide / Red
sails / Wide / to leeward, swing on the heavy spar"; put on a royal face
in "Beating oars / The stern was formed / A gilded shell"; grew abandoned in "I raised my knees / Supine on the floor of a narrow canoe";
turned piercing in "O Lord Thou pluckest me out." Consider! The
protagonist now asserts a masterful perspective on the whole subject

3. Erich Neumann, *The Origins and History of Consciousness,* trans. R. F. C. Hull
(Princeton: Princeton University Press, 1970), 253.

of being (in Augustine's words) "proudly doting, exceeding carnal," and implies his own readiness to submit the vessel of his soul to the direction of the Wind.

Forgot the Cry of Gulls (Mimesis)

Here, now, is a drowning of the "sense" opposite to the one suffered in the perfume-choked room, and a "burial" that cannot lead to any objectionable sprouting. So the rhythm is eased, empathy is released, the protagonist enjoying a sort of fellow-traveling with his drowned alter ego, even as he cautions against so empty a life *and death*. It is this curious empathy with the undersea experience—the very one, again, that the passage ends by warning us against—that disposes one to look, after all, for those pearls that were his eyes. But they are not to be found unless in the protagonist's anticipation of what might await the *right* death by drowning—a voluntary one—at full fadom five.

What he dreads, like a primitive, is the brute entanglement of things, the thicket of the senses. Hence his practice of—in Worringer's sense—an art of abstraction. Again, lilacs in *his* lines have no odor or color—nothing that would stand in distracting excess of his structural need of them, nothing outside his peculiar control. And so with the river's sweat, or the decadent allurements of the violet hour. His practice is to isolate and frame contingencies, and where he fails, as in the opening passage of "A Game of Chess," his "sense" openly drowns, overcome by the surreally shifting objects densely colluding together in space. Similarly, he has presented others, and often himself, as types that can be formulated in a few phrases. So it is again with Phlebas the Phoenician; but here, since there is only death in impersonal water to dread, something by now far less horrifying than life, with its hell-fires, its sinister organic plots, here, where the senses are, after all, being unraveled into the negative purity of nothingness, he is freed to imagine a desensitizing activity with a kind of sensory fidelity.

So the rhythms, again, are eased of anxiety. Although the "Ph . . . Ph" pattern at the outset (in "Phlebas the Phoenician") is superficially imposing as two masts, the rhythm of the line is almost rappingly happy, relieved: *Phleb*as the Phoe*ni*cian, a *fortnight dead*. And where is the dread in the to-the-side interruption, "a fortnight dead"—so matter of fact compared to the drum-rolling approach to "a handful of dust"? Then, too, in the second line, the iambic swing of "For*got* the *cry* of *gulls*" lulls like waves. And what led the narrator to place three strong stresses to each side of the caesura in "Forgot the cry of gulls, and the deep sea swell" was empathy with the balance and sway of sea swell after sea swell The contiguity of the final three stresses (*deep sea swell*) causes the entire line to swell, with the sound of "gulls" half-echoed in "swell" like a returning lift. The prosody evokes the wearying, tireless, periodically cresting cyclicity of natural life, only to imply how delicious it is to enjoy it an absolvingly *final* time, passively, with the perfect abandon of a corpse. What equanimity, to forget the surface swell and all profit and loss and yet to be under the cradling influence of undersea currents, to rise and fall with them a while, before entering the whirlpool of liberation. As the first sentence trails on in a series of *and*s ("and the deep sea swell / And the profit and loss"), it conveys the flux and multiplicity gradually being left behind, the gradualness of the letting go after a fortnight (Phlebas might have only *just* forgot the cry of gulls, and so on, according to the syntax).

Indeed, the protagonist so feels himself into the Lethean currents that they, in turn, inundate and disperse the structure of his quatrains. Each quatrain is picked apart in the middle of a line (in the third and second line respectively). The first linear and stanzaic drift and dispersal begins with the term that would logically most attract it: "A current." The iambic sway of "Forgot the cry of gulls" is resumed in "A current under sea." (The intervening anapestic rhythm of "And the *prof*it and *loss*" had suggested instability and evanescence.) The iambs seem quiet enough to entertain whispers; yet the trochaism of "*Picked* his *bones* in *whis*pers" sets up a macabre witch-murmur of counterpoint. The rhythm suggests the concentrated, hard-pulling activity of picking, as does the hush-hush assonance of the short *i* in "Picked his . . . in whispers." Yet the leisurely rising rhythm of "As he *rose* and *fell*" carries no after-dread, and leisurely, unalarming, is the spacious, balanced measure of "He *passed* the *stag*es of his *age* and *youth*." Then all is over, sympathy shuts down, only the terrible plunge of "*Ent*ering the *whirl*pool" remains. Mercilessly, the last syllable, "pool," waterily swallows the sound of "youth."

Here the second stanzaic rupture occurs as, the narrator's empathy with drowning having gone as far as it dared to do, or for its purposes needed to do, his imaginative ear now concentrates on the muscular strain of turning a wheel: "O *you* who *turn* the *wheel* and *look* to *wind*ward," and the mental strain of considering: "Con*sider Phle*bas." The decision to shift gears from narrative to sermon creates a more decisive break than the one effected with "A current"; and yet "Gentile or Jew" whirls out of the sounds of "whirlpool" as with the threatening possibility of being sucked back into its sonal vortex. "O you who" keeps within the same phonemic field. And soon "wheel" harks back to "whirl." And so for the ear, the resolute rupture indicated typographically by the gap and twist between "whirlpool" and "Gentile or Jew" lacks—by design—any comfortable impression of leading to a point of safety. Still, the potential difference between you, the living, and Phlebas is honestly indicated, do with it what you will.

"Whom Thou fillest," says Augustine, "Thou liftest up."[4] Only so would life cease to be the labor implied by the struggling monosyllables of "O you who turn the wheel and look to windward." Through his empathy with a drowned body, the protagonist has displayed or developed, for the first time in the poem (despite the lounging idyll of Lower Thames Street), a feeling for a will-surrendered peace that eventually will mature into his chant: "Shantih shantih shantih." Out on the sea of His will, there are no disturbing archaizing women, no abject mirages of mortal beauty. The accents of "Once handsome and tall as you" may betray a nostalgia for phallic pride (even the tall consonants in "handsome and tall" seem to emulate it), but the fate of such pride has been uncompromisingly indicated. In the excised sea adventure of part 4, the protagonist, one night on watch, seeing in the cross-trees three women with streaming white hair, heard from them a song that charmed his senses. He was horrified. But, he thought, "now, when / I like, I can wake up and end the dream."

4. Saint Augustine, *The Confessions of Saint Augustine*, trans. Edward B. Pusey (New York: Washington Square Press, 1960), 196.

WHAT THE THUNDER SAID

AFTER THE TORCHLIGHT

After the torchlight red on sweaty faces
After the frosty silence in the gardens
After the agony in stony places
The shouting and the crying
Prison and palace and reverberation
Of thunder of spring over distant mountains
He who was living is now dead
We who were living are now dying
With a little patience

Epochal Speech (Heteroglossia)

The first paragraph of part 5 is not its true beginning. The paragraph looks back and states what had not been articulated before, but only felt: the religious disappointment that accompanies and fails to alleviate the romantic disillusionment in the waste land. Not only love is missing, the All is missing, and death is, on the other hand, all too near. This first paragraph serves as a gray foil against which the line "Here is no water but only rock" at the beginning of the next paragraph shines with the glare of a fiercely and freshly released spiritual agony. Doing a voice (*the* voice) of post-Christian depression, a voice past individual outcry, expressing a pale group affliction, the protagonist in effect draws a line with it, saying: This is the delusory disillusion, the limit, that I shall now step across with allegorical boldness and with familiar, astonishing reserves of faith.

More frayed, older by centuries than the collective voice at the beginning of the poem, this one stretches over the frame of the entire Christian dispensation, if like rotting canvas in an abandoned campsite. In contrast to Tiresias' infinitely eked-out consciousness, this almost equally long mind summarizes a particular epoch. It springs out of the appalled immediate pain of the disciples of Christ at one end and, at the other, subsides toward the Beckettian view of birth as given astride the grave.

Through concrete montage—images of torchlight, silence, agony, shouting, crying, thunder—this voice evokes the story of man's betrayal of Christ only to conclude that Christ, in turn, failed man. At the same time, it generalizes this spiritual turmoil and wastefulness,

through the plural "gardens" and "stony places," the floating specificity of shouting and crying and thunder and so on. As for the protagonist's own experience of an inhuman silence in or near a garden,
his fear of frost in Stetson's, his pain amid stony rubbish, his expectation of perfidy ("waiting for a knock upon the door"), his inner shouts
and cries—the door is open for all of these to enter, though out of
modesty they should perhaps hang back, since the protagonist is at
best only a pale and sorry copy of Christ, even if here the latter is only
the Hanged Man who in dying takes everyone with him into death.

This voice tells all there apparently is to tell in one doomful sentence, testifying as if merely for the sake of the record. The sentence is
cruelly structured as an inexorable but nonetheless disappointing anti-
climax: "After . . . After . . . After . . . now dead . . . now dying."
The speech impulse itself seems to die away within the paragraph,
mustering strength enough at the end only for the brief line "With a
little patience," where the slacks outnumber the stresses. Tiredly, the
voice waits upon its own extinction. It is less elegiac than just short—
infinitely short—of posthumous.

True, the sentence is rather remarkably full of movement. The focus
first contracts, then expands, turns inward and then outward.
Torchlight falls on the faces of the mob, then a frosty silence riddles
Christ. Then an agony that rises within and is private as stone, as hard
to see into. Then another mob—shouts of enemies commingling with
the bewailing cries of friends. Then the pseudo-crowd noise, really
anti-crowd, of the thunder, like the "agony" hard to spell.

With almost cinematic vividness, the protagonist first brings before
us the red sweaty faces (the more reddened and sweaty for the
torchlight), an image conflating earlier images of red, sweat, and fire,
only to turn with a montage artist's instinct for loaded contrast to "the
frosty silence in the gardens" (after "the silence," a frosty silence
seeming more dreadful, somehow, than a frosty garden). The paragraph progresses like a furiously edited film, concentrating on, and
concentrating, the serial claustrophobic confinements and tortures of
a particular martyrdom, till suddenly the scene opens up mercifully, if
ambiguously, to distant mountains, the emotions to the advent (still
painfully far away) of spring.

All the same, and all along, certain factors "fade out" the once-
immediate events. For one, the diffusion in the plurality already noted.
For another, the anaphora, the gramophonic nick nick nick of repetition in initial position, indicating a static in the soul. Hitherto, anaphora had not been in much demand, for the poem had been largely built
on dramatic disjunction (as it still is even here), and repetition had

been needed only for local effects, such as the neurotic verbal tics of the woman in "A Game of Chess." Anaphora belongs with the endlessness of waiting for the end (as the couple in "A Game of Chess" half dread to do, it is so final, and half want to do—it would mean that desire would be dispatched, they'd find rest). Anaphora belongs equally to the endlessness of faith, though there it is stilled and simplified into powerful repetition, as at the very end of the poem.

Here at the beginning of part 5 "After the" inflicts its dying fall at the beginning of three lines in a row. Here, too, all the terminal words expire softly in audibly perishing accents ("faces," "gardens," "places," etc.), except for the too briefly reverberant "dead," that stark monosyllable with a blunt chiselstroke at each end. "Dead" refuses echo, is lithically uncopulative. By contrast, "patience" reverberates with "faces" and "places," and even "reverberations." Crafted for suspense, surprise, and pathos, the sentence ends with the word "patience" as if with the faintest last rumble of the thunder struck into the sky so many centuries ago, a quiver now past all expectancy, exhausting itself quickly in two syllables.

The beauty of the many turns and returns of the sentence may be the best face of patience, the repetitions its slow pulse. Still, wryness is not repudiated. Toward the end we find a figure of repetition-and-variation, one aligned with anaphora, a graph of what has been twisted awry:

> He who was living   is now dead
> We who are living   are now dying with a little patience

The variation of course jars. There is a touch of both exasperation and weariness. The extra breath needed to break the grammatical parallel and the ambiguity as to whether "a little patience" is mild precision or acerbic wit (betraying impatience) convey over something unforgiving in the speaker, if something almost mute, too discouraged to make much of a noise.

HERE IS NO WATER

> Here is no water but only rock
> Rock and no water and the sandy road
> The road winding above among the mountains
> Which are mountains of rock without water
> If there were water we should stop and drink
> Amongst the rock one cannot stop or think
> Sweat is dry and feet are in the sand
> If there were only water amongst the rock
> Dead mountain mouth of carious teeth that cannot spit

Here one can neither stand nor lie nor sit
There is not even silence in the mountains
But dry sterile thunder without rain
There is not even solitude in the mountains
But red sullen faces sneer and snarl
From doors of mudcracked houses.
                              If there were water
    And no rock
If there were rock
And also water
And water
A spring
A pool among the rock
If there were the sound of water only
Not the cicada
And dry grass singing
But sound of water over a rock
Where the hermit-thrush sings in the pine trees
Drip drop drip drop drop drop drop
But there is no water

Allegorical Mountains (Heteromodality)

As readers, we cannot be insensitive to the possibly benign (if awe-inspiring) eschatological implications of that thunder of spring over distant mountains, nor would the protagonist have us be. Emerging from out behind the depressed voice of reluctant disbelief, he himself will go on to seek a renewal symbolized by rain-bearing thunder-clouds.

At first blush, "Here is no water but only rock" seems consonant with the group mood articulated in the preceding paragraph. But as we read on we see that it contains an impatient meaning: there *ought* to be water, faith requires it, is athirst.

An unwanted yet wanted, loose yet unshakable faith has all along kept the protagonist from either peace or despair. Proof of the divine shattered his wits and put out his eyes and tongue, in mock castration, near the Hyacinth garden, exposing a faith that he apparently did not know he had, a lion faith that sprang on and devoured the poor dying parts of him. Now, however, that faith has become more friendly to consciousness, more a part of it, decisively seconded by it. The payment is a strenuously pursued course of asceticism, a willful and blessed "Emptying [of] the sensual with deprivation," in the words of "Burnt Norton."[1] This sensory dryness would create an oasis for the

1. T. S. Eliot, *The Complete Poems and Plays 1909–1950* (New York: Harcourt, Brace & Co., 1952), 120.

spirit, force the release of its water from the baked red rocks. Asceticism may seem to the skeptic a mere "religion of autotherapy," in Eliot's own denigrating phrase. "But we can be healed," Eliot adds, "only if our faith is stronger even than our desire to be healed."[2]

The protagonist begins for the purposes of autobiography an allegorical ascent into allegorical mountains: in other words, he figures an inner ascetic ordeal and search in terms of a parching trek along a white road winding upward toward clouds big with rain and with mighty, repressed utterance. Mimesis (and its paper copies of the unreal world) no longer appeals to him. Even in the opening paragraph of part 5 mimesis seemed skittish, for it requires an animal trust in things, a warm remembrance of the mother. Time had crumpled for it, and here time-and-space have been discarded like waste paper; the protagonist erects in their place *admitted* paper mountains, assured that they at least represent something real, because intangible: the elevation possible to the soul. *Naturally* he turns to allegory, if discourse he must, since, as György Lukács says, "Allegory is that genre that lends itself par excellence to a description of man's alienation from objective reality."[3]

"Thou were more inward to me, than my most inward part," said Augustine, and the protagonist, knowing what he means, elects the magically inward genre of allegory to chart his own inward progression.[4] To be sure, the poem continues to be multimodal even in part 5, the protagonist introducing this section with a fabulous historical consciousness before turning to a pop-up Gothic world of dry mountains like carious teeth and red sullen faces, and suffering various generic permutations to occur further on (Apocalypse-painting, myth, naturalism, fable, a catalog drawn from nursery rhyme and lyric poetry and scripture). Allegory has nonetheless come to dominate and to stay, for allegory is to representation (in its traditional externalistic mimetic sense) what asceticism is to the senses, a discipline of deprivation and a cleansing, a humbling almost unto dust.

These mountains rise, then, from a harsh new concentration of spirit, an overriding desire for the rain of renewal. The "Here" in "Here is no water" is not a place to which the protagonist has strayed. His straying days are over: it is a place he has sought out in order to undergo an *askēsis*.

2. *The Idea of a Christian Society and Other Writings* (London: Faber and Faber, 1939), 188. Eliot uses the phrase "a religion of autotherapy" to dismiss D. H. Lawrence's "religion of power and magic."

3. György Lukács, *Realism in Our Time: Literature and the Class Struggle*, trans. John and Necke Mander (New York: Harper & Row, 1964), 40.

4. Saint Augustine, *The Confessions of Saint Augustine*, trans. Edward B. Pusey (New York: Washington Square Press, 1960), 37.

No sooner does he appear to start, however, no sooner does he enter what might be called the foothills, than he encounters hostile human figures. What do these "red sullen faces" represent? As Angus Fletcher points out, "ascetic habits induce visions of daemons, which are projected needs, desires, and hates," and if the mountains themselves are internal to the protagonist, so are these faces.[5] They correlate with the part of him that resents having come even this far, and will go no further. Materially heavy, they halt where they are. They are the suffering and unrewarded and unexpectant flesh, its *ressentiment*. The red of these faces suggests rancor but also the reason for anger: they seem baked, parched. They look out from doorways as if stubbornly and even perversely—and quite hopelessly, for the doorways are made of mud—clinging to the logic of a nourishing material enclosure taught them by their mothers.

So the red faces of history give way to those of inner demons.

History was always under erasure in the poem, its function merely documentary, its details subject to infinite substitution. The writing from the start veers toward a world-rejecting interiorization—toward the nonconditioned, the anticontingent, the *glance elsewhere* of metaphor, not the nicks and knick-knacks of metonym. Now verticality begins to subdue horizontality, the axis of consciousness swings upward into heights and downward into depths (the protagonist will again take to fishing, this time in earnest).

Ritual Thirst

Again, the protagonist's chosen desiccation would be as Moses and fetch water out of the rock. "O God," he virtually says with the psalmist, "my soul thirsteth for thee . . . in a dry and thirsty land, where no water is" (Psalms 63). Also relevant is Jeremiah 2:13: "My people have forsaken me the fountain of living waters, and hewed them out cisterns, broken cisterns, that can hold no water"—a passage alluded to in line 385 of the poem: "And voices singing out of empty cisterns and exhausted wells." Again: "Except a man be born of water and of the Spirit," Jesus said, "he cannot enter into the kingdom of God" (John 3:5). Pertinent, too, is "whosoever drinketh of the water that I shall give him shall never thirst: but the water that I shall give him shall be in him a well of water springing up into everlasting life" (John 4:14).

In keeping with the protagonist's newly reverential relation to

5. Angus Fletcher, *Allegory: The Theory of a Symbolic Mode* (Ithaca: Cornell University Press, 1964), 35–37.

water (Spirit), to what is sorely absent but ardently desired, the verse now becomes all but liturgically formal, enacting the repetitions and circlings of obsession, the scratchy swallowings of extreme thirst, the doggedness of even a sun-crazed faith. Verbal repetition is turned again and again like a screw. "Water" recurs eleven times, "rock" nine times, and "no" and "the sound of" and "mountains" and "drop" and "If there were" and "dry" and "only" are also repeated, and all in the space of twenty nine lines. (The prophetic desert passage in part 1 anticipated this one with its dry rehearsals: "And the dead tree . . . And the dry stone" and so on.) Metonymic naturalism and pseudo-naturalism give way to ritualistic artifice, a structure of enforced inclusions and exclusions, a self-mortification of language and verse. A chiastic, pinching pattern of repetitions in the first two lines— "no water . . rock . . . / Rock . . . no water"—lies like a small box inside a somewhat damaged larger one, as the italicized words in the following diagram will indicate:

		no *water*		*rock*	
Rock		no water			*road*
	road				*mountains*
		mountains		*rock*	*water*

(or *water rock road road mountains mountains rock water*).

There is no punctuation to lend fluidity, the relations among the lines are dry and crumbly. Parataxis seems to bring back an empty cup, line by line, from the dried-up well of syntactic discourse. Each line is a separate, irritable, arid consideration. Stupefaction sounds in the monosyllabism and lurching syntax of "Sweat is dry and feet are in the sand" (a dazed variant of "My feet are at Moorgate, and my heart / Under my feet"). "Dead mountain mouth" almost stops the line and mouth on the mouthing repetition of "mou-." The physical disgust conveyed by the imagery thus erupts, as if irrepressibly, into the oral character of the line. In all, an effect of sun-drilled stupidity, as still another abstract of reeling repetition will illustrate:

If there were water	stop	drink
Amongst the rock	stop	think

If there were water amongst the rock

spit

sit

Thought itself seems about to suffer a stroke, or to be looking for a place to sit.

The five lines still remaining in this blocky-looking subsection re-hearse a sullen pattern. Negation ("not even . . . / But") keeps pointing exascerbatingly at what is missing. There is "not even" silence in the mountains, "not even" solitude there. Instead of the first, there is *x*, and instead of the second, *y*. "Not even" is rather whiney. Then, too, "sneer and snarl" conjoins two nose-crinkling verbs and sullenly concludes a grammatically ill-tempered denial of parallelism:

There is not even silence in the mountains	But dry sterile thunder without rain
There is not even solitude in the mountains	But red sullen faces sneer and snarl

The verb withheld from the as-yet ungiving thunder is added as a snarl to the sneer. The sour sibilance of "sullen faces sneer . . . snarl" is then replaced by dull dry sounds, "From doors of mudcracked houses," though "houses" almost nestles in the remembered sonority of "moun-tains" much as the mudcracked hovels huddle among the mountains.

Then, as the protagonist begins to meditate on the possible presences of water, shifting from its absence to its hypothetical appearances, from "no" to "if," the lines quicken like hope, or like a thirsty animal that smells a water hole. A wishful and rather hard-working attempt at mirage-making begins with "If there were water," which is placed at the far right as if to escape the gravitational pull of the earlier water-denying lines. The conditional "if," used five times in this second sub-section, fumbles to loosen the tight knot of the negative.

The protagonist dwells in a multiple possibility, churning out per-mutations of the "if." If there were water without rock—or water *and* rock—or water in the form of a spring—or of a pool; or if there were at least the sound of water (and *not* the sound of the cicada or of dry grass singing)—or the sound of water over rock in a certain context, complete with hermit-thrush and pine trees—or perhaps even just the drip drop drip drop drop drop drop of the thrush's water-song. But there *is* no water—a fact stated, however, dully, in a reasserted hard discipline of near patience: "But there is no water."

In the fourteen lines of this subsection, "water" recurs with vari-ants seven times, not counting the drips and drops, and thus forms its own extended pattern of drip drop drip drop drop drop drop. All told, an eager imagining of water or several such imaginings ripple shal-lowly over an underlying and irremovable negative. Conditionals spurt up as if through cracks forced in impossibility, as indicated in the left-and-right oppositions below:

> If there were water
> *And no rock*
> And also water
> And water

A spring
A pool among the rock
If there were the sound of water only

> Not *the cicada*
> And *dry grass singing*

But sound of water over a rock
Where the hermit-thrush sings in the pine trees
Drip drop drip drop drop drop drop

> But *there is no water*

Longing tries the cheat the gruff grammatical negatives by clustering lines in its own favor. This process culminates in the multiplication of only two reluctantly liquid words, *drip* and *drop*. Naturally, after that, the imagination collapses back into the confession that "there is no water," having grown tired of its own willfulness and monotony.

For their purpose, these short lines on the desire for water are undeniably well wrought. Yet is it the highest sort of purpose, this deliberate spell-binding that is also spell-denying? F. O. Matthiessen thought Eliot had them in mind when commenting on D. H. Lawrence's dictum that "everything can go, but this stark, bare, rocky directness of statement, [for] this alone makes poetry, today":

This speaks to me [Eliot stated in 1933] of that at which I have long aimed, in writing poetry; to write poetry which should be essentially poetry, with nothing poetic about it, poetry standing naked in its bare bones, or poetry so transparent that we should not see the poetry, but that which we are meant to see through the poetry. . . . To get *beyond poetry,* as Beethoven, in his later works, strove to get *beyond music.* We never succeed, perhaps, but Lawrence's words . . . express to me what I think that the forty or fifty original lines that I have written strive towards.[6]

Yet to me "You gave me hyacinths first a year ago," or "Unshaven, with a pocket full of currants," or "Trams and dusty trees" is more "naked" or "beyond poetry" than is, say, "If there were the sound of water only / Not the cicada / And dry grass singing / But sound of water over a rock." This last is comparatively a formal, artful arrangement. I do not see through the words (but why would a *poet* care to aim for this?), or hear through them; instead, I hear *them.* And I note that they seem to want to do a number on me, just as the protagonist tries to make them do on him. Then, too, while others have found something of what Eliot calls the "exquisite modulation" and "purity and sweetness of tone" of a hermit-thrush's song in the line "Drip

6. F. O. Matthiessen, *The Achievement of T. S. Eliot: An Essay on the Nature of Poetry* (New York: Oxford University Press, 1959), 90.

drop drip drop drop drop drop," what I find is a cartoon- or childlike literalistic rendition—appropriately faintly comic, not exquisite.

Eliot reputedly told Ford Madox Ford that the twenty-nine lines of the "water-dripping song" are the only "good lines" in *The Waste Land*. This judgment is on a par with Eliot's other pronouncements on his great poem, all of which cloud its nature and merits. Why would he have thought these self-consciously ritualized lines supreme? Perhaps only because they are the most mathematically modulated lines in the poem, the least of a give-away of his personal "grouses," the least owned of his grumbles. There is nothing here to have embarrassed Eliot the man later on.

"Eliot emerged from his juvenilia," writes Bush, "into a period where music and internal monologue were held in a powerful but precarious balance. But starting with the 'water-dripping song,' music—the tendency in post-symbolist verse toward a 'musical pattern of sound and a musical pattern of the secondary meaning of the words which compose it'—began to tip the scale." Bush adds that "after *The Waste Land* Eliot's writing, though it did not abandon the effort to map small movements of feeling and thought, did lose its keenness to dredge up the mind's subterranean reaches."[7] I find this statement excessive at both ends. The later verse to my mind seldom substitutes "musical pattern" for thought: *Four Quartets* is frankly thoughtful for large stretches. On the other hand, the early verse does not so much "dredge up" the mind's depths as evoke their severe repression. A dramatic versus discursive distinction strikes me as more sound, thought being apposite to both, and music rising or falling at intervals in either mode.

Who Is the Third

Who is the third who walks always beside you?
When I count, there are only you and I together
But when I look ahead up the white road
There is always another one walking beside you
Gliding wrapt in a brown mantle, hooded
I do not know whether a man or a woman
—But who is that on the other side of you?

Allegory and Obsession

The earlier parts of the poem constitute an unsettled, mixed form of discourse—anxious, restive, mischievous, Menippean. They belong to

7. Ronald Bush, *T. S. Eliot: A Study in Character and Style* (New York: Oxford University Press, 1983), 76–77.

what might be called the hysterical phase of the protagonist's spiritual story.

Hysteria is a neurotic form of empathy. It sports—but ungovernably, wildly—with imitating the symptoms of others. It substitutes sympathy for sexual contact, so Freud diagnosed, but more, it unfurls like a many-webbed fan all the wrinkles of personality, its possibilities. Hysterics "fill all the parts of a drama with their own personalities." They are, then, playwrights or novelists on the instrument of their own personality, foregoing an "impersonal," representational medium.[8] Absorbing everyone around, the hysteric is a gesticulating crowd.

The protagonist as ventriloquist or impromptu performer of roles was the aesthetic counterpart of a hysteric: his "identity" a stage on which many actors walked the boards, an echo chamber in which many voices rang.

In part 5, a change occurs. Just as allegory begins to dominate over the Menippea characteristic of the first three parts, so obsession begins to still, to put to bed in a darkened room, the earlier hysteria. Obsession translates here into a dogged and valorous quest—an underlying anxiety may be assumed—for the reality concealed behind the superficial, kaleidoscopic play of roles and identities.

In *Totem and Taboo* Freud notes that, just as hysteria corresponds to artistic creation, with its emotional absorptions and imitations, its gesturing multiplicity, so obsession, or compulsion, corresponds to religious observance, and paranoia to the defensive rigidities of philosophical system—the three neuroses serving, in short, as distorting mirrors of instincts and practices on which culture smiles:

> In one way the neuroses show a striking and far-reaching correspondence with the great social productions of art, religion and philosophy, while again they seem like distortions of them. We may say that hysteria is a caricature of an artistic creation, a compulsion neurosis a caricature of a religion, and a paranoiac delusion a caricature of a philosophic system.[9]

Fletcher (who quotes this passage) observes that allegory "is the most religious of the modes, obeying, as it does, the commands of the Superego, believing in Sin, portraying atonements through ritual."[10] From an artist manqué, the protagonist has begun to transform himself into

8. Sigmund Freud, *The Interpretation of Dreams,* in *The Basic Writings of Sigmund Freud,* trans. A. A. Brill (New York: Modern Library, 1938), 227. See also Fletcher, *Allegory,* 283n.

9. Sigmund Freud, *Totem and Taboo,* trans. A. A. Brill (New York: Random House, 1946), 96.

10. Fletcher, *Allegory,* 283n.

a religious adept, of which the "agent" of allegory is the facilitative literary convention, the role that the artist in the protagonist (undying, after all) instinctively appoints for his God-self. This progression from the caricature-spree of hysteria to the sober intensity of the obsessive, from drama to allegory, from "doing" others to discovering the inmost part of oneself, in fact observes what Lacan calls the genetic order of ego defences, which "situates . . . hysterical repression and its returns at a more archaic stage than obsessional inversion and its isolating processes," the latter in turn serving as "preliminary to paranoic alienation."[11]

Ferociously single-minded, yet divided, withal, into hierarchical daemons, "agents" good and bad, the protagonist forces a march up the winding white road, in effect possessed by a voice that says, over and over, *someone will die of thirst if water is not found,* and again, *avoid crowds and women* (those crowds). Paranoia, which often buttresses obsession, lends its accents to this voice, these compulsions; paranoia unfolds before the protagonist the nasty surprise of those sneering and snarling red faces. But can paranoia explain the mysterious "third" who, in keeping with the usual logic of allegory, as the agent's serial encounter with various aspects of himself, now walks to the side of him and an unnamed figure in between, much as the risen Christ walked beside the two disciples on the road to Emmaus— Christ being at first unrecognized and rebuking his disciples with the words, "O . . . slow of heart to believe all that the prophets have spoken!" (Luke 24:25)? Or is this figure not, rather, the equivalent of the work of grace—the right, the sought fruit of an obsession with purity itself?

In a note, Eliot cites the "journey to Emmaus" as one of the chief themes of "What the Thunder Said," whereas he could have cited, instead, its image-shadow, "the account of one of the Antarctic expeditions . . . the delusion that there was *one more member* than could actually be counted." He thus showed his hand. The protagonist may be an ambiguous cross between the disciples and the Antarctic explorers, but it is a cross in which the experience of the latter is transmuted into metaphysical vision by association with the former—as who should say, the protagonist, if not a Christian disciple, is nonetheless a religious novice able to summon up out of a supernatural cache in himself, or out of the thin air, a miraculous spiritual presence, a "projection" if you will of the subtlest registers of his faith and his being.

11. Jacques Lacan, *Ecrits: A Selection,* trans. Alan Sheridan (New York: W. W. Norton, 1977), 5.

Now somewhat further up the road into the Spirit than where the sullen faces projected the hostility of his own flesh to the new obsessive goal, the protagonist has won through to an apprehension of the opposite of such gross abjection, and objection: the Inapprehensible rendered in the somehow apprehensible form of an aethereal shape, a shape more image than body, more motion and color than even the figment of flesh, for no face is indicated, no limbs are made to account for the "gliding." According to 1 Corinthians 15, "There is a natural body and there is a spiritual body, . . . and as we have borne the image of the earthy, we shall also bear the image of the heavenly." The "third" corresponds to this heavenly body and as well to the "subtle body" of Eastern religion, it cannot be caught in the coarse grid of sight, anymore than it appears actually to touch the earth, foot to ground, matter to matter. It might almost be precipitated out of the light striking the brown earth, though the "brown" of the mantle is perhaps best accounted for by the association of brown with monkish garb.

Under some pressure, even this "third" yields up the ambivalence that, so Fletcher states, invariably pervades allegorical quests.[12] Entertain the possibility that something other than the Absolute-in-the-man is engaged in projection, here, and the brown hooded figure may begin to take on other meanings. Recall that the phallus as a fetish (to quote Lacan again) always "slips through the fingers." And that in the earliest, magical phase of consciousness it seems to belong indiscriminately or equally to both father and mother ("I do not know whether a man or a woman"). In the fiction of "transcendence," of the heavenly body, can the phallus with its ability to mime transcendence be far away?

Or dwell on the curious "brown" of the mantle, a color so mundane for the context, together with the disquieted sidelong glance, and excrement may come to mind, the superego having pitched its mansion, after all, in excremental abjection. Fletcher reminds us that the compulsive is fast in the grip of an authoritarian figure "since this particular neurosis has its source in the period of strictest parental disciplining, the toilet-training period, when the child is first learning to control his own excretory processes."[13]

Still, it is clearly the spiritual meaning that receives the strongest inflection. The difficulty of getting a fix on it (at least the protagonist's difficulty) seems to lie more in the nature of the numinous than in the repressions of the unconscious. The pun on "wrapt" is significant, and

12. Fletcher, *Allegory*, 301.
13. Ibid., 299.

so is the placement of the "third" to the other side of an apparently ordinary (if undrawn) human figure walking next to the protagonist. This "second" is of course a legacy of the "journey to Emmaus" paradigm, but, more, and specifically, it suggests, with its very lack of specificity and its position, the spiritual part of the protagonist himself, the side nearest the Absolute, as opposed to the self-willed human part with its irritable reachings after fact, its childlike pestering questions ("Who is the third who walks always beside you?"; "But who is that on the other side of you?"). The ego, so Lacan suggests, wants always to be master (it is a case of ego versus death *to the death*),[14] and so it is here with the speaker, who only counts when he counts (rationally numbers differences for reasons of security). Whereas his spiritual imagination is delicately divinatory, his conscious mind is surprisingly dull. His questions sound stupid; he cannot really expect anyone to take them up and answer them. He treats his own difficulty in grasping the "third" as if it might be some quirk of his own; this is obtuse, if made so primarily for purposes of caricaturing the upstart human mind and used as a rhetoric to goad the reader into attention. In a sense there *are* just two, the protagonist as human and as other, the "third" being only a projection of an intimate otherness and as such not recognizable, at least by the self-centered ego, as really part of the human individual himself. It remains as it were unclaimed, whether for reasons of territorial jealousy or of modesty, or both. When the protagonist counts, there are only two, and when he doesn't count, there are still only two, or equally only one, for then he no longer counts as an *agonist*—a competitor, debator, or actor. Once the disciples' eyes are opened and they "know" Christ, he vanishes from their sight. The moral of Eliot's variation on the biblical journey is the same: "God is a spirit: and they that worship him must worship him in spirit" (John 4:24). Eyesight is irrelevant; something else looks into the heart of light.

Just as the Absolute cannot admit distinctions, so this "third" could be either a man or a woman, or neither. Only the human part of the protagonist would even be curious about classifying it as to gender. Still, his uncertainty may reflect a genuine androgyny in the figure (or figment of a figure). "Androgyny," writes Mircea Eliade in *Myths, Dreams and Mysteries*, "is an archaic and universal formula for the expression of *wholeness,* the co-existence of the contraries, or *coincidentia oppositorum.*" The figure of the divine androgyne suggests more than "sexual completeness"—it symbolizes "the perfection of a

14. Lacan, *Ecrits*, 5–6, 308–9.

primordial nonconditioned state."[15] While Tiresias experienced the sexes as coexistent, the protagonist may here experience their fusion or ground, an original undifferentiation.

Even if the protagonist had not raised the question of gender, the third would still have struck us as androgynous in the sense that its sexual identity is both elusive and divided. A suggestion of feminine grace in that glide, of feminine modesty in the hoodedness, the wraptness, a suggestion of maternal *attending*—these accompany and balance, perhaps more than balance, a suggestion of patriarchal authority (as in "mantle of") and of paternal aloofness and *superintending*. Not that this third is "daddy-mommy," in the caricature phrase of Deleuze and Guattari ("the ego . . . is like daddy-mommy . . . the schizo has long since ceased to believe in it").[16] It seems, rather, daddy-mommy in a sprung form, a numinous flowering of this Oedipal entity in which each parent transforms the other and at the same time becomes indistinguishable from the son, as in the androgynous figure of Christ. The spirit is in sympathy with the schizoid shibboleth, "Expand your own territory by deterritorialization."[17]

Christ and the Holy Ghost, Jung says, are "symbols of the self [that] cannot be distinguished empirically from a God image." Certainly this "third" evokes the doctrine of homoousia or "unity [of man] with the substance of God"—its human clothing, so much insisted upon, being metonymic for "man" even as it covers the nakedness where the flesh would be (the flesh itself being naked in a different, an abject and intolerable sense). If the "red sullen faces" are Jungian shadows, this third is the opposite, a luminescence turned down, as by a tender hand, to a degree where the protagonist can apprehend it. "The individuation process," Jung adds, "is invariably started off by the patient's becoming conscious of the shadow, a personality component usually with a negative sign. This 'inferior' personality is made up of everything that will not fit in with, and adapt to, the laws and

15. Quoted in Fletcher, *Allegory*, 356n. Elaine Pagels notes that many Gnostic Christian texts "speak of God as a dyad who embraces both masculine and feminine elements." The poet Valentinus "reasons that silence is the appropriate complement of the Father, designating the former as feminine and the latter as masculine because of the grammatical gender of the Greek words." Silence receives the seed of the Ineffable Source. Other gnostics, however, stressed that such gender terms are only metaphors, since the divine is neither male nor female. See *The Gnostic Gospels* (New York: Random House, 1979), 49–51.

16. Gilles Deleuze and Félix Guattari, *Anti-Oedipus: Capitalism and Schizophrenia*, trans. Robert Hurley, Mark Seem, and Helen R. Lane (Minneapolis: University of Minnesota Press, 1983), 23.

17. Gilles Deleuze and Félix Guattari, *On the Line*, trans. John Johnston (New York: Semiotext(e), 1983), 23.

regulations of conscious life."[18] The third, by contrast, is precisely *obedience,* and in a self-illuminated form. Jung turns religion into a figure of self-making; Eliot in a reverse alchemy turns the self into religion.

So it is that, for the first time since the implicit presence of the Divine in the urgent quotation "O Lord Thou pluckest me out," the protagonist knows the Absolute. Here, in contrast to the illumination near the Hyacinth garden, he seems more blessed than punished by a mystical apprehension. Eliot's own reluctance to surrender himself to "Another"—inferable from "The Love Song of J. Alfred Prufrock," "Gerontion," and "The Hollow Men"—a hesitation so at odds, on the surface, with his almost reckless surrender of his own "voice" to the voices and words of others (though more to the latter than to the former) may explain why so many readers of *The Waste Land* seem ill prepared to recognize the indications, which I find very strong, that the protagonist makes several partially or beautifully absolving submissions of himself to the Absolute. Here, perhaps partly as a result of his fragile psychic health at the time that he wrote the poem, Eliot risked, however vicariously, the terror of such a surrender. Religion is "frightening," Eliot said, "frightful and scandalous to [the] secular mind which we are all compelled to some extent to share," but "it is . . . important really to feel terror."[19] The terror will appear signed by lightning and thunder later in the poem, just as earlier it was signed by an inability to speak, see, etc.; here it is comparatively subdued, not so much an imaginative shock treatment applied to the poet's *abulia* as a soothing if tantalizingly impalpable hand.

Chronotopes

The chronotope of part 5, as of allegory generally, is that of the road, the hermeneutic journey.

Defined by Bakhtin as one or another temporal-and-spatial image of man, *chronotope* refers to the organizing principle for a set of narrative events. It is the way space becomes charged with and responsive to time, the way time "thickens, takes on flesh."[20] The image of man is always intrinsically chronotopic, but the basket of narrative contains spool after spool of such images: the agricultural idyll, the work idyll, the family saga, the adventure tale, biography, and so on.

18. C. G. Jung, *Psychology and Western Religion,* trans. R. F. C. Hull (Princeton: Princeton University Press, 1984), 93–94.

19. Eliot, *The Idea of a Christian Society and Other Writings,* 188.

20. Mikhail Bakhtin, *The Dialogic Imagination: Four Essays,* ed. Michael Holquist, trans. Caryl Emerson and Michael Holquist (Austin: University of Texas Press, 1981), 84.

In the chronotope of the road, time flows in space, forming the road, which is conceived of both as a point of new departures and as an open extension where events may find their resolution, the soul its rest. In allegory—for instance, *Pilgrim's Progress*—the road becomes a figure for a serpentine course of life; more, as in the picaresque tradition, it is the scene of a series of encounters between the hero and representatives from different walks of life or corners of the earth, even if in allegory these are pieces of the hero himself.[21] Eliot's protagonist is, again, first put to the test by representatives of the sensual self, then graced by a hierophany of the spiritual self, the Super-self. He has not so much left behind him the biographical chronotope dominant in certain earlier parts of the poem, with its "time that discloses character," as suffered its transformation into a chronotope of the road where time still discloses character but in a simplified and schematic way, like a Sunday school story told with cut-out felt figures applied one by one to the blackboard.

A peculiarity of modernist works (works, unfortunately, that the brilliant and balanced Bakhtin does not address) is that they are often multichronotopic, fitful chameleons of chronotopes. Lawrence's dyad *The Rainbow* and *Women in Love*, for instance, goes through nearly every chronotope named by Bakhtin, from the agricultural, work, and family idylls to the provincial idyll and the biography of a developing protagonist (first Ursula), plus the chronotope of the crisis or "break" in life, only to end by facing toward the paradisal chronotope of Man the Walking Flower, in which the generative time of the earliest agricultural idyll has been internalized and declared a miracle. *The Waste Land* is almost as rich in chronotopes, almost as restive with them, even if it *is* only 434 lines long. It begins with a famous resistance to "blossoming" time and shows no liking for space, either: time and space will both be redeemed only as they flow together in the allegory of the road, a road leading toward a fulfillment far beyond each. From its initial antichronotopic position, the poem modulates, via an elegiac chronotope of reminiscence (of and by Marie), to the biographical chronotope—the protagonist's courting, his consultation with a fortune teller, his holding down a job, marrying, and his wanderings near the Thames, his little voyeuristic holidays. Virtually falling out of a provincial chronotope (his early association with a garden) and losing his *ingénue* status, the speaker becomes urban, worldly, soiled, bitter, following the pattern of romantic disillusionment anatomized by Lukács in *Theory of the Novel*. In its own way the middle portion of

21. Ibid., 243–44.

the poem performs what Bakhtin calls "one of the most basic tasks for the novel, the laying-bare of . . . conventionality, the exposure of all that is vulgar and falsely stereotyped in human relationships."[22] Only a reversion among the lounging fishmen to the antiquated work idyll seems to afford the protagonist any relief.

Then a break occurs, the chronotope of the threshold (at its most dramatic, a short-lived and self-destructing chronotope) springs up with "Burning burning burning burning." At last the biographical chronotope itself becomes marked by the *energeia* that is a staple of Plutarchan biography and that endows the individual with active force. Readying himself for the chronotope of the road, the protagonist then portrays human life as a sea voyage, before turning to its variant, the mountain road, as to which he might have taken for epigraph a verse from Galatians 5: "This I say then, Walk in the Spirit, and ye shall not fulfill the lust of the flesh."

What Is That Sound

What is that sound high in the air
Murmur of maternal lamentation
Who are those hooded hordes swarming
Over endless plains, stumbling in cracked earth
Ringed by the flat horizon only
What is the city over the mountains
Cracks and reforms and bursts in the violet air
Falling towers
Jerusalem Athens Alexandria
Vienna London
Unreal

A woman drew her long black hair out tight
And fiddled whisper music on those strings
And bats with baby faces in the violet light
Whistled, and beat their wings
And crawled head downward down a blackened wall
And upside down in air were towers
Tolling reminiscent bells, that kept the hours
And voices singing out of empty cisterns and exhausted wells.

Those Hooded Hordes

The protagonist next sees, has a vision of, or imagines—in this allegorical mode the distinctions cease to matter—the waste land he has left behind. In turning back toward it, he seems to shift into the surreal

---

22. Ibid., 162.

mode that began to overtake his description of the room in "A Game of Chess." The dregs of his phobias are stirred up. Yet he keeps a certain detachment, even so, and the nightmare seems less what he suffers than what he sees as, all distant, all removed, he subjects the catastrophe of secularism to an x-ray vision. Having ascended higher into those mountains—the awareness of the "third" was itself a sign of considerable elevation—he has gained a vantage point of insight into the abandoned secular realm, recognizing now its vast geographical expanse and its race toward Apocalypse. The list of great cities— "Jerusalem Athens Alexandria / Vienna London"—writes *fini* to former intellectual and spiritual capitals of Europe and the Near East: all are now falling towers of authority. The cities even suffer (in the protagonist's visionary sense of them) a nightmare of accelerated mutability. The hooded hordes seem to be deserting them, but for what? Unlike the protagonist, who is watching from mountains (mountains of the mind), these hooded hordes are not quickened by metaphysical aspirations, ringed, as they are, by a flat horizon *only*.

Eliot in a note refers to Hermann Hesse's *In Sight of Chaos*, a pamphlet in which Hesse pictures European hordes returning back to Asia, to the source, where Nothingness and the All collapse together in Dionysian abandon. A comprehensive "LAISSEZ-FAIRE," Hesse says in demagogic capitals, "is the new and dangerous faith" that Dostoyevsky's Elder Zossima announced: a renunciation of moral aversion, the ideal of man as "the God-Devil, the Nothingness and the All," an ecstatic creature of "monstrous soul-stuff" who can "only go under." The "'Russian Man' . . . rules half Europe . . . Europe is tired . . . Europe wants to turn homewards. . . . Europe wants to be recreated, reborn."[23] Naturally "those who cling definitely to the past, those who venerate time-honored cultural forms, the knights of a treasured morality, must seek to delay this downfall . . . for them the Downfall is the End, for the others it is the Beginning." Again, "for one party, Europe and its soul constitute an entity once and for all, foreordained, inviolate, a thing fixed and immutable. . . . They see the Downfall of Europe coming as a horrible catastrophe with thunder."

Eliot adopts Hesse's apocalyptic vision, but radicalizes it metaphysically, shows sympathy for neither clinging definitely to the past nor the lemming-rush to destruction. Whatever complicity in Dostoyevskian hysteria the protagonist may have previously betrayed— Alyosha, Dmitri, Fyodor, and Ivan in *The Brothers Karamazov*, notes

---

23. Hermann Hesse, *In Sight of Chaos*, trans. Stephen Hudson (Zurich: Verlag Seldwyla, 1923), 13–46.

Hesse, "are not to be identified with any single character but with a readiness to adopt any and every character"—he now has the savage singleness of a knight, only a knight not of "treasured morality" but of the Ineffable. For him, what is imperative is not one more cultural rebirth, one more attempt to distend the human toward the divine, but *contemptus mundi,* the severe abdication of the natural and human orders, the cleansing of affection from the temporal. "Already half Europe, at all events half Eastern Europe, is on the road to Chaos," says Hesse in the words Eliot quotes in the original German. "In a state of drunken illusion, she is reeling into the abyss and, as she reels, she sings a drunken hymn such as Dmitri Karmazoff sang. The . . . saint and seer hear it with tears."

Whether or not we regard the "endless plains" as an image inspired by the Russian steppes and "hooded" as intimating the inscrutable Asiatic "Man" or soul, the *sacred* meaning of the mountains imposes on the plains below the negative value of the *secular:* the endlessness of the plains is that of a life without hope of conclusion, the flatness that of an unconscious despair of the bracing rigidities of the hierarchical. The protagonist's own relative freedom and breadth of sight makes the hordes' hoodedness seem roughly equal in meaning to the narrowness of vision of the City workers, each with eyes fixed "before his feet." The image of *swarming* suggests the often-sounded modern intellectuals' horror of the leveling of culture under the combined weight of untrained minds—indeed, minds hostile to training. "Swarming" carries the overtone of instinctual and collective sex drive, and "hooded" in the allegorical context intimates a cowering of the human mind below the *denied* reaches of the sublime, a cowardly retreat into animal darkness. By contrast, "hooded" in the "journey to Emmaus" passage had intimated the unsearchable wisdom of the divine. The word had harked back phonetically and all but punningly to "ahead." Here it acquires guilt by association with "hordes," significantly a word of Mongolian origin—a word huddling even further from the redemptive aspect of organization (metaphysical or other) than does the word "crowd." A crowd is composed of individuals; it is hard to say what a horde is supposed to be made up of.

The stumbling of the hordes on cracked earth may bring to mind Isaiah 59:10: "We stumble at noon day as in the night." Or those who, disobeying Christ, are said to "stumble at the word" (1 Peter 2:8). In Job 12:25, as apparently here, both the "chief of the people" and the people alike "grope in the dark without light, and . . . stagger like a drunken man." "Stumbling" has even the double-edged suggestion of a disturbed, fainting, and obfuscated relation to both the supernatural and the natural. In *The Idea of a Christian Society* Eliot was to comment:

> We may say that religion, as distinguished from modern paganism [industrial secularism], implies a life in conformity with nature. It may be observed that the natural life and the supernatural life have a conformity to each other which neither has with the mechanistic life: but so far has our notion of what is natural become distorted, that people who consider it 'unnatural' and therefore repugnant, that a person of either sex should elect a life of celibacy, consider it perfectly 'natural' that families should be limited to one or two children. . . . We are being made aware that the organization of society on the principle of private profit, as well as public destruction, is leading both to the deformation of humanity by unregulated industrialism, and to the exhaustion of natural resources. . . . I need only mention, as an instance now very much before the public eye, the results of 'soil-erosion'—the exploitation of the earth, on a vast scale for two generations, for commercial profit: immediate benefits leading to dearth and desert . . . a wrong attitude towards nature implies, somewhere, a wrong attitude towards God, and . . . the consequence is an inevitable doom.[24]

The "cracked earth" image—together with the earlier one of "the human engine"—seems to anticipate this very explicit criticism, made seventeen years later, of "a mechanized, commercialized, urbanized way of life." Like "Little Gidding," it recognizes "the death of earth," which derides "The sacrifice that we denied." At the same time, Eliot's determination to thin "nature" out to agreement with "a life of celibacy" betrays his uneasiness—and not only at that later time—with the hot darkness of the flesh. If *The Waste Land* indicts human indifference to the life of the earth, it is as a side note to its horror of the indiscriminate desiccations of ennui, in particular the breaking of the cisterns of reverence for the Invisible One within the All.

Maternal Lamentation, the Maternal Lamented

Doubtless the "maternal lamentation" alludes (in the dying wake of "Palace and prison and reverberation") to the women who followed the condemned Christ to Calvary, betrayed and unconsolable. Yet it should be noted that Jesus addressed to these women the words, "Daughters of Jerusalem, weep not for me, but weep for yourselves, and for your children. For behold, the days are coming, in the which they shall say, Blessed are the barren, and the wombs that never bare, and the paps which never gave suck. Then shall they begin to say to the mountains, Fall on us; . . . For if they do these things in a green

24. Eliot, *The Idea of a Christian Society and Other Writings*, 80–81.

tree, what shall be done in the dry" (Luke 23:28–31). Yes, in the waste land maternal grief must have sickened into this, into regret for fertility itself, despair of the "green tree" of pagan generation, lamentation over the dried tree of the senses (the Thames-daughters had addressed themselves to this obliquely: "Trees and dusty trams"). The mothers on the endless plains, mothers anywhere, must weep for the disinheritance of their children from the Life of the Spirit. Their multitudinous cries reach the womanless protagonist even up in the mountains of Life, but only as a wailing sublimity of the negative, a sound that by numbers and by grief carries high into the air without, it may be, piercing into the Aether, or affecting the heart of light.

The second of the two paragraphs on the barren life left behind begins with a manically and even maniacally self-absorbed woman fiddling whisper music on the strings of her hair. Is she too a mother? The polysyndetic flow of the syntax pours from her to "bats with baby faces" almost as if along a well-known and irresistible current. This nightmarish female narcissist *would* have monstrous, Boschian children. As if driven out of sheltering dark female enclosures by an indifferent and even hostile feminine principle, the bats crawl "head downward" in a parody of birth on a "blackened wall," victims of a holocaust of the "natural," horrid little infantile Count Draculas each and every one. Already they creep restively, already they seem astray. What is being exposed here? The sense that narcissistic mothers make their children feel like unnatural parasites, blood-suckers who go hungry and are forced to crawl? Both Eliot and his wife Vivien carried on like the unmirrored, unechoed, unnourished offspring of narcissistic mothers (as analyzed by Alice Miller in *Prisoners of Childhood*),[25] Vivien through her physical ailments (including swellings) and loud hostilities and Eliot through his depressions, including feeling shaky after his mother had concluded her visit to London in 1921, the mother he had felt he *must* "see" again if he was ever to be happy (but had he himself not been seen?).[26] Add, too, his giftedness; for, as Miller concludes, the child who occupies an outside place in his mother's universe (in *the* universe) may round up uncanny powers of sensitivity in order to read and try to meet his mother's needs, as well as engines of ambition with which to compel (like little Paul in Lawrence's "Rocking-Horse Winner") her reluctant admiration.

25. See Alice Miller, *Prisoners of Childhood: The Drama of the Gifted Child and the Search for the True Self*, trans. Ruth Ward (New York: Basic Books, 1981), 30–63.
26. See T. S. Eliot, *The Waste Land: A Facsimile and Transcript of the Original Drafts Including the Annotations of Ezra Pound*, ed. Valerie Eliot (New York: Harcourt Brace Jovanovich, 1971), xviii–xxi.

However that may be (the information we have been given on Eliot's childhood is hardly conclusive), this uncaring woman is ironically seen through a virtual close-up that privileges her as an object of sight and sound, singling her out from among the undifferentiated masses of the waste land. The protagonist thus betrays his lingering need for a woman's attentions, if also his rage at feeling essentially a perennial outsider to woman's exclusive self-preoccupation (Prufrock's lament, in part, and a complaint ready to spring on the woman with fiery hair, and even on Marie, the hyacinth girl, Madame Sosostris, and the typist). This woman's playing of her hair absorbs her even more than the act of brushing hair had absorbed the upper-class woman. There is a marked and unforgiving progression, an incremental horror of female vanity and of a suffering female abandonment, from hair unteased and wet (the hyacinth girl's) to hair brushed into electric points and, finally, to hair held fixedly tight and made to yield a dry whisper music. The upper-class woman's hair was spread out like a net or web to catch attention; the hair of this woman in the Cities of the Plains—hair unreflectingly black—is an autoerotic means of satisfying a need, grown psychotic, for the illusion of being a physical source of enchantment.

Bursts, Stumbles, Whispers (Mimesis)

These two verse paragraphs, related as a panel to a detail or a distance shot to a close-up, differ formally.

To begin with, the first rides paratactic questions, the second, polysyndeton. The initial question "What is that sound high in the air" is followed by what may be more description than answer, the hauntingly worded "Murmur of maternal lamentation." The discourse is already patchy. The next question, "Who are those hooded hordes," goes unanswered, for whatever reply might have suggested itself is crowded out by the exigent *further* question, "What is the city over the mountains." The subsequent list of five cities both over- and under-answers this question, providing four too many names and too few by an incalculable number. To Eliot, with his ruthlessly reductive view of secularism, all earthly cities must seem virtually one, "Unreal."

By contrast, the clauses in the second paragraph are beaded on a string of *And*'s and *and*'s. Where the syntax in the first had hovered and trembled in preparation for collapse, with clauses like buildings held upright by the momentary pitch of interrogation, here the roll and rumble of the unstoppable catalog of horror and chaos is quasi-biblical and out of the mouths of anathematizing prophets. The period after the last word, "wells," acknowledges that the paragraph follows a single mad impulse and needs reining in. (It is the first period since the caution-confirming one in "Consider Phlebas, who was once handsome and tall as you.")

Then, too, the first paragraph is not in "form," while the second seems to try to keep, despite its pell-mell catalog, to a certain measure. The first permits itself noticeably, and enactively, short lines: "Falling towers" and "Unreal," the latter seeming both a displaced adjective tumbling fragmentarily from the falling cities and an austere summary and indictment. The accentual norm of four beats in this paragraph, not at all firm to begin with, cracks and finally bursts into pieces, of mostly two beats ("Falling towers"; "Vienna London"; "Unreal"). In still other actings-out, the swarming of the hordes is marked by a run-on: "hordes swarming / Over endless plains"; "stumbling" by a caesura: "Over endless plains, stumbling"; and "Ringed" and "by the flat horizon only" through inclusion in the same nasally restricted line. Syntax itself breaks down in "What is the city over the mountains / Cracks and reforms and bursts in the violet air": lost in the crack between the lines, as it were, is the "that" or "It" expectable after "mountains." Fittingly, "Falling towers" is unshored by syntax, and the ticking-off paratactical list of cities is a remorseless trashing technique, as is, again, the dismissive placement of "Unreal." Incidentally, the last six words, from "Jerusalem" to "Unreal," all rumble with the reverberation predicated in "Falling," each vibrating with a nasal *m* or *n*.

In contrast, the second paragraph keeps to lines of middle or long length and holds, as well, to a rhyme scheme (*abab, cddc*), falling as it does into two rough quatrains. It is, after all, a paragraph about the "music" of disaster, with its references to fiddling, whistling, tolling, and singing. The pace-setting first three lines, and the fifth, are in iambic pentameter ("A *wo*man *drew* her *long black hair* out *tight* / And *fid*dled *whis*per *mu*sic *on* those *strings*," and so on), whereas only three lines in the first paragraph could be construed as or constrained into iambic pentameter: the second, "*Mur*mur of ma*ter*nal *lamenta*-tion," the sixth, "*What is the ci*ty over the *moun*tains," and the seventh, "*Cracks* and *reforms* and *bursts* in the *vi*olet *air*" (and two of these pretty decidedly contain only four beats). And while the only terminal rhyme in the first paragraph is the poverty-announcing one of the repeated "air," a rhyme emphasizing the disappointed and vacated hierarchy of space and a mere vanishing point, all the lines of the second paragraph end in rhyme words, and in full rhyme at that, except for the muffled chime of "wall" and "wells," which, however, is internally half-repaired by the sound of "bells." As the passage from

Hesse quoted in Eliot's note would have it, Europe *hymns* on its way to destruction, but here some of its music is mere echo of its once more melodious past, the bells merely "reminiscent" of the peals once carried from still-standing white towers (and otherwise perhaps merely keeping the hours, fatally, like those of Saint Mary Woolnoth).

Here as most elsewhere in the poem prosody is a body submersed in musical speech and so purified into meaning. An assured and sensitive skill produced the *heard* elevation of sound in the kinetic and stressed monosyllabism of "that sound high" and, as well, the local swarming of the *or* sound in "hordes swarming / Over" and the swarming *s* in "those . . . hordes swarming / . . . endless plains, stumbling." The urgent, obsessive assonance in "What *is* the *city*" is delicately piercing. "Violet air," which almost reads "violent air," echoes with appropriateness the sounds of "high in the air," and the same sounds appear demonically reversed in "hair out tight." "Long black hair out tight" is of course mimetically tightened by contiguous stressed monosyllables. "Fiddled whisper music" has a faintly falling music. The interlinked sounds in "bats with baby faces" add their almost horridly cute persuasion to the image. The upside-down word order of "And upside down in air were towers" is right, as is the muted sibilance of "voices singing" and the emptying duple tilt of "empty cisterns."

IN THIS DECAYED HOLE

> In this decayed hole among the mountains
> In the faint moonlight, the grass is singing
> Over the tumbled graves, about the chapel
> There is the empty chapel, only the wind's home.
> It has no windows, and the door swings,
> Dry bones can harm no one.
> Only a cock stood on the rooftree
> Co co rico co co rico
> In a flash of lightning. Then a damp gust
> Bringing rain

Dry Bones Can Harm No One

The protagonist has by this point shown his mettle in withstanding the sullen faces of disbelief. And his capacity for apprehending a subtle spiritual reality. And his inner distance—if one convertible to merciless close-ups—from his former habitat, the waste land. Now further up the road to salvation, he must meet the test posed by the Chapel Perilous (Eliot's clearest adaptation of the myth of the Fisher King and the Grail quest, even if stripped of the macabre trappings—the Black Hand, the Devil, and so on—detailed by Jessie Weston in *From Ritual to Romance*).[27] Fear emptiness, says the chapel; dread death. Where God might be, feel the Void. The Grail knight, bolstered by the courage of faith, passes unscathed beyond this spectral mirage of nothingness or the cunning of evil; heals the Fisher King; renews the land. The protagonist, a knight unto himself alone, is no less successful—the heavens flash for him, the first breath of rain reaches his soul.

In faint moonlight—virtually the opposite of the heart of light, a sickly luminescence of decay, the dead skin of glory—the protagonist comes upon a place of graves. In a hole. With an empty chapel. No reassuring signs of worship, let alone of the Lord's presence. Should he then despair? No, dry bones can harm no one. A seemingly abrupt conclusion, swinging into place, as it does, on the hinge of a comma, after "It has no windows, and the door swings." Well, this only shows the better that the protagonist has seen through the harm imaged by the chapel, passed right through its phantasmal barrier to the truth, about which he is resolute. The spirit is inviolable, he knows that, enough of this charade, especially since it is, in its way, an effective one.

That there is no welcoming and inhabiting "flock" cannot signify to a nondenominational worshiper like the protagonist, a spiritual loner, phobic to crowds. His search is inner—Eastern, individual, driven. Should he attain salvation, it will be carved out of his own agony, by eyes that cannot see. True, a community he has, even teachers; but—not discounting the functional assumption of community with the reader—this intelligent society is transtemporal, consisting (readers aside) of voices in a supernatural line of inspiration: the Buddha, Augustine, Dante, the Shakespeare of *The Tempest,* even Wagner and Verlaine, among still others. "In the form of writing," notes Hans-Georg Gadamer, "all tradition is simultaneous with any present time . . . it involves a unique co-existence of past and present, insofar as present consciousness has the possibility of a free access to all that is handed down in writing."[28] The protagonist's own chapel is a structure of open books: the Bible, the *Rig-Veda,* Frazer's *Golden Bough,* Weston's *From Ritual to Romance,* and so on.

Nor can it signify that the chapel has no windows. Does this mean that the chapel was built without them? No matter. Windows were effectively an architectural superfluity in the waste land—a convenience for hanging "combinations"—yet even so, the protagonist was

27. See Jessie Weston, *From Ritual to Romance* (Garden City: Doubleday, 1957), 175–82.

28. Hans-Georg Gadamer, *Truth and Method* (New York: Crossroad, 1975), 351.

able to look into the heart of light, there, his sight failing. And that the chapel is "only the wind's home" cannot put off one who has shown a fascination with the wind before now, as if expecting something from it (and indeed it is about to blow on him the first smell of renewing rain).

Dry bones can harm no one, because death cannot destroy the soul, I shall feel no fear in a handful of dust. Dry bones are even safer than living bodies, white bodies naked on the low damp ground. Beyond the disturbance of woman, if not of the rat's foot. Woman is evoked here, if faintly as moonlight, by the moonlight, her aura; by the decayed hole; by emptiness;[29] and by grass singing like a demented Ophelian nymph over the tumbled graves, cousin to the woman fiddling whisper music on her hair. She is evoked also by the swinging door, sign of an overused and essentially futile passageway. And not least by the prepositions of spatial relations, those words of depression and smothering and ambush: *in, among, over, about.* The protagonist's talisman against the annihilation of life signifed by woman, she who is the "empty" bearer of life, is, for the moment, the cock crowing "on the rooftree," a vigorous phallic presence, transcendent over the graves with its air-shaking and hailing music. Music the opposite of the low grass's singing, the antithesis of "reminiscent."

The cock as weathercock is associated with climatic change, as crowing cock with the heralding of a new day, a new start—even, like Hades' cocks, with chasing off specters. The crowing seems directly consequent on the protagonist's discovery—caught between surprise and adamancy—that he does not fear carnal death. The "Only" of "Only a cock stood" comes to exorcise that of "only the wind's home" (though, in another sense, the cock and the wind are allied). Then follows, like a crow of the sky itself, the flash of lighting, a violent corrective to the moonlight, a repudiation of faint heartedness as from the very heart of light.

Tumbled and Crowing Syntax (Mimesis)

Having come this far, the protagonist knows what to expect, his self-reliance (or faith) is almost a nonchalance ("Dry bones can harm no

---

29. In Yukio Mishima's novella *The Sailor Who Fell from Grace with the Sea*, a thirteen-year-old boy—murderously idealistic and "certain that life consisted of a few simple signals and decisions," and thus a sort of caricature of Eliot's protagonist—believes his "friends were probably right when they called it [a woman's sex] a pitiful little vacant house. He wondered if that had anything to do with the emptiness of his own world" (*The Sailor Who Fell from Grace with the Sea*, trans. John Nathan [New York: G. P. Putnam's Sons, 1965], 8).

one"). Similarly, the reader is by this point prepared to negotiate the ambiguities and deceptions and malignant mazes of the grammar. The protagonist's syntax at first reflects his sense of being in a den of snares for faith. The five prepositional phrases in the opening sentence form a syntactic serpentine. The "in," which is itself in an "in," a "hole," one the more potentially confining and otherwise menacing for being "decayed," turns into an "among" that relativizes the "in" even while burying it in finite horizons. This "among" then recedes before another "In," the one formed by the moonlight. The moonlight is a steepness, a height and, because descending, a depth that dwarfs the height of the mountains and the depth of the hole. Relativity of position—as in "A Game of Chess"—afflicts description like a nausea. The moral? Guard against being taken "in."

What is "In . . . among . . . In" is the grass, which, peculiarly, is "singing" (drily, presumably, as earlier in the water-dripping song). The wind perhaps rustles this music out of it, a stupid music as reflexive and meaningless as that of the voices singing out of empty cisterns and exhausted wells. Faith will stop the protagonist's ears against these vegetal Sirens, this lyricism of decay and emptiness (the lyricism some wrongly credit as Eliot's achievement, though certainly he mimes it well, evokes it hauntingly). The grass is singing (in the fourth prepositional phrase) "Over the tumbled graves," or, in another relative bearing, "about the chapel." So, then, the grass is singing *in* a hole *among* the mountains *in* the moonlight *over* tumbled graves *about* the chapel. The spatial arrangement of things is here curiously reluctant to present itself whole and clear. The verse plants it down piece by piece as if working out a jigsaw puzzle. A metonymic wind blows us on from point to point before focusing our attention on the singing grass and then drawing it away toward the chapel, which is perhaps the real, the true, the dread object of interest in the scene, so much so that the syntax seems to have to sidle up to it. "There is" in "There is the empty chapel" points almost as if to something expected, even as it makes a fascinated, circling return to "the chapel." "There is"—and then a series of notations that add up to a "nothing much," or even "nothing."

So, then, does everything that comes within the force field of this decayed hole, including a description of it, start to faint, swing, tumble, deteriorate? No, the decisive tone of "Dry bones can harm no one," a line couched with the forceful assurance of a proverb, springs up from an interior source of strength, as a spurt and defiance of monologue. Here is a thought that, like the cock crow, sends ghosts packing. The period at the end of it terminates anxiety; and even the ambiguity of "no one" (the self-abdicated ego, or no one who is part of the One?—but these are much the same thing) must relieve the burden of personal alarms. The monosyllables of the line create an effect that is carefully deliberate—they are firm, precise. So it is that the oblique "showing" of the protagonist's deep uneasiness before the morbid strangeness of the scene is succeeded by a direct showing of the thought that dispels it.

This turning point having been reached, the writing grows more brisk. The syntax of "Only a cock stood on the rooftree" is intimate, swift, intuitive—we are to understand what "Only" indicates here without its being explained. Then "Co co rico co co rico" is less the work of narrative than an eruption into narrative—an eruption parallel to that of "Dry bones can harm no one." It breaks headlong and parenthetically into the sentence "Only a cock stood on the rooftree . . . / In a flash of lightning," as if impatient of delay, and the effect is of a virtual synchronicity of visual and aural impression, a soundtrack in sync with a cinematic image. As intrusion, the formalized sound conveys the startling abruptness of the crow; as unmarked continuation, it strives to be thick and fast with the visual depiction.

As for the capitalized "In" of "In a flash of lightning," it countermands that of "In the faint moonlight" just as the "Only" in "Only a cock stood" rises triumphantly over the lowercase, discouraged and discouraging "only" of "only the wind's home." And as for "Then" in "Then a damp gust / Bringing rain," it is rare, in this poem, in both its capacities: as a chronological connective and as a hinted indication of a consequence. The directional thrust of "Then"—a heart-word of the chronotope of the road—effectively brushes away the earlier syntactic circlings-round like a tired cobweb.

A new alertness, an erectness of expectation, is finally conveyed by the enactive break after "gust," a self-suggestive word that seems the more brisk for its open position. "Bringing rain," with its singing resonance, its lightest and springiest of pingings, is set off not as what is delayed, exactly, but as what is incipient, indicating something fresh in its very essence with beginnings, indeed with the beginning of beginning.[30]

---

30. The editors of *The Norton Anthology of Modern Poetry* remark that "the efficacy" of the cock's cry "is made doubtful by Eliot here." But I suggest that "damp gust / Bringing rain"—the first happy conjunction of wind and water in the poem since the Elizabethan passage—is promise enough. See *The Norton Anthology of Modern Poetry*, ed. Richard Ellmann and Robert O'Clair (New York: W. W. Norton, 1973), 470n.

GANGA WAS SUNKEN

Ganga was sunken, and the limp leaves
Waited for rain, while the black clouds
Gathered far distant, over Himavant.
The jungle crouched, humped in silence.
Then spoke the thunder

DA

Datta: what have we given?
My friend, blood shaking my heart
The awful daring of a moment's surrender
Which an age of prudence can never retract
By this, and this only, we have existed
Which is not to be found in our obituaries
Or in memories draped by the beneficent spider
Or under seals broken by the lean solicitor
In our empty rooms

DA

Dayadhvam: I have heard the key
Turn in the door once and turn once only
We think of the key, each in his prison
Thinking of the key, each confirms a prison
Only at nightfall, aethereal rumours
Revive for a moment a broken Coriolanus

DA

Damyata: The boat responded
Gaily, to the hand expert with sail and oar
The sea was calm, your heart would have responded
Gaily, when invited, beating obedient
To controlling hands

The Jungle Crouched (Heteromodality, Diegesis, Mimesis)

To ease his adaptation of the Hindu Fable of the Thunder into the poem, the protagonist first provides it with a naturalistic jungle setting, a literalistic counterpart to the allegorical landscape (though Grover Smith finds in this last a literal allusion to Sinai) of dry mountains and white road—the chief and obvious parallel lying in the common need for rain. So natural a storyteller is the protagonist (so natural if also so frequently baulked by the judgments of "the silence") that he supplies the fable with what it lacks in the original (*Bridhadaranyaka* Upanishad 5.2.3), namely a naturalistic world, a scene of drama, metonymic reverberations. For this man so unhappy with the world, everything must be, at least for poetic purposes, worlded, strong with an element of immediate experience. Even quotation seems to be sensuous for him, and now with nothing less than thunder-speech to report he is happy, his imagination races. Despite his use of the past tense, he virtually imagines himself part of the expectancy of the crouched jungle, hearing thunder as if not from fable but from terrifying air and responding as passionately and instantly as if his brilliant mediations had been startled out of him.

Once again thunderclouds over distant mountains. A region quailing below a hierarchical presence, the terrorizing power of the beyond. The throaty *a* of "Gathered far distant, over Himavant," the premonitory "-ant . . . -ant" rumble, the recurring short *i* and two bracketing capitals—these oppress, are heaped up, menacingly concentrated. So what appears to be a telling is again a showing. The winding repetition of contiguous terminal stresses in "Ganga was sunken, and the *limp leaves* / Waited for rain, while the *black clouds*" builds tension till by contagion the clouds themselves seem ready to explode.

This jungle crouches like a frightened but recalcitrant beast endeavoring to lie low and avoid the lashings of the coming storm. It assumes a spinal hump of defence and resistance, a brute response captured in the grunting *u* of "jungle" and "sunken" and "humped." The caesura before "humped" ("The jungle crouched, humped in silence") is of course the right preparation for a sudden close-huddled and self-shutting word. Visually, "humped" is a rough reversal of "sunken." Odd that "thunder" too should shake around the same vowel. This shared sound seals the fate of the jungle. It is a fate, moreover, that the jungle actually desired, for, like Gerontion, the "limp leaves / Waited for rain." The pain of renewal is dreaded yet renewal is sought—the protagonist's own "story," in a breath. His soul, like the leaves, became tired of an apathetic existence (as caught in the monotonous alliteration and flattening accents of *limp leaves*) and wanted, and still wants, to spring erect.

Then Spoke the Thunder (Heteromodality, Heteroglossia, Diegesis, Mimesis)

The past tense acknowledges that the fable to be introduced from this naturalistic base, from these lines that break and pause so beautifully, has descended to the protagonist from written tradition. In this sense, the naturalistic setting emerges as literary, though intrinsically cutting against this classification, while the allegorical landscape dominant in part 5 is equated with a fraught immediacy of experience. Eliot prepares for the fable as if it were not fabulous but as literal as the word

"Ganges" or "Himavant." But in fact the original fable, with its *three* sets of interpreters of the thunder's speech—men, gods, and devils— would not conscionably fit into the jungle setting; and Eliot's intention to dispense with the narrative structure of the Upanishad—with Prajápati, or the intelligent heart of the universe, approving in turn the varying interpretations of the gods, the men, and the demons—is already signaled by the introductory "Ganga was sunken."

All that survives is DA, repeated three times, and its three Sanskrit glosses, which, literal-minded, take "Da" as the clue to a particular word starting with the same letter. Gone are the gods who, because they are naturally unruly, and using their bad conscience as a hermeneutic guide, think that the thunder must mean "Control yourselves," *damyata*. Gone, too, the race of men who believe the thunder must mean "Give," *datta*, so prone are men themselves to avariciousness. And gone the demons who, generally injurious to others, believe that the thunder (Prajápati) means "Be compassionate," *dayadhvam*. Gone, also, Prajápati's response in each case, "Yes, you have understood."[31]

In keeping the three glosses while eliminating the gods and devils, Eliot implies that all three commands are equally applicable to human beings. (Similarly, Sri Sankaracharya, an eighteenth-century philosopher, thought that "it is human beings who should be guided by the three instructions," for unruly men are gods, and cruel men, demons.)[32] And in further eliminating "mankind" and leveling the thunder-speech at the lone figure of the protagonist, who by now is far inward on a solitary and holy quest, Eliot, through his protagonist's own bias of interpretation, also implies that the instructions all bear primarily on the relations of the human soul to the divine—that they have nothing directly to say about *civilized* control, or *humanist* sympathy, or *romantic* giving. Give oneself to the Absolute, sympathize with it, be controlled by it (for Eliot's translation of the Sanskrit words, "Give, sympathize, control," significantly drops the reflexive "yourself" that the last, coming from *damyata*, technically requires)— so the protagonist's own bad conscience, his own intelligent heart, leads him to understand the divine Ur-syllable to say.[33]

31. See *The Upanishads, a Third Selection: Aitareya and Brihadáranyaka*, trans. Swami Nikhilananda (London: Phoenix House, 1957), 321–22. The text concludes: "That very thing is repeated [even today] by the heavenly voice, in the form of thunder, as 'Da,' 'Da,' 'Da,' which means: 'Control yourselves,' 'Give,' and 'Have compassion.' Therefore one should learn these three: self-control, giving, and mercy."

32. Ibid., 322.

33. Compare Elizabeth Schneider's argument that "the virtues subsumed under DA are humanist virtues, whatever their language"; that *The Waste Land* is "an English poem . . . not mystical" (*T. S. Eliot: The Pattern in the Carpet* [Berkeley: University of California Press, 1975], 67n).

The instant effect of each Sanskrit interpretation, as if a response to inward thunder pealing against the protagonist's spiritual ear, is to release a heartfelt understanding—a flood of intuition, enlightenment by way of figuration. One could say, "It is just what the protagonist's prior account of himself would lead one to expect," but in fact it is eloquent even beyond expectation, a thunder-*quickened* speech, an act of the acutest self-examination. For we learn that the protagonist has experienced more of spiritual terror and joy than his broken narrative (much as it was a showing) has indicated up till now, perhaps more, indeed, than he had consciously realized or been prepared, minus a freeing if fearful startlement, to recall, let alone divulge. Like divining rods, the Sanskrit words release springs of feeling and realization hitherto hidden in his soul. *Contra* David Spurr, who sees this vividness of response as an earthy imaginative rebellion against the severity of the instructions, I find in it the very ecstasy of acquiescence and understanding.[34]

The thunder's speech and the Sanskrit interpretations are (re-)told; the protagonist's responses are shown. The thunder is a thing of fable, the protagonist an allegorical agent, at this point, representing a "live" character-narrator. The thunder utters one "syllable," the protagonist a rush of narrative commentary. The thunder is an authoritarian monologuist, while the protagonist is in passionate, persuasive dialogue with a "friend" or a "you" or assuming his commonality with others in a "We" even in the allegorical fiction of a locked cell, where the fiction itself excludes an addressee. Then, too, the thunder speaks in ur-Sanskrit, the protagonist in English. At no earlier point in the poem has the concurrence of heteromodality and heteroglossia, as of diegesis and mimesis, been so marked (even the meditations on the commands vary in mode, as shall be detailed). Or so happy, either, and harmonious. The protagonist has attained to an altitude where every speech knows its relation to God.

Where the Hindu fable begins with *damyata* (again, "control yourself"), the protagonist begins with *datta* ("give"). For "Give" is the most terrifying of the commands: the all-changing one that makes "control" possible, the one that sympathy with the Absolute waits to hear spoken, as lightning waits upon thunderclouds, as being hooked through the gills may follow upon nibbling at the bait. Hence the question, "what have we given"? And the answer? "My friend, blood

34. "The speaking of the thunder dramatizes a conflict, implicit throughout Eliot's work, between a willed form of order and the creative moment, which independent of the will has its own internal order. The unresolved nature of this struggle generates the deliberate confusion of the final eleven lines, where the discordant strains of the poem are brought together in ultimate cacophony" (David Spurr, *Conflicts in Consciousness: T. S. Eliot's Poetry and Criticism* [Urbana: University of Illinois Press, 1983], 43).

shaking my heart / The awful daring of a moment's surrender / Which an age of prudence can never retract / By this, and this only, we have existed."

The familiar interpretation of this aswer is that the protagonist admits he failed to come into existence through love for another human being (the hyacinth girl usually springing first to mind). But I think this a romantic sentimentalism that the passage itself rules out (as does the entire thrust of the poem). By what logic or superiority to logic should one human being "surrender" himself irrevocably to another? What was the hyacinth girl that she could command such a gift? The notions of giving and surrender are—outside of the mists of romanticism— terrible and radical ones, and scandalous in any context but the supernatural. Clearly the protagonist finds "giving" awesome and clearly the supernatural is the largest and final and determining context here—the one that decides the real, the existent.

The protagonist says, not that he failed to give, but that, on the contrary, he knows "the awful daring of a moment's surrender / Which an age of prudence can never retract"—knows it now in memory, knew it once in fact, "blood shaking my heart." This personal acknowledgment forces itself in wonder on a man, and a sentence, that would surely prefer to retain an impersonal air, to belong to a "we," and so the change to the latter pronoun in "By this, and this only, we have existed" is easily accounted for; it is that almost blurted admission, "blood shaking my heart," that is so movingly unexpected in its first-person exigency. (Earlier, even the first-person pronoun in "O Lord Thou pluckest me out" had been, after all, a quotation.) Now, the protagonist had been unable to "surrender" to the hyacinth girl, except phallically, if first through floral surrogates—and the reason for this withholding was not, so I suggested, some failure, as is often said, but precisely a success *elsewhere,* the first indicated surrender (appalling? ecstatic?) of the protagonist's ego to God. Later, too, when the protagonist cries "O Lord Thou pluckest me out / O Lord Thou pluckest," he must know, blood shaking his heart, what an existence-through-giving is. But his statement refers to no single event we can absolutely identify—as if, again, there might be more to his story than he had earlier told us, or than he knew. In any case, his very journey into interior mountains is posited on such a giving, even while balancing out the theological melodrama of a moment of "awful daring" by portraying it as subject to perpetual renewals, or as a process.

The kind of giving that shakes the heart is—so the protagonist specifies—alien to, and even unaffected by, such matters as obituaries. Nor is it the sort of gift one bequeaths to heirs; it has nothing to do with hungry solicitors. (In fact, giving to others is figured as essentially morbid, as death's spoils, by the image of the reading of a will: "seals broken by the lean solicitor / In our empty rooms," as against the seven seals on the backside of the book of God—Revelation 5:1.) Deathless, this sublime is also terribly inward, no one else is even likely to suspect it—indeed, the protagonist himself seemed to relegate to his own subconscious his cataclysmic experience of the heart of light, the silence, so that he had to journey toward self-knowledge before he could journey toward God.

As for *dayadhvam,* "sympathize," it too turns the protagonist round toward his own past (the commands appearing to act as litmus tests of his spiritual history). "I have heard the key / Turn in the door once and turn once only," he says, making it, however, turn twice through the verbal repetition, in resistance to his own declaration. This response does indeed sound "negative" (Grover Smith finds all three responses so): how can the protagonist sympathize with others if he is locked in the prison of his body (*soma,* jail)? The only subsequent detail in the passage that answers to "sympathy" is "aethereal rumours": "We think of the key, each in his prison, / Thinking of the key, each confirms a prison / Only at nightfall, aethereal rumours / Revive for a moment a broken Coriolanus." These "aethereal rumours" are mumbles of the thunder, not human sounds; they are perhaps of the Aether, Dantean. "By 'sympathy,'" as Lyndall Gordon says, "the thunder means"—at least the protagonist understands it to mean—"not so much human sympathy as a kind of receptivity to intimations and signs."[35] Just so the "third" became known to the protagonist earlier through the seismic power of his own sympathy, his disposition (even divine predisposition) to feel adjacent—that, at least—to the purely spiritual (as rehearsed in Lower Thames Street, when he watched the fishmen near St. Magnus Martyr). In the allegorized instance of the "third," he overcame his natural egoism, much as Shakespeare's Coriolanus did his when, moved by the appeals of the women of his family—oh, women!—and saying, "it is no little thing to make / Mine eyes to sweat compassion" (*Coriolanus* 5.3.195–96), he returned to the currish city that, so the women insisted, needed his leadership, only, once there, to be betrayed. Sympathy with man does not "save" one, sympathy with the divine can at least revive the soul, however momentarily. The brokenness of the passage is enforced by a medial caesura in each of the three lines beginning "We think of the key, each in his prison," and by initial uncertainty, first, as to where "Thinking of the key" belongs, whether with "each in his prison"

35. Lyndall Gordon, *Eliot's Early Years* (New York: Oxford University Press, 1977), 114.

before it or "each confirms a prison" following it, and, second, as to where "Only at nightfall" belongs, whether to "each confirms a prison" ahead of it or "aethereal rumours / Revive" after it; the answer lying, in each case, with the latter, for the lines are forward-looking, along with the reviving protagonist. At last all this brokenness is repaired, a bridge erected, through the strong run-over from "aethereal rumours" to "Revive," the verb triumphantly knowing its function and its place.

So it is that the protagonist puts a case, if a bare and minimal case, for "receptivity to intimations and signs." The soul can extend only so far, the walls of its prison house are thick, and the jailer seems to have lost interest and gone far off, the clouds discussing this disappearance in words that cannot quite be made out.

This Gnostic low point in the protagonist's reflections succeeds to a response that overrides its strong but not total element of negativity. Rapturously meditating on the third command, the protagonist evokes a relation to the divine that goes far beyond "sympathy," one that is strong, direct, hands-on. Yes, he seems to have first-person knowledge of the *extasis* of having the vessel of the heart or soul piloted by the supernatural. In the calm sea of His Will, the boat responded gaily, when invited, to the hand expert with sail and oar—a reminiscence from out of what imageless moment of beatitude in the protagonist's past? But is it *his* past? If not, he is faking in a way that the stern presence of the thunder (however imaginary) would surely discourage. "The boat responded / Gaily," he begins, without ceremony, already in deepest sympathy with the image, the line break giving giddiness to "Gaily."

Here is an image that places and rebukes all the earlier images of boats in the poem, that fleet of unholy loves, from the one on which the sailor in Wagner sings of love's woe and the one not yet visibly bearing Isolde to Tristan, to the ships at Mylae and the gilt-barge-like "Chair" in "A Game of Chess" and the gilded shell bearing Elizabeth and Leicester, the two long smoldering, to the narrow canoe in which the Thames-daughter raises her knees supine, to the boat in part 4 being willfully piloted windward. God is vastness, says the image, but his love is the finest navigational skill. Clearly control, here, means not self-control, but the abandonment, precisely, of all such calculating prudence, of self-possession, joy in letting Another take the wheel.[36] It is the ego that creates death, beatitude and life lie beyond it. We can

36. This even though Eliot's source, Paul Deussen, has "wir sollen uns bezahmen." See Paul Deussen, *Sechzig Upanishad's des Veda* (Leipzig: F. A. Brockhaus, 1905), 489. Elsewhere in Deussen we find "damyata! datta! dayadhvam! (be self-restrained, liberal,

see why *damyata,* "control," had to be placed last, for here the heart, with "blood shaking," is disciplined, though not self-disciplined, into "beating obedient."

"Your heart would have responded / Gaily"—here is a sweetness of generosity that might not have been expected from the hero of *The Waste Land,* apart from the marvellous *maturing* of his reflections made under the impetus of Divine Speech. (It marks a near development from "my friend" in the first response, which in turn marks a development from "mon frère" in part 1.) His depression has lifted, and along with it all meanness of self-preoccupation. Communal as well as eager for a repetition of the experience is the iteration of "responded . . . / Gaily . . . responded / Gaily." Still, this passage *is* almost predictable from the earlier depression, it signifies and releases what the depression had been in lieu of, what was missed, guiltily kept back. The overflowing of beatitude, not simply to Another but to another, is the overflow, at last, of the great poet's capacity for empathy that is manifest earlier at every point, save the most satiric; and as an imagining of the very height of feeling, it effectively crowns and completes the range of religious feeling depicted in the poem.

Chronotopes

What results in the back and forth, which is not yet an interchange, between the authoritative speech of the thunder and the interpretative, persuasive speech of the protagonist is a unique para-chronotope, that of reanimated and extended written tradition—"reanimated" in that the protagonist's contributions seem spontaneously oral, with a backflow of the effect of live utterance to the thunder itself. Authoritative speech, again, does not admit of dialogue; it just *is,* it exists as fiat. But a sort of dialogue—*heard only on one side*—takes place between English and Sanskrit, as between Eliot's "Eastern" absolutism and the "Western" humanism of the Upanishad, and again between the protagonist and the reader (objectified a little in the section as "friend" or the pronoun "you"). Dialogic speech assumes and adjusts to an audience (actually, authoritative speech does this as well, by virtue of being pitched to be grasped, or at least instituted and heeded: and "DA" is, as syllable, already a compromise between the speechless One and

---

pitiful)." See Paul Deussen, *The Philosophy of the Upanishads,* trans. A. S. Geden (Edinburgh: T. &. T. Clark, 1919), 365.

Perhaps needless to say, self-control is a precondition of Divine control—the Ved declaring, in Thoreau's words: "A command over our passions, and over the external senses of the body, and good acts . . . [are] indispensable in the mind's approximation to God" (*The Portable Thoreau,* ed. Carl Bode [New York: Viking Press, 1947], 466).

the babbling Many). Only the protagonist's adjustments, only *his* persuasive techniques, are in evidence, yet he is *all response*. It is across virtual great reaches of time that he responds, across the spatial divide between India and the West, across the generic difference between fable and allegory, and across the seeming distinction between sacred scripture and prompt human speech.

Within the three responses rise three subnarratives, narratives subordinate to, but independent of, that of the fable. Of the three, the first is the only one that could plausibly be called naturalistic, treating in almost bewilderingly direct terms, as it does, a break in life and conforming to what Bakhtin calls the chronotope of the crisis or threshold. This recall of an earlier chronotope in the poem, this further comment on it, adds a variation to the chronotope of encounter, the broad chronotope of which that of the road is an instance: here the encounter with the Divine, through an unbearably palpitating heart, is unmediated by allegory, even if the language soon reverts to types (lean solicitor, empty rooms) in a retreat from the embarrassments of self-disclosure. (Similarly, the relational play of speaker and friend adds social density to the otherwise anchoritic chronotope of the white road.) The chronotope of the crisis and break here glows blindingly against a foil formed by the dun terminal stuff of the biographical chronotope, with its expectation of eventual obituaries and the reading of a will in vacated rooms.

The second bit of narrative is at the antipodes of the chronotope of the threshold, the key having been heard to turn in the door "once only." No break-out seems planned. The jail image, developed into an allegorical fable, also develops backward, as it were, out of the image in the preceding, naturalistic reference to "empty rooms." There is here too much brokenness to allow for a "break," or so it first appears: in fact the chronotope of the threshold is virtually reinstated in "Only at nightfall, aethereal rumours / Revive for a moment a broken Coriolanus." Implicit here is the truth that "sympathizing," like "giving," can hardly be narrated; in both, time itself surrenders quiveringly to the supernatural. In any case, "Revive for a moment" admits that even sympathy is fleeting at best, a harkening to remote words in another language, if language is at all an appropriate image; a step toward a threshold that is instantly withdrawn.

At least the experience of feeling subject to "controlling hands" is happier in duration, so much so that the allegorized chronotope of the road is called in to represent it, only in the variant form of the sea-path (formerly used in part 4, "Death by Water"). A beatific sail under expert hands becomes a mini-subplot to the main journey-plot of part 5, a sudden metaphorical intensification and even advance, the image

of an "arrival" that is nonetheless still a traveling, a motion beyond
the human power either to emulate or understand.

DA (Heteroglossia)

The protagonist has at last encountered a "voice" he cannot merely
listen in on, as to some degree he could even with Madame Sosostris's
fortune-telling (the parenthetical interruption, there, suggesting both
involvement and detachment). For the first time, his antiphon is not
begrudged: it fountains internally, and it reveals him, both to himself
and to us, if not idealizes him, as completely as language can. It even
overflows, as noted, into gregarious secondary dialogue ("my friend,"
"your heart").

The Eastern sounds are so strange that, like thunder-speech, they
arrest the ear and the mind of hero and reader alike, and roll on lead-
ingly with significance, at least for the protagonist. With the monosyllable DA and its three Sanskrit amplifications (watery flowerings as
from folded paper) we move away from the decadence of European
civilization and come to the "East" as to a sanctuary in which spiritual
renewal is still possible (it helps that the jungle, like most of the allegorical landscape through which the protagonist passes, seems unin-
habited by man). The Sanskrit is presented in an august manner that
requires the reader to puzzle out the meaning from the protagonist's
brilliantly metaphoric comments on it, interpreting, so to speak, the
protagonist's own interpretations: the reader, too, is thus shocked into
discovery. In the English and European context, the Sanskrit ambigu-
ates the message of spiritual salvation as if protecting it from vulgar
and facile assimilations, as from the indifference that familiarity
breeds. Wisdom is removed from common gabble, even if it risks
sounding like foreign babble in the process. Mad Hieronymo dug it
out of a German translation of Hindu scripture, and intends us to get
lost in translation: "All is translation, / And every bit of us is lost in it
(Or found . . .)."[37] The Sanskrit words are like gliding hooded forms
amid the more recognizable Western words, seeming to bear the secret
of Life and prepared to reveal it only to those who delight, as the
protagonist does, in sibylline listening.

Reached for, as it were, across continents, the Sanskrit words are
the most flagrant instance of the heteroglossic restiveness of the poem.
On the other hand, they promulgate a beatific condition that the-
oretically transcends language (tapping into what is prior to it, a pre-
formal fluent fullness). The protagonist can evoke it for us, and

37. James Merrill, "Lost in Translation," in *From the First Nine: Poems 1946–
1976* (New York: Atheneum, 1984), 352.

meditate on it, only if he uses language—his own words becoming a beautiful multiplication in English of the few Sanskrit words, themselves, again, wordy versions of "Da." "The silence" itself cannot be represented in langauge, even if only language can designate it "the silence"; the divine, on the other hand, can be allegorically represented in speech as the intelligent heart of reality (of light) in the form of a "speech" that exceeds ordinary human discourse in its mighty resonance yet propagates such discourse by requiring interpretation (here first in Sanskrit, then in English, in a ripple of hermeneutics). The thunder is the authoritative "word" of what is in the last analysis, and beyond analysis, Silence, but because of its very authenticity (one allowed by a devout fiction), the human mind cannot understand it except through an inspired act of interpretation. It would seem to spawn heteroglossia anew, except that it *will* be understood by those earnest for instruction, leading to "shantih" or the peace that passes understanding. On the one side, "Da"—as the threshold where the sacred enters language—sanctifies linguistic symbolicity as a medium of discourse about the divine. On the other, as a nonword, a dark phoneme, it draws the linguistic mind toward its resistance to speech.

Modernism and Terror

In 1917, Rudolf Otto, in *Das Heilege,* aroused extraordinary interest—as later reported by Mircea Eliade in *The Sacred and the Profane*—through his stress on the irrational, frightening side of religion: on God as force, not as idea. Otto isolated *terror before the divine* as the true religious "mode." In lieu of received religious opinion, many modernists were seeking, at about the same time, the *one reality* of religious terror: inexplicable ontological power.[38] There arose the fiction of the sacred blow—the assumption that the divine could not manifest itself to man except through a violence of passage, a rude impact consequent upon the disparity between the divine as efficacy and the human as what pathetically cries out for efficacy. "Come," cry the modernists, and the god comes and leaves them or their surrogates—Leda, Adela Quested, Nellie March, Joseph K., the Rilkean elegist, the blind and dumb protagonist who is neither alive nor dead—staggering, disorientated, terrified, *killed.* "I think," Yeats said famously, "profound philosophy must come from terror. An abyss opens under our feet; inherited convictions . . . drop into the abyss . . . We cry with the Indian Sacred Book: 'They have put a gold-

38. Mircea Eliade, *The Sacred and the Profane: The Nature of Religion,* trans. Willard R. Trask (New York: Harper & Row, 1959), 8–18.

en stopper into the neck of the bottle; pull it! Let out reality!' "[39]

Modernism was a *bursting out* from the intolerable claustrophobia of positivism, Duty, science, social democracy, Huxley, Darwin, Mill . . . a vertical explosion that in one direction reopened the "unseen" and in the other the abysmal. God and the Unconscious (where antithetical, not consubstanial), once again, and more explicitly than before, marked the poles of existence. At the same time, the nineteenth-century analysis of social and historical life, of the horizontal axis of experience, continued, enriched by flashes overhead or fire-shadows cast from below. As I see it, modernism is a Greek cross of vertical and horizontal axes meeting in crisis, as crux.

To the modernist, the "inspired condition" (in Yeats's phrase) is, then, a state of fertile terror: art is traffic with the gods, it lets out reality. Forster in *A Passage to India*, Lawrence in *The Rainbow* and *Women in Love*, Yeats in "The Second Coming" and "Long-Legged Fly," Eliot in *The Waste Land*, Pound in the "Grecian" Cantos, even Virginia Woolf, as in "The Moment: Summer's Night" ("to be part of the eyeless dark, to be rippling and streaming, to feel the glory run molten up the spine, down the limbs, making the eyes glow")—all found reality more in what ravishes, makes one shake, induces a heavy waking sleep, burns one down, than in the "presuppositions of . . . thought" (Yeats). Terror and exultation were their watchwords; even Stephen Dedalus, as he meditates on his name, and Bloom orgasmic on the Hill of Howth, and both through guilt in Nighttown, catch, from their more commonplace positions, some of the *other light* of the bright and dark gods.

Lawrence and Yeats in particular attempted to oracle a new hierophany: they persisted in it with sublime confidence that art could be a world-bearing woman to the gods. Eliot was more prudent, and in *The Waste Land* almost disguised his hierophanies beyond recognition, what with the "play" of quotation and a surface of ambiguity. Still, even after *The Waste Land* he did not cease to evoke the divine in accordance with his own sense of its peculiar grace of terror, however Anglican his presuppositions may have become. Like Yeats and Lawrence, who sought to replace the sickly hierophany that was Christ with the harsh, masculine, and surgical power of the divine, Eliot praised a deity of terror, a force appalling above all because, like those of the Emperor-God in Yeats's nighttime Byzantium, its flames flew to the soul's impurities, to all unrealities of abjection.

Kristeva notes that

39. William Butler Yeats, *Essays and Introductions* (New York: Macmillan, 1961), 502–3.

in a world in which the Other has collapsed, the aesthetic task—a descent into the foundations of the symbolic construct—amounts to retracing the fragile limits of the speaking being, closest to its dawn, to the bottomless 'primacy' constituted by primal repression. Through that experience, which is nevertheless managed by the Other, 'subject' and 'object' push each other away, confront each other, collapse and start again. . . . Great modern literature unfolds over that terrain: Dostoyevsky, Lautréamont, Proust, Artaud, Kafka, Céline.[40]

If this means, as Kristeva suggests, an attempt "to give back a memory, hence a language, to the unnameable and nameable states of fear," then *The Waste Land* unfolds over the same terrain. It takes a position—with *The Golden Bough,* with *The Rite of Spring*—at the "place" where art, philosophy, and religion all spring from terror; where "the Other" seems to interrogate the abjectness of human existence as if it were still a phenomenon of the jungle and knowledge of redemption had still to be wrested out of the lowering clouds. Eliot's structural avant-gardism (including his heteromodality and heteroglossia) *is* his "descent into the foundations of the symbolic construct," his attempt to retrace "the fragile limits of the speaking being, closest to its dawn"; and his provisional choice of epigraph, "The horror . . . the horror," from Conrad's *Heart of Darkness,* signed his recognition that his protagonist was in his own way a Kurtz, a man who had gone to the end of abjection (an urban and cosmopolitan terminus, a rats' alley). There language shatters into fragments of what others said when saying still had credence and renewal lies in climbing above this debris to confront—as "subject" before an "object" that is the Self-Other denied by primal repression—the terror of the Silence.

The Greek cross of modernism enforced a change in the techniques of evocation and representation, a more explosive procedure consonant with the abruptnesses of the *terrific:* peremptory and cryptic metaphors, ellipses, metastases—in short, "mimetic" disruptions of the formal expectations of written discourse—and arrangements of related images (motifs) left like a trail of blazes disappearing into a darkening wood. The modernists (beginning, perhaps, with the Melville of *Moby-Dick*) altered literary form so as to make it accommodate to the utmost a plurality of possible constructions to be put on experience, a plurality one with a new-felt sense of "the fragile limits of the speaking being," and with a new-felt terror of naked exposure before the *x* of the Other—resulting in collapses and new starts, rejections and confrontations. The literary modernists tried to get around the limits of

40. Julia Kristeva, *Powers of Horror: An Essay on Abjection,* trans. Leon S. Roudiez (New York: Columbia University Press, 1982), 18.

speech by extending the powers of arrangement, around words through structure; but of course the structures themselves were relations of words, and for Eliot even terror could be properly (or not improperly) mediated through the most conventional of deific emblems, the thunder, and the seemingly dullest of sounds, "DA."

Eliot's interest in the myth of the Fisher King lay in its intimation (derived from primitive religious observance) that the path to purity winds through a landscape of terror. Then, too, purity means, for the human being, not a natural change, but a violent transformation, so abject is the human being to begin with; and transformation entails dread and awe, as in the protagonist's touchstone of religious transformation, "Those are pearls that were his eyes," and in his touchstone of artistic transformation, Philomel. The first tells of losing the flesh in the incorruptible and precious, the second of losing speech in song, or language in an inviolable music of transcendence.

Certainly of all the modernists Eliot was the one most driven to escape the flesh—in fact, in the main modernism was an attempt to rescue Eros from the suffocating sentiments of the Victorians, and in this light Joyce was the more representative modernist of the two, *his* experimentations all in the service of a ludic principle more favorable to the obsessive yet spontaneous god. Eliot, like Conrad, was afflicted with an awareness of abjection and unlike Conrad he took the fact of abjection's shadowy unreality—that *horror*—as a subrevelation that reality (for must there not somewhere be a reality?) is purely metaphysical. To him, our choice appears to lie between the fire of the senses and those of purgatorial suffering, for "We only live, only suspire / Consumed by either fire or fire"; but in truth there really is no choice, or so Eliot came to believe (and so his *Waste Land* protagonist already illustrates):

> Love is the unfamiliar Name
> Behind the hands that wove
> The intolerable shirt of flame
> Which human power cannot remove.[41]

I SAT UPON THE SHORE

> I sat upon the shore
> Fishing, with the arid plain behind me
> Shall I at least set my lands in order?
> London Bridge is falling down falling down falling down
> *Poi s'ascose nel foco che gli affina*

41. Eliot, *The Complete Poems and Plays, 1909–1950,* 144.

Quando fiam uti chelidon—O swallow swallow
Le Prince d'Aquitaine à la tour abolie
These fragments I have shored against my ruins
Why then Ile fit you. Hieronymo's mad againe.
Datta. Dayadhvam. Damyata.
          Shantih   shantih   shantih

Tenses (Diegesis, Mimesis)

After the chronotopic digression (or road extension) of the Fable of
the Thunder, the protagonist resumes his allegory of a journey away
from the waste land—resumes it in order to conclude it, in a provisional way, and for purposes of poetic closure.

Closural intention is signaled right off: "I sat upon the shore / Fishing." Why the past tense? Not simply because the ear would reject "I
sit upon the shore / Fishing," which would prompt in us the response,
"What a transparent piece of fiction," whereas "I sat upon the shore /
Fishing" is an acceptably faked one; but also because we are to think
that the protagonist has for some time now enjoyed a welcome alleviation of his quest-goading anxiety (the anxiety typical of allegory and
compulsion)—perhaps as a result, in part, of having found in the registers of his memory experiences answering to the thunder's soul-
thrilling exactions.

Of necessity, the allegory has up to this point been largely conducted in the present tense, since the protagonist is *only now* in search
of shoring for his soul. In part 5 he had used the past tense on but two
occasions before its traditional narrative use in presenting the fable.
The first was the passage beginning "A woman drew her long black
hair out tight." There, the sudden closing in on specific scenes in the
plains far below was counterdistanced by a shift to the past tense, lest
we seem to have regressed, along with a backsliding protagonist, into
the ambience of the waste land. The familiar explanation for the
shift—that the protagonist is recollecting a nightmare—is plausible
but not, to my mind, compelling. But certainly he seems to experience
a vision that involves horrifying magnification and distortion, and the
past tense functions as the long, somewhat reassuring tube of this visionary telescope.

Of the second use of the past tense—the one in "Only a cock stood
on the rooftree"—Stanley Sultan comments: "The effect is to suggest
the powerful significance for him of that experience. It brought his
question to a conclusion."[42] The cock's crow does indeed mark a begin-

---

42. Stanley Sultan, *Ulysses, The Waste Land, and Modernism: A Jubilee Study* (Port
Washington, N.Y.: Kennikat Press, 1977), 57.

ning, if not a conclusion, in that it memorializes the moment when the protagonist finally proves free enough of the fear of death to receive instruction on the necessity of "surrender." The adoption of the past tense makes of the moment an instantaneous reference point in his spiritual progress. To avoid suggesting that a conclusion has been reached, to suggest that the instant is one of a series in an infinite series of new starts (for as long as the soul is entrapped in the flesh it can only demonstrate a *preparedness* to depart), the protagonist reinvokes the discovering present in the perfect presentness of "Co co rico co co rico"; and the participle in "Bringing rain" promisingly extends it. The two combine to erase the momentary narrative distancing of "stood"— are even now advancing.

Even in the last paragraph, the protagonist effects a rapid withdrawal from the narrative past tense (from "I sat"). This begins with "Fishing," which, dominantly placed like "Bringing," casts its long presentness over the line. "Shall I at least set my lands in order?" is unmistakably and vigorously of the moment. And the sing-song presentness of "London Bridge is falling down falling down falling down" adventitiously heightens the feeling of instancy, even as it ironically places earthly being in invisible quotation marks. In truth, the passage is undecided between closural summary and still further present enactiveness. Again, "Shall I at least set my lands in order" clearly instances the last, while "These fragments I have shored against my ruins," indicating that the lands *have* been set in order, as if just now, hovers between the note of readying and the note of closure, unable to choose between them, and not really needing to.

Fishing

That the protagonist is now sitting and fishing rather than ascending still higher among the mountains suggests that he is indeed ready to set his soul in order—that the necessary composure has been wrestled from out of his suffering. No doubt he has attained the perspective Eliot was later to articulate in his essay "Second Thoughts about Humanism":

Man is man because he can recognize supernatural realities, not because he can invent them. Either everything in man can be traced as a development from below, or something must come from above. There is no avoiding that dilemma: you must be either a naturalist or a supernaturalist. If you remove from the word "human" all that the belief in the supernatural has given to man, you can view him finally as no more than an extremely clever, adaptable, and mischievous little animal.[43]

43. T. S. Eliot, *Selected Essays* (London: Faber and Faber, 1958), 485.

The expression *set one's lands in order* sounds merely preparatory to consigning the lands to one's heirs. But what is implied is not so much resignation as a realistic acknowledgment of the limits of human perfectibility, and an ever-present sense of exigency ("HURRY UP PLEASE ITS TIME"). As for the former, "Second Thoughts" is again germane:

The modern humanistic view implies that man is either perfectible, or capable of indefinite improvement, because from that point of view the only difference is a difference of degree—so that there is always hope of a higher degree. It is to the immense credit of Hulme that he found out for himself that there is an *absolute* to which Man can *never* attain.

Man is a wretched creature, said Hulme, "who can yet apprehend perfection." The protagonist's act of fishing suggests a concerted effort at such an apprehension—an act that, ipso facto, places the aridity of secularism at his back.

Fishing proves an optimal closural image in its fusion of quietness with quest. It is far from the crowd. It is slow expectation. If the protagonist shows an anal compulsion to set his lands in order, to retrieve "fragments" and shore them against ruin, he also knows, as his mental cinema on sailing gaily has just revealed, the joy of *not* acting as, indeed the joy of an unhesitating submission to, a conserving authority; and fishing, as an activity, lies about midway between, as an attempt at providing for oneself and at the same time an ascesis of patience.

The protagonist has come to a shore that, unlike the banks of the Thames or the dull canal, borders on the real: a boundary he cannot cross at will, perhaps, though the boat metaphor in the lines just preceding hints that he can go forth upon the deep when invited. There is a substance, an area, from which he is always permitted to hope to draw sustenance. Something of the Other that he can hope to incorporate. The fish is not bodiless like the wind, the lightning, the thunder (other symbols common to *The Waste Land,* the Bible, and the Upanishads); but, again, it suggests both the potential of the human soul to be raised out of darkness into light, out of the sensual sea into a breathless sphere, out of separateness into Absolution, and, almost conversely, the possibility of eating God, so as to have him in one, as one's power, one's immunity to destruction. Just as "we are a part of the substance of our mother who has borne us, and whose milk nourished us," as Freud says, so sharing a meal of and with one's God (as in totem feasts) expresses the conviction "that one [is] of the same substance as he." Eating from nature is abjection, eating God, salvation.[44]

44. Freud, *Totem and Taboo,* 175.

These Fragments (Heteromodality, Heteroglossia)

The line "Shall I at least set my lands in order?" will support an emphasis on "my," so as to enforce a distinction between these lands and "the arid plain" now at the speaker's back. The protagonist cannot hope to set the waste land itself in order (for, although Eliot himself would later promote the idea of a Christian society, the protagonist has discerned no fructifying suffering in others but, at best, as in the Thames-daughters, only a sensory disillusionment that hides the soul); but *at least* he can set his own lands in order. And to set one's lands in order is both to prepare for death and to be granted further life, or so suggests the allusion to Hezekiah, king of Judah, who, warned by God that his end is near, and that he should set his house in order, nonetheless gains fifteen more years of life when he argues, movingly, that "the grave cannot praise thee." In any case, for the protagonist, setting his lands in order is perhaps proof of his intention to live before the divine like Hezekiah "in truth and with a perfect heart" (Isaiah 38).

But what are his "lands"? What "property" can he claim as his? His lands are at once his "ruins" and whatever he can shore, from out of them, against them. And what are his ruins? His memories (including his reading) and their evidence of his abjection? "Shored against" implies that the ruins must not be allowed to decline any further, into altogether meaningless stony rubbish. What counters the feeling of abjection is, to begin with, writing itself, as a pledge of symbolic bodilessness and, second, the defensive and righteous act of surrounding oneself with talismans, all the better for being drawn from the abjection-eschewing writing of others. Again, "discourse," as Kristeva puts it, is "substituted for maternal care, and with it a fatherhood belonging more to the realm of the ideal than of the superego."[45]

So the natural ruin of the protagonist's aggressive drives is to be defended against by fragments of cultural ruin, the latter ruin the purer of the two by virtue of its removal, such as it is, from the flesh— this in the absence of a coherent and living supernatural tradition (but then *The Waste Land* intimates an Absolute incommensurate with any, even the severest, "tradition"). Appropriately, the paratactic list of fragments under the rubric of "lands" begins and ends with references to architectural destruction: London Bridge and the Aquitanian tower. Eliot once cautioned that tradition "cannot be inherited, and if you want it you must obtain it by great labour." The protagonist has performed this labor; it underlies the dispatch with which he conducts his inventory of spiritual touchstones.

45. Kristeva, *Powers of Horror*, 45.

These "fragments" are presented as just that, and appear makeshift, not as a triumph of neoclassical or neometaphysical architecture. This last paragraph perpetuates—in almost impertinent, illustrative fashion—the flash-form, pluralistic tenor of the poem. Something of Hieronymo's own mischievousness, his deliberate web-spinning, if nothing of his mad malice, lies behind this last display of heteroglossia (the farrago of voices from the Bible, Mother Goose, Dante, Latin poetry, Tennyson, Gérard de Nerval, Thomas Kyd, and the Upanishads) and of hetermodality (allegorical narrative, self-address, nursery rhyme, lyrical poetry, dramatic dialogue—"Why then Ile fit you"—scriptural fable—"Datta. Dayadhvam. Damyatta"— and scriptural ritual—"Shantih shantih shantih"). Yet, despite this appearance of a growing Babel, the protagonist is now more than ever the master of his multiple discourse. Here his polytonality has the rationale of (1) a deliberately constructed maze that only those favored by the Ariadne of the poem, namely, sympathy with the supernatural, or at least intelligence of his plight, can find their way through, and (2) a quickly got up, heterogeneous shoring of quotations. He does not so much flash from identity to identity (Ferdinand, the Fisher King, Hezekiah, a wise child, Dante and his Arnaut Daniel, Venus longing for Adonis and spring, the Prince of Aquitaine in his ruined tower, vengeful Hieronymo), he does not so much stray, as situate himself where all assumable poses are consciously inadequate, at least as taken singly, to articulate both his abjection and the inexplicable reality of which he is finally (in both senses) part. We know him best not through any of these flash-identities but through his formidable ability to marshal and pass through them, toward the silence and the light.

Then, too, the protagonist is orderly enough to arrange these fragments (his own, won from his reading and his suffering) as a sort of mandala that will align him, and continue to realign him, with his deepest knowledge. He begins chronologically with a fragment from childhood, a quasi-obsessive line of rhyme. For the American Eliot, London was probably first of all the London of Mother Goose—of "London Bridge is falling down" and, perhaps, "Gay go up and gay go down, / To ring the bells of London Town," of which a trace may possibly be found in "Flowed up the hill and down King William Street" and the bells of St. Mary Woolnoth.[46] (The link between destruction and gay women in the first—"London Bridge / Is Broken down /Dance over my Lady Lee"—would also satisfy the young

---

46. See *The Annotated Mother Goose*, ed. William S. Baring-Gould and Ceil Baring-Gould (New York: Bramhill House, 1962), 253.

poet's sense of the inevitable association between ruin and women.) This apocalyptic fragment must serve to remind the protagonist of the inevitable transitoriness and collapse of earthly things—the chant "falling down falling down falling down" even sounding, in keeping with Hesse's evocation of the intoxicants of destruction, glad and vindictive. (Certainly the lack of punctuation falls in with the theme of chaos.) The fragment also situates poetry, unresolvedly, as on the one hand regressive and irresponsible, a rhythmic gay togetherness with the mother, a sensual rejoicing despite catastrophe, and, on the other, clear-sightedness.

Opposite in orientation, dialectically placed, is the next fragment, "*Poi s'ascose nel foco che gli affina*" ("Then he hid himself in the fire that refines them"). At the crudest level of contrast, this line directs us to heights, not depths—to the Mount of Purgatory, and Arnaut Daniel, the Provençal poet who, not least as a representative of his scribbling tribe, has abjection to atone for, purity to seek: "In grievousness I see my follies past; / in joie, the blistful daie of my preparing"[47] (*Purgatorio* 26.143–44). "In their suffering is their hope," Dante says of those in purgatory. The flame is torment, but not death. The gulf between carnal terror and purgatorial pain is as that between a fall into water and an ascent into driest mountains, or as that between a nursery jingle and Dante's sweet, poised gravity.

After catastrophic abjection and the hope that lies in suffering, a further step: the blissful day of preparing, which the protagonist, the poet as much as he is the seeker or saint, figures (in keeping with his earlier choice of Daniel) through a line from Bion's "The Vigil of Venus," "*Quando fiam uti chelidon*" ("When shall I be like the swallow?"). For the poet, to sing (with inviolable voice) is equivalent to rejoicing in Love, which takes the form of the "inspired condition." If the protagonist almost recklessly chooses for touchstone the words of a goddess hungry for the love of a god (the poet, said Yeats, is a woman), the reason is that he too would be moved to effortless utterance by Love. Again, in Kristeva's words, art is "rooted in the abject it utters" yet "by the same token" purifies it and thus "appears as the essential component of religiosity, . . . destined to survive the collapse of the historical forms of religions."[48] "She sings," says Venus of the nightingale, "I am silent—When will my spring come? . . . In this silence the Muses have left me—Apollo is gone." Yet what the nightingale

47. *The Purgatorio*, trans. John Ciardi (New York: New American Library, 1961), 269.

48. Kristeva, *Powers of Horror*, 17.

voices is Philomel's "complaint of a brutal husband."[49] To sing of suffering in a voice purified by suffering is the religious poet's prayer.

Is this protagonist ambivalent, then, about submitting to "the silence"? "I could not / Speak"—is this a condition to be preferred to Philomel's? It is not (compare "My Soul" in Yeats's "Dialogue of Self and Soul": "Only the dead can be forgiven; / But when I think of that my tongue's a stone"); and Eliot in his own way chooses for theme "original sin"—and by virtue, in the first place, of being a poet. "The lion and the honeycomb," the sweetness that can be housed and garnered in corruption, is that of which he sings; and yet his heart would not be "unchristened," as Yeats in "Vacillation" roundly and backingly declared of Homer's: Eliot is torn, rather, between the probable bad faith and the possible good faith of his art; and what Alvarez calls his "world of formal perfection," a world that "lacks the dimension of human error," is his attempt to achieve the dubious, the infinitely to be desired, goal of a christened poetry, in which the poet's heart beats obedient to controlling hands.

As for Tennyson's "O swallow swallow," it forms an echo of Bion except that, in contrast to Bion's swallow, Tennyson's is not a Philomel but, instead, a sky-traveler, knowing that while "bright and fierce and fickle is the South, . . . dark and true and tender is the North," and instructed by the speaker to fly to his beloved and say, "I do but wanton in the South, / But in the North long since my nest is made."[50] So it is that, perhaps more out of his belief in the transmuting power of poetry than out of nostalgia for sexual love, the protagonist again uses the sensual as a typology for the spiritual. He would follow the swallow "flying from the golden woods" to where "all the woods are green." "O tell her, brief is life but love is long." The protagonist relies on the reader to catch something of this longing for a renewal that is also a homecoming—his "O swallow swallow" touching this off as if with a brush of its wing.

This fragment climaxes the implicit movement that organizes the first four. As for the fifth fragment, it restates the rationale for seeking and shoring up these touchstones of fear and longing. A prince in a ruined tower ("*Le Prince d'Aquitaine à la tour abolie*")? The ruined tower (like Yeats's in "Dialogue of Self and Soul") suggests the inevitability of both physical and cultural decay; nor can we have missed the protagonist's propensity (shared by Gérard de Nerval, author of

49. *Bion's Elegy for Adonis and the Vigil of Venus,* trans. Peter Jay (Santa Barbara: Unicorn Press, 1968), unpaginated.

50. Alfred Tennyson, *The Princess,* in *Poems of Tennyson,* introduction by T. S. Eliot (New York: Thomas Nelson and Sons, 1936), 288.

this fragment) to identify with royalty. What remains among the disin-
heriting ruins of secularism is princely, the soul.[51] The problem is to
choose the right stony rubbish in which its roots may stir, its branches
grow. So this fragment embraces the others. There is more method in
Hieronymo's "madness" than first meets the mind.

Why Then Ile Fit You (Hetermodality, Heteroglossia)

"Why then Ile fit you" implies that the protagonist is meeting and
baiting something or someone—is it us?—as a strategist, and is not to
be outdone. Hieronymo in Kyd's *The Spanish Tragedy* was out to
delude and kill the villains who hanged his son. Who has hurt the
protagonist so direly that he should compare himself to "mad" Hieronymo? No one, surely, unless in the secret scenarios of Oedipal fantasy; but he would seem to be almost beyond those now, however
metaphysically castrated. Still, he *is* in a position to have enemies, and
he might well say with Hieronymo, "Take my tongue, for never shalt
thou force me to reveal / The thing which I have vow'd inviolate."
What he will not say out directly and betrayingly is that he *believes*—
more, that his God is the Unnameable, and that he would forsake the
whole earth for a single drop from the clouds huddling near the
Absolute.

Eliot's protagonist all but confesses that he has constructed an elaborate trap for those inimical to his purpose, a sticky-paper poem of
confusion, full of a distracting if bewildering "variety," as of appearing, disappearing, and reappearing motifs; and that he has done this so
as to be in a safe and cunning position of mastery, the better to protect
what to him is inviolable, in part by affecting, like Hieronymo,
"milder speeches than [his] spirit affords," and in part, as intimated,
by mystifying readers hostile to the metaphysical with a "strange and
wondrous show"—one in which their doom is sealed, and without
any pity from the poet, by their own deductions of despair ("Yes,
contemporary life *is* a heap of broken images, we *can* connect nothing
with nothing, there is rock and no water, it is just as the poet says").

The protagonist, in short, would not be easily found out. How
laugh at his medieval metaphysicalness if it can scarcely be made out
in the din of diverse voices and the harlequinade of generic kinds? Let,
even, people take him for mad (in the way that Harold Munro spoke

---

51. Robert Emmet Jones links Nerval's ruined tower to the tarot cards: "The six-
teenth card of the Major Arcana—the Lightning-struck Tower, or, as it is called in
France, La Maison Dieu—signifies the fall of the Angels or the fall from both physical
and spiritual grace" (Robert Emmet Jones, *Gérard de Nerval* [New York: Twayne Publishers, 1974], 67).

of "The Love Song of J. Alfred Prufrock" as "insane"): better this bitter ignominy than that his faith should be vulgarized by common discourse, its originality obscured by the frayed curtains of tradition, its deferrals to silence lost in the small talk of connectives and transitions and its terms like the last bled bits of coughdrop on tired tongues.

Terry Eagleton suggests that "behind the back of this ruptured, radically decentered poem runs an alternative text which is nothing less than the closed, coherent, authoritative discourse of the mythologies which frame it."[52] Leaving aside the question of which mythologies these might be, and of how *mythologies* can be authoritative, one might argue that, on the contrary, everything recognizably closed and coherent is "madly" referred, in this poem, to what is radical and central, the One Alone as an open coherency that is scarcely conceivable and that justifies nothing except absolute conformity to itself (certainly not what Eagleton finds as a lining of the poem's avant-gardism, the "conservative values" of a "ruling minority"). Reading the Eliot of *The Waste Land* as if the poet were the Christian philosopher of the later criticism, Eagleton has hold of the wrong Hieronymo.

The Traditional Blueprint

As Gordon observes, "Eliot could safely expose the heart of darkness to a modern audience," but the "traditional blueprint [of conversion] had to be subdued. To the intellectuals of Eliot's generation it would have seemed an anachronism." Hence his Hieronymo-like indirections, his multiple tongues. The tactic, however, backfired, for (as Gordon puts it) readers "fastened hungrily" on the signs of despair, and even on the erudition, "and ignored the fact that these were subsidiary to an exemplary life." So Eliot was "forced to rewrite his saint's life in more explicit terms in 'Ash-Wednesday' and *Four Quartets*."[53]

Skepticism still rules the criticism of this fundamentally unskeptical poem. It is taken as a text of despair, or if a salvational thrust is descried, stress is laid on the fact that the protagonist merely comes near his goal, as if spiritual success were ever anything more than this *coming near*.

At the one extreme, Alvarez sees the poem pointing toward "the impossibility of finding any solution."[54] In the same key, Eloise

---

52. Terry Eagleton, *Criticism and Ideology: A Study in Marxist Literary Theory* (New York: Schocken Books, 1978), 150.
53. Gordon, *Eliot's Early Years*, 119.
54. A. Alvarez, *The Shaping Spirit: Studies in Modern English and American Poets* (London: Chatto & Windus, 1967), 27.

Knapp Hay remarks: "*The Waste Land* . . . can now be read simply as it was written, as a poem of radical doubt and negation."[55] Taking a middle position, A. Walton Litz observes that critics "have discerned a set of moralistic judgments on life [in *The Waste Land*] where nothing was intended but a delicate balance of attitudes."[56] Somewhat less neutral, Elizabeth Schneider finds that, although the poem "expressly looks toward some alternative to Gerontion's whorl of fractured atoms," it "does not actually explore [subjective] change."[57] Again, Ronald Bush infers that Eliot may have had "some kind of short-lived religious illumination during the process of re-envisioning the fragments of his poem"—but, not taking this possible illumination seriously, Bush concludes that the poem nonetheless "survived" its consequent reshaping.[58] Again, David Spurr, in a view harmonious with Bush's inference that the poem is not the work of a "classic" temperament but under the control of Eliot's "demon," grants a "presiding consciousness" in the poem (a protagonist) but finds it rebellious against ascetic salvation: as in Yeats's "Dialogue of Self and Soul," here, Spurr says, "a judgmental Soul demands, but cannot compel, renunciation and purgatorial assent from a self obsessed with the earthly joys of imagination."[59]

Even those who posit the predominance of puritanical motive in *The Waste Land* disagree as to what final view to take of it. Gregory Jay concludes that "the first three sections of the poem constitute a kind of preparation of the soul and heart for reception of the Word, adopting from mystic literature their climactic call for a prerequisitive purification or celibacy before the final approach to the mystery."[60] But the Christian concept of "The Word" jars with the importance that the poem ascribes (in Eastern fashion) to "the silence." The incarnational aesthetic of the poem as such is out of rhythm with its metaphysics, in which salvation might be imaged as, in Ricoeur's words on Orphism, "an excursion from the body, . . . a voyage in the other world" ("The boat responded / Gaily, to the hand expert with sail and oar / The sea was calm").[61] Still reflecting Christian thought, Jay

55. Eloise Knapp Hay, *T. S. Eliot's Negative Way* (Cambridge, Mass.: Harvard University Press, 1982), 48.
56. A. Walton Litz, "*The Waste Land:* Fifty Years After," in *Eliot in His Time: Essays on the Fiftieth Anniversary of the Waste Land,* ed. A. Walton Litz (Princeton: Princeton University Press, 1973), 7.
57. Schneider, *T. S. Eliot: The Pattern in the Carpet,* 67.
58. Bush, *T. S. Eliot: A Study in Character and Style,* 72.
59. Spurr, *Conflicts in Consciousness,* 25.
60. Gregory Jay, *T. S. Eliot and the Poetics of Literary History* (Baton Rouge: Louisiana University Press, 1984), 155.
61. Paul Ricoeur, *The Symbolism of Evil,* trans. Emerson Buchanan (Boston: Beacon Press, 1969), 287.

states that "the poem leaves us at the edge of purgatory but still far distant from paradise, lacking that loving logos that moved the constellations of Dante and that returns in the brightest moments of the *Quartets.*" Jay goes so far, in fact, as to ascribe to the poem a "negation of transcendence."[62] By contrast, A. D. Moody unguardedly finds the work justified in "its hidden claim to have ended a dead era." "To end 'What the Thunder Said,'" he remarks, "with the Sanskrit invocation is to imply that it has been a form of Upanishad; and to imply also that it has been aspiring to the state of final blessedness in which the individual being is consumed within the All."[63]

The poem, I think, does not claim to have ended a dead era, but it does indeed depict a conversion in which the dead land of one soul is reclaimed, and by fertilization not from the Word but from the Eternal Silence, which is too pure for words. It would invoke radical surgery for its own acute reaction to the crisis of heteroglossia in the hysteria-inducing, hyperhistorical awareness of modern culture. Contrary to Schneider's opinion that the rain of salvation in the poem must surely fall on the waste land itself, that the protagonist cannot simply have turned his back upon humanity, I suggest that a Hieronymo is not in a position to view the torturing world about him with so much generosity.[64] The protagonist is like the Hinayana Buddhist who goes apart from others to save his purity, as opposed to the Mahayana Buddhist who would establish a Pure Land for the many.

The important qualification to this last is built into the poem—it is the hard-to-determine degree of generosity implicit in Eliot's resolution to disseminate, through his poem, the good news of an exemplary life.

Shantih (Heteroglossia and Silence)

Significantly, only one of the fragments, the one from Dante, is squarely in the Christian tradition. And it is chastened and offset by the super-fragment "Datta. Dayadhvam. Damyatta," which is chill as with a wind off the Himalayas, and which escapes the inventoried status of the others and comes in climactically—after the preconclusion of "These fragments I have shored against my ruins"—as the very consummation of wisdom. The "fragments" address a longing that the Sanskrit has helped show the protagonist how to satisfy.

Again, Prufrock could not bring himself to risk the faith that might

62. Jay, *T. S. Eliot and the Poetics of Literary History,* 155, 158.
63. A. D. Moody, *Thomas Stearns Eliot: Poet* (Cambridge: Cambridge University Press, 1979), 106.
64. See Schneider, *T. S. Eliot: The Pattern in the Carpet,* 60–62.

be required, or exposed, by "the overwhelming question" (he was perhaps terrified of a rich transformation); and Gerontion apologizes to Christ for not acting on a faith he begrudgingly holds (or, rather, one that holds him and, baulked, depresses him). The *Waste Land* protagonist actually acts on his faith, but *his* faith is not quite Christian in its orientation or description. Eliot's earlier absorption in Buddhism at Harvard, under Irving Babbitt's sympathetic guidance, has finally and profoundly been reflected in his poetry; the notion of the divine as *purely* spiritual, of the spiritual as *non*human as well as nonnatural, has straitened his Christian sensibility.

This last, however, woven of the Bible and his mother's verse and his readings in Augustine and Dante, together with untold other things, is still vivid and strong, particularly in his disposition to imagine sin turning "around into living beauty," in Kristeva's words, as illustrated by the progression from the purgatory image to Bion's poem, which trails the refrain, *"Tomorrow let there be love for him who never has loved"*; as earlier in the progression from a "broken Coriolanus" to "your heart would have responded / Gaily, when invited." By means of the beautiful, so Kristeva remarks of the New Testament, "the demoniacal dimension of the pagan would be tamed":

Christian sin, tying its spiritual knot between flesh and law, does not cut off the abject. . . . Meant for remission, sin is what is absorbed—in and through speech. By the same token, abjection will not be designated as such, that is, as other, as something to be ejected, or separated, but as the most propitious place for communication—as the point where the scales are tipped towards pure spirituality.[65]

Christian conversion transmutes, as from eyes to pearls. It is not the emptying-out constituted by the Eastern solution. It is rejoicing song, not the sweet sanctity of the silence.

As religious *poet*, the protagonist would sing, be "Christian." By contrast, as a seeker after the ultimate in its paradoxical *austere* fullness, he would imitate the *Stithaprajna*, the man of equanimity, and, instead of turning evil into inviolate music, transcend the polarities altogether by concentrating on *Omkāra*, the eternal silence. *The Waste Land* ends in a tension between these alternatives, a tension resolved, and perhaps as much for reasons of poetic as of theological closure, but only just resolved, in the ritualistic final line, "Shantih shantih shantih." In his notes Eliot provides even for this—the for-

---

65. Kristeva, *Powers of Horror*, 127.

mal ending to every Upanishad—a Christian equivalent, curtailing Phillipians 4:7, "and the peace of God, which passeth all understanding, shall keep your hearts and minds through Christ Jesus," to "The Peace which passeth understanding." This somewhat brusque paraphrase, however, with its omission of any reference to Christ, virtually reifies "Peace" and thus faces it in the direction of the Orient, where the peaceful soul becomes all but indistinguishable from the One that *is* Peace; simply, there is only Peace.

Already silence seems to invade the intervals between the thrice repeated word "shantih," which is spaced out as in Hindu practice. The word seems willing to be swallowed up by the Eternal Silence, if invited. Further, repeated as it is, it shuts down discourse in simple, discontinuous recurrence and a passivation this side of syntax. Its redundancy would free the mind from the virulence of thought, or free the soul from the mind. In the Upanishads, the repetition is prefaced by "Om," the syllable evoking eternal silence, as in the following peace chant:

> Om. That is full; this is full. This fullness has been projected from that fullness. When this fullness merges in that fullness, all that remains is fullness.
> Om. Peace! Peace! Peace!

"Shantih," or "Peace!" thus would spring up within the Silence itself as a would-be post-word, a self-vacated verbal form, a crypt in which Babel (together with Hieronymo's "Babylon") has dwindled to a trace.

The penultimate line, "Datta. Dayadhvam. Damyata." has the clear closural function of a reprise, while the final line, in being self-reprising, reduces all language to one word that means, in its thrust, "Beyond words!" The first series of Sanskrit words telescopes once, twice, and still a third time, out of a single syllable, in a reluctant parody of wild earthly proliferations as well as of the abundance of the One Alone. At least the words are assonantally and alliteratively akin, they seem to come from one and the same fount of Wisdom. "Shantih" then repeats the same dominant vowel, *a,* as if in sign of its intention to close discourse, which is based on tireless difference, in a redundancy of the same.

So it is that, by the mildest of means (the violence of Eliot's disjunctive method having come by this point to seem a spirit-glancing lightness), the protagonist tilts the emphasis back toward "the silence," away from inviolate song, turning language almost against itself in order to evoke the Unnameable. This is the maximum theological close and it is perfectly achieved—the more readily, of course, in that "Shantih" is a word that baffles the English ear even as, through its reiteration, it seems to insist on its own finality.

Hieronymo ironically said of his play in which "Each one of us / Must act his part in unknown languages," "the conclusion / Shall prove the invention and all was good." Minus the irony, so it is with this poem in which secular heteroglossia windingly seeks its own consummation, its sacrificial death, in the eternal silence. And this consummation is indeed *performed,* if only through words and their silence-invoking arrangments. The poet in the protagonist is not, after all, silenced at last, except by his own choice and through his own evocation of attaining to the brink of silence: a silence too full to heed the prison-wall scratchings of language, a silence that has never heard anything but itself, in a tautology that stops the tongue. The protagonist does not claim to hear this silence (though he once, as it were, heard into it), nor does he permit us to hear it, since what we hear is, precisely, still another quotation from world literature. The actual close of *The Waste Land* is poised between the protagonist's listing of still one more, and now the ultimate, spiritual touchstone, and his magical effort, which lovingly seizes on the closural dynamics of the poem, to make his final line seem cessative not only for the poem but for language and consciousness themselves: a self-transcendence attained by both a self-forgetting hero and a self-forgetting art.

Perhaps no poem in the language seems more self-aware than *The Waste Land,* yet none seems nearly so other-conscious at the same time, so eager to wing off of others' words to the one true sphere. The protagonist's last such effort borrows from the oldest surviving scripture, as if endeavoring to go back to language at its pristine source, prior to its degeneration into babble. This gesture on the one hand sanctions written "tradition," if a syncretic tradition garnered from far and wide, and, on the other hand, given the denotation of "shantih," a word that appears to vanish immediately into the ethereal reaches of connotation, it implies that all discourse, scriptural or secular, written or spoken, is as nothing compared to the silence of the One: at best a selective resource for a defence against its own broken accumulations. A defence of which *The Waste Land* itself, in its entirety, is proffered as a hard-won and would-be-inviolable example.

INDEX